D1808229

CLASSIC NEW ZEALAND
MOUNTAIN BIKE
SEVENTH EDITION
RIDES

CLASSIC NEW ZEALAND
MOUNTAIN BIKE
SEVENTH EDITION
RIDES

Simon Kennett
Jonathan Kennett
Paul Kennett

Kennett Brothers

Published by
KENNETT BROTHERS
PO Box 11 310, Wellington
Phone/fax +64 4 499 6376
info@kennett.co.nz
http://www.kennett.co.nz

7th edition copyright © 2008 Simon Kennett, Jonathan Kennett and Paul Kennett.

ISBN 978-0-9582673-3-5

Cover photo	www.jumpingjimflash.com
Editing	Bronwen Wall
Maps	Sarah Drake, Alex Revell
Cartoons	Corey Harbrow
Design	Paul Kennett
Wardrobe	Ground Effect
Print broker	Printciple Source, Sydney Australia

Groundeffect

Acknowledgements

We appreciate the assistance of staff from Department of Conservation, Councils around the country and Bike NZ for all their help and information.

Thanks also to private landowners who provide some of New Zealand's best riding areas.

For their hospitality, encouragement, information, and riding company we'd like to thank:

Queenstown–Lance Brown, Jim Davies, Hugo Gladstone. Wanaka–David Drake & Jennie Taylor, Doug Hamilton. Central Otago–Matthew Sole. Dunedin–Julian Cox, Ant Green, Gareth Hargreaves, Pam Jackson, Hamish Seaton. Mosgiel–Scott Farmer. Hokitika–Mark Dawson, Cathy Hammer. Greymouth–Tony Coll. Westport–Tim Sikma. Christchurch–Lisa Carter, Shailer Hart, Rob Hoult, Dave Mitchell, John Mote, Vivienne & Laurence Mote, Craig Tregurtha, Guy Wynn-Williams, Richard and Trudi Zawodny. Takaka–Brent Hartshorne, Martin and Marie Langley. Nelson–Chris Mildon, Stew Thorpe, Martin Cleland, Andrew Cavill, Dianna Parr, Susan Shaw, Paul McArthur, Rob Kay and the guys from Stewarts; Niel, Mitch and Chris. French Pass–Danny Boultan. Wellington–Selwyn Andrews, Oli Brooke-White, Murray Drake, Sarah Drake, Duncan Fyfe, Stuart Edwards, Graham Hare, Andrew McLellan, Mark and Rachel Kent, Jo McKenzie, Patrick Morgan, Darryl Neal, Carl Patton, John Randal, Jonty Ritchie, Mark Soanes, Greg Thurlow, Bronnie Wall, Rosie Wall, Ben Wilde, Ginny Wood, Andrew & Sally, Hamish & Eleanor, Dave Venables, Carla Wellington. Wanganui–Doug@The Bike Shed. Palmerston North–Phil Etheridge. New Plymouth–Graeme Lindup. Turangi–John Carmen. Taupo–Thomas Schwarz and Greta Donaldson. Clive–Bernie Kelly and Paula Kibblewhite. Napier–Carl Larsen. Gisborne–Norm Graham, John Harris, Freddy Salgado, Annett Robinson. Rotorua–Nick Lambert. Tokoroa–Matt Gisby, Mark Nicolas. Opotiki–Mike Houghton, Jim and Nikki Robinson. Whakatane–Andy High, Kim van der Aa. Waitomo–Pete and Kieran Chandler. Auckland–Ryan@Freeriden, David Benson & Donna Wynd, Clark Smith. Whangarei–Brent Love, Grant Tavinor.

And many helpful bike shops and internet users.

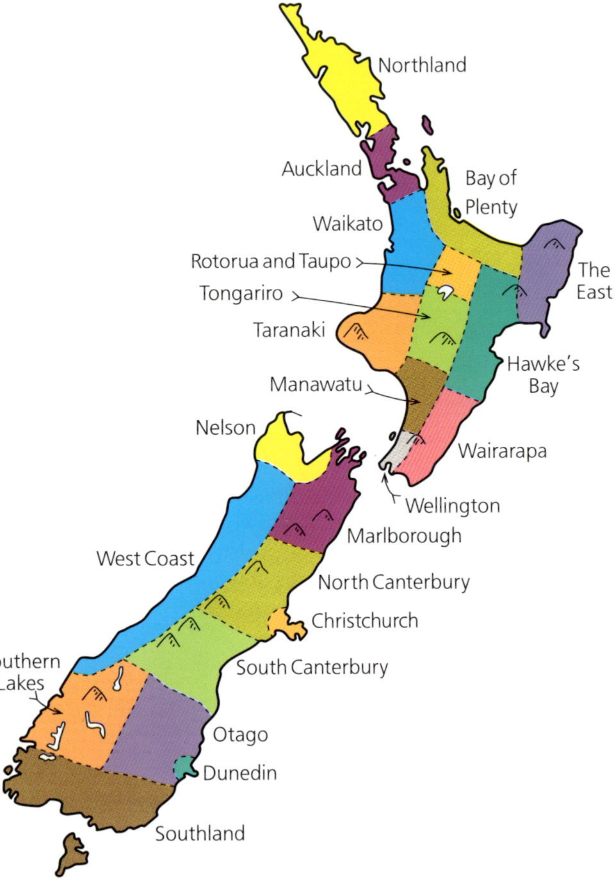

Northland

Auckland

Bay of
Plenty

Waikato

Rotorua and Taupo >

Tongariro >

Taranaki

Manawatu >

The
East

Hawke's
Bay

Nelson

Wairarapa

West Coast

└ Wellington

Marlborough

North Canterbury

Southern
Lakes

Christchurch

South Canterbury

Otago

Dunedin

Southland

Key to maps

Single track	Native bush	Buildings
4WD track	Exotic forest	Town/city
Gravel road	Tussock/grassland	Info centre
Sealed road	River/stream Lake/sea	Campground

Contents

Dedication

To the hundreds of mountain bikers around New Zealand who have volunteered their time and skills to build tracks and lobby for land access. Without their remarkable generosity, many of the rides listed in the following pages would not exist.

Preface

It gives us a great sense of satisfaction to bring you the seventh edition of *Classic New Zealand Mountain Bike Rides*. As you'd expect, doing the research rides was a dream job—it always is. There's no shortage of sweet riding in this country. This time we also got huge pleasure from redesigning the book; adding colour maps and photos throughout.

We hope you'll enjoy the new look—if it inspires you to discover a new favourite ride (or two), then we're happy. If it simply reminds you of an old favourite you'd almost forgotten, then we're also happy. Just reading about a brilliant ride sparks our enthusiasm–we're confident it will spark yours too.

Pedal on!

Simon, Jonathan and Paul

Intro

Things change

This book is the definitive guide to mountain biking in New Zealand—400 rides ranging from the sublime to the ridiculous.

Over time, new tracks are built, old ones become overgrown, signs are vandalised and landowners change. Since the last edition, we've added 140 new tracks, deleted 45 rides and significantly revised over half of the rest. It's a dynamic scene.

If you know of any changes, please email info@kennett.co.nz or write to: Kennett Brothers, PO Box 11 310, Wellington. If it's a change we haven't heard of, we'll send you a chocolate fish.

Terms we've used

To differentiate between vertical and horizontal; **'m'** refers to vertical height, and **'metres'** refers to horizontal distance.

The heights shown on elevation charts are metres above sea level and were measured off topomaps at 500-metre intervals throughout the ride. This method tends to eliminate small hills. Be wary of using elevation charts for route finding.

Laurence appreciates the difference between vertical and horizontal.

Rating the rides

After vigorous and lengthy debate, we've rated every ride in the book based on our love of adventure, appreciation of scenery and appetite for flowing single track:

★ ★ ★ ★ A fantastic slice of mountain bike heaven.

★ ★ ★   Highly recommended rides, which we really enjoyed.

★ ★   Loads of fun with good mates on a fine day.

★   Enjoyed by locals but not worth a special trip.

👎   No way we'd go back for these duds.

Notes We really rate rides that take us places, and we're happy to walk a bit if we're rewarded with a sweet descent or stunning landscape. Also, we prefer big hills to big jumps.

Four star, grade-5 riding at Seven Mile, Southern Lakes.   www.jumpingjimflash.com

Gradings

This mountain bike grading system is based on those used for kayaking and climbing. It is now used by DOC and is similar to the International Mountain Bicycling Association (IMBA) grades. Most tracks are a grade or two harder when wet.

Grade 1   Fairly flat, wide and smooth track or gravel road; suitable for all first-time riders.

Grade 2   Mostly flat with some gentle climbs on smooth tracks with easily avoidable obstacles, such as rocks, tree roots or pot holes.

Grade 3   Steeper grades on a loose surface; trickier obstacles may be present but are avoidable; may be some exposure at the outside edge of the track.

Grade 4   A mixture of steep climbs, loose track surfaces and obstacles that are tricky to avoid or jump over; generally exposed at the outside edge of the track. Most riders will find some sections easier to walk.

Grade 5   Prolonged steep climbs; generally exposed at the outside edge of the track, with technically challenging obstacles and sharp corners. The majority of riders will need to walk some sections.

Grade 6   Downhill or free-ride specific tracks; extremely steep sections with large drop-offs and other unavoidable obstacles; may include huge man-made structures and jumps.

Stuff to take

Don't ride alone; always take a buddy and a tool kit. Let someone know where you're going and when you'll be back. If there's a chance you'll be caught out overnight, take a small survival kit (including an emergency blanket, torch and extra food).

There is a gear list at the end of the book for you to check all the usual stuff that experienced riders take.

First aid

It's almost inevitable. Sooner or later you or one of your buddies is going to wipe out big time. Blood, stress, shock, broken bones, deep gashes ... maybe worse! Don't panic! Do a first aid course and take a first aid kit.

Food and drink

Drink early and often. Once you start to feel thirsty, your energy levels are already dropping. The best drinks for your body are water, diluted fruit juice and sports drinks.

On any ride over two hours long, take something to eat. Some of our favourite 'inner tube fillings' are fruit, muesli bars, scroggin and bananas.

Access koha

Farmers in general, and especially those who live a long way from shops, are very appreciative of a little koha. Take any small thing that is hard for them to get regularly, such as a local newspaper or perishable foodstuffs. Trust us; you'll be doing a great service for land access.

Maps

Don't go into any seriously wild country without a good map, such as a 1:50,000 scale topomap. We've listed the map you'll need at the end of each ride's write-up.

A compass or GPS may also be useful—and for some rides essential. Remember to stand clear of steel bike frames before checking directions with a compass, and don't expect a GPS to work well when under a forest canopy.

In late 2009, the entire 1:50,000 Topomap series is being completely re-published with a new format and projection that is more compatible with GPSs. This means that the map names in this series will change and the existing maps will become unavailable over time.

Murray Drake

"I'm sure there's a trig around here somewhere."

Cell phones

Over the last few years, several lost or injured bikers have used cell phones to contact Search and Rescue (phone 111 and ask for Police). Although reception is unreliable in the valleys, it's still worth taking one if you can. Make sure it's fully charged.

Attitude

To help keep tracks open to mountain bikers, try to ride dual-use tracks as 'diplomatically' as possible. Avoid startling other track users, call out a friendly 'hello' well before reaching walkers and accept that really popular dual-use tracks won't be worth biking at busy times such as national holidays.

Weather reports

We often check both of these sites before heading into the hills—they have the most up-to-date weather reports:

www.metservice.co.nz/forecasts/

www.metvuw.co.nz/forecast/

All other things being equal, expect the temperature to drop a degree for every 100 m height you gain.

Stuff to leave behind

Rock Snot

Cleaning your bike not only helps it last longer, it also stops invasive species such as Didymo and African Clubmoss spreading from one area to another.

Ripping it up

The impact of a mountain biker is usually on a par with that of a walker, unless the biker is skidding, in which case, the erosion is several times greater. It takes just a little skill to be able to roll rather than skid those tyres. Go easy on the back brake and enjoy the tracks for years to come.

Nick Lambert

Sabrina Wilson slipping into a fresh rut at Wairakei MTB Park, Taupo.

Trains, planes and buses

If you're short on time, want to do a through trip or simply don't like cars, the best way to get to and from a ride is by public transport.

Contact details

Tranz Rail (train) and Interislander (ferry)	0800 802 802
Bluebridge (ferry)	0800 844 844
Air New Zealand	0800 737 000
Auckland public transport (buses and trains)	(09) 366 6400
Wellington public transport (buses and trains)	(04) 801 7000

Smaller operators are mentioned in the relevant ride notes.

Bike bags

A bike bag usually gets your treadly on buses, trains and ferries for free! It's not a bad idea to unbolt the rear derailleur (or its hanger) and tape it to the frame to give it more protection, and pack something between the rear drop-outs to prevent the frame from being squashed. You can buy a bike bag from Ground Effect (www.groundeffect.co.nz).

Fees for unbagged bikes

City to city buses and trains charge $10 for an unbagged bike. Bus operators often ask that you remove the pedals and wrap the chain.

Wellington and Auckland commuter trains no longer charge for bikes, but space can be limited—first in first served.

Commuter buses don't take bikes yet (bike advocates are working on them, and there's a trial taking place in Christchurch).

The Interislander ferry charges $15 for a bike. You ride it on and off the ferry. Bluebridge Cook Strait Ferries only charges $10 for a bike.

Air New Zealand does not charge for bikes but does charge for your second bag/item ($15 for a bag up to 25 kg). They expect you to pack your bike well or at least wrap the chain and cogs in newspaper, remove the pedals and turn the handlebars.

Qantas charges $20 per bike and sell bike boxes for $25. If your bike weighs more than 15 kg, there may also be an excess luggage charge!

The cost of travel

Like any human activity, the sport of mountain biking is impacted by the rising cost of fuel. To help reduce your travel expenses and carbon emissions, we've given you the actual driving distance from the nearest main town for every ride. You can then estimate your costs for the ride.

In 2008, AA estimated that (taking into account fuel, tyres, maintenance, etc) an average car costs 74 cents per km to run. A large or fully loaded car is more than $1 per km.

Landcare Research estimated that an average-sized car will emit 1 tonne of CO_2 for every 4,000 km driven—larger cars emit much more.

To reduce costs and emissions, pack your bikes inside your car and share your trip with others. Maybe check out the public transport options. And the best solution? Cycle to and from the ride.

Jonathan Kennett

You'll need to wear more than a helmet to survive in the mountains.

Northland

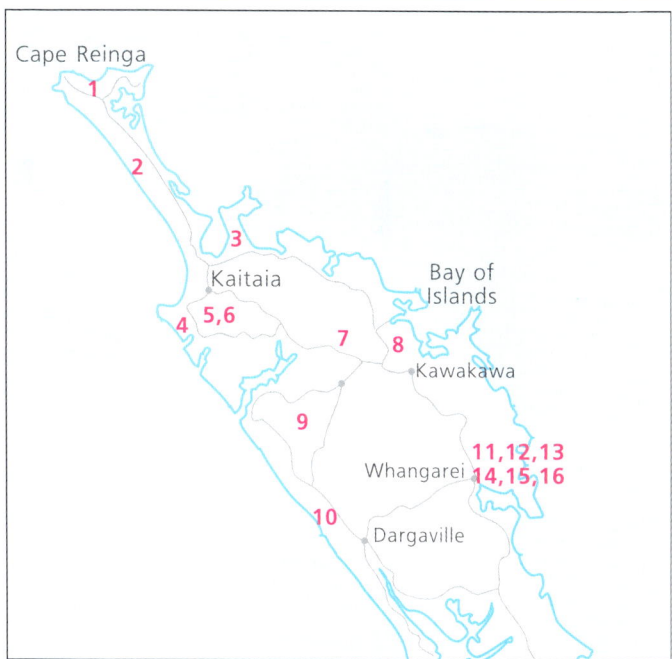

1	Pandora–Spirits Bay	**9**	Waoku Coach Road
2	Ninety Mile Beach	**10**	Kaiiwi Lakes
3	Tahanga Trail	**11**	Glenbervie Forest
4	Tutu Trail	**12**	Whanui Loop
5	Kaitaia Walkway	**13**	Western Hills
6	Takahue Saddle	**14**	Parihaka Loop
7	Puketi Kauri Forest	**15**	Mt Tiger
8	Waitangi Forest	**16**	Waimahanga Track

NORTHLAND HIGHLIGHTS

The centre of Northland's mountain biking is Whangarei, where Glenbervie Forest has the best purpose-built trails in the region. Further north, beautiful beaches and tropical weather provide the setting for four cruisy coastal rides.

1 Pandora–Spirits Bay

North Cape

Grade 3, 2–4 hours, 15 km return or 40-km loop ★ ★

Spirits Bay, to the east of Cape Reinga, is an incredibly beautiful spot, made all the more so because cars can't drive to it.

How to get there   The start of the track is signposted 11 km north of Waitiki Landing.

Route description   A 4WD track leads north on a gentle ridge, reaching a 'Kauri Bush Walk' sign after 2 km. It's a worthwhile half-hour walk to New Zealand's northernmost remnant of kauri forest—no bikes allowed. Riding on past the bush walk, you soon reach a locked gate, beyond which the road drops steeply down to the stunning Pandora Bay 3 km away.

From Pandora Bay most people return the way they came.

Alternatively, if you're keen on doing a round trip, and the tide is low, you can ride and walk 7 km along Te Horo Beach (Spirits Bay), to a camping area from where there is a gravel road leading back to Waitiki Landing (the route is well signposted). Don't follow the walking track through the dunes. We got to the beach 3 hours before low tide and had to walk about half the distance.

Notes   There is a garage and general store at Waitiki Landing. Swimming at Spirits Bay can be dangerous.

2 Ninety Mile Beach

North Cape

Grade 1-, 4–6 hours (no headwind), 93 km ★

Riding the big beach is like crossing the Sahara; desolate, stunning and windswept: it helps to follow the prevailing north-westerly wind.

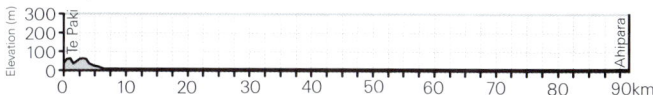

Route description This is the ideal ride for fit beginners. From Te Paki, 24 km south of Cape Reinga, cycle down Kauaeparaoa Stream (also called Te Paki Stream) to the northern end of Ninety Mile Beach. From there, it is 86 flat kilometres south to Ahipara, which lies 14 km southwest of Kaitaia.

During low tide, the beach surface is as hard as concrete—easy but boring. Ride with an entertaining bunch of friends. Try cycling with your eyes closed. Even better is no hands with your eyes closed. Check tide times at Waitiki Landing or Information Far North in Kaitaia, phone (09) 408 0879.

Other users Tourist buses (they all come through from Kaitaia within about 20 minutes of each other) and the odd car.

Notes Waitiki Landing and Ahipara are the first and last places to buy food, so stock up. Food isn't sold or allowed to be eaten at Cape Reinga because of the spiritual importance of the site. Bikes should be thoroughly cleaned of salt and sand straight after the ride.

3 Tahanga Trail

20 km from Kaitaia

Grade 2, 2–3 hours, 40-km loop   ★

This unique beginners' trip whets the appetite with an interesting exploration of Karikari Peninsula.

Route description Head 20 km northeast of Kaitaia and turn left off Highway 10 onto Inland Road and cycle past Lake Ohia, a dried-out lake full of 300,000-year-old tree stumps. After 3.5 km, turn right onto a gravel road (Ramp Road) and ride down to Tokerau Beach, then head north along the sand to Tokerau village near the end of the beach (leave the beach when you are right next to a couple of Norfolk pines). This ride can only be done during low tide; any other time, you'll have to miss out the beach section and take the road to Tokerau village.

From the Tokerau Reserve picnic area, ride out to the main road 1 km away. Turn right here, then after another 800 metres, turn left onto Waimango Road. After 4 km, you'll hop over a gate onto a major gravel road. Veer left and ride round, past the Rangiputa turn-off, to Wallace Road, where you should turn right. This soon becomes the Tahanga Trail and leads you across old gumfields on a gravel road/4WD track back to Highway 10 about 4 km southwest of the Inland Road turn-off.

Track conditions   A little bit of everything

Notes   Refer to Terrainmap 1 North Cape.

4 Tutu Trail

INTERMEDIATE

Ahipara, 14 km southwest of Kaitaia

Grade 3+, 4–6 hours return, 27 km   ★ ★

One of the most interesting and scenic rides of Northland. Make sure you get the tides right and go prepared for blazing sun and sand.

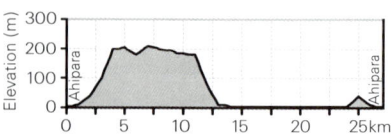

Route description   You must return along the coast during low tide—before departing, ring Information Far North, (09) 408 0879, for a tide timetable.

From Ahipara beach, ride southwest past the changing sheds and up the hill. Veer left at the first Y-intersection (1 km from the changing sheds) and, after another kilometre, right at the second Y-intersection. After about 30 minutes, you'll reach a plateau. Follow the metal Gumfields Road until you come to a group of corrugated iron buildings on the left side of the road—one of them is a museum featuring relics from the gumfield days. At the museum, turn hard right onto a sandy clay track. This is the Tutu Trail.

Not far down the Tutu Trail, you may notice a small set of steps cut into a bank on your left. They lead up to the gumfields. Continue past them down the main track. After about 3 km, there is a minor turn-off on the right leading up to a lookout spot and then a few hundred metres later a minor turn-off on the left, which is the Erewhon Trail. This used to be the main route to the coast but is now overgrown.

Continue following the main track out to the top of the sand dunes another kilometre away. If you really love your bike, turn back here (or carry your bike down to the coast). If you're not too fussy, glide down the sand dunes to the coast. Follow the main set of quad bike tracks. Wandering off the main track will exacerbate erosion, and you might get lost.

At the coast, turn right and ride on firm sand, where you can find it, back towards Ahipara. As you get close to Ahipara, you'll encounter flat patches of rock, and the sea will force you to ride close to the cliffs. This section is only passable during low tide.

Track conditions 5% sealed road, 25% gravel road, 20% 4WD and single track, 40% coastal rocks and hard sand, 10% semi-ridable sand

Notes If the tide conditions are not right for this ride, then just check out the gumfields and the view from the top of the dunes before riding back the same way. Drinking water is scarce—take an extra bottle. Clean your bike thoroughly after the ride—salt and sand are murder on metal components. Please remember that sand dunes are a fragile environment and avoid riding over any vegetation.

The beach at Ahipara is great for body surfing. Topomap N05 Herekino is useful for working out where to ride in the gumfields.

5 Kaitaia Walkway

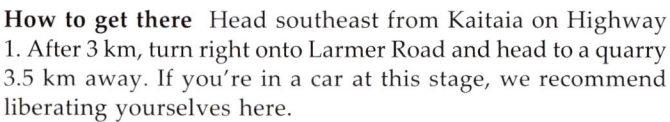

7.5 km from Kaitaia

Grade 3, 1–2 hours, 12 km   ★ ★

This is a fun, but short, single-track ride through native forest.

How to get there Head southeast from Kaitaia on Highway 1. After 3 km, turn right onto Larmer Road and head to a quarry 3.5 km away. If you're in a car at this stage, we recommend liberating yourselves here.

Route description Follow the narrow gravel road that drops down to the right from the quarry and ride 2 km to the start of the Kaitaia Walkway (signposted). A former bullock track, the walkway passes through native bush at an easy gradient. After about 30 minutes, pass a short detour to a kauri grove (unrideable but worth the 10-minute walk). Another few minutes takes you to another side track, this time to a lookout point 30 metres away. From there, turn round and follow your tyre tracks back to the quarry.

Track conditions 30% narrow gravel road, 70% single track

Notes The track from the lookout to Diggers Valley is partly overgrown and mostly unrideable.

6 Takahue Saddle

19 km southeast of Kaitaia

Grade 2, 2–3 hours, 38-km loop   ★

This is an easy ride based around an old public road that is no longer driveable.

How to get there Head southeast of Kaitaia on Highway 1 for 11 km and turn right at the 'Takahue 8 km' sign.

Route description From Takahue, take Takahue Saddle Road southeast for 10 km through to Broadwood. It goes like this: about 2.5 km from Takahue, where Warner Road begins following the river, veer right up the side valley. About 350 metres later, you'll cross a small stream and sidle up around the hills to the saddle (380 m). Just keep following the main sidle track and ignore

Jonathan swings through to Broadwood.

the turn-offs. The track follows an old road to Broadwood, so the gradient is mild.

At Takahue Saddle, go straight ahead and after about a 10-minute downhill you will have to scramble around a slip to a gate. One hundred metres from the gate, you will pop onto a gravel road next to a 'No Vehicle Access' sign. Cruise down the scenic gravel road to Broadwood. At the very end, take a short cut across a swing bridge on your right to get to the Broadwood general store.

To return to Takahue, turn right when you hit the sealed road, ride 13 km, before turning right again onto Waiotehue Road and pedalling another 15 km back to the start.

Refer to Topomap Rawene O05 or Terrainmap 1 North Cape.

7 Puketi Kauri Forest

15 km west of Kerikeri

Grade 3-, 2 hours, 20 km return   ★

A few 4WD tracks provide access to some huge kauri trees. Great scenery but boring riding.

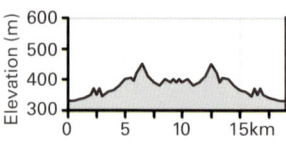

How to get there   From Kerikeri, drive 4 km northwest to Waipapa. Then follow Highway 10 north for 1 km before turning left and following the signposts to 'Puketi Recreation Area' 13 km away.

Route description   At the recreation area car park, check out the map board and then head up Pirau Road. This soon becomes a good 4WD track that climbs up and down, but generally up, Pirau Ridge into tall kauri forest.

After almost 10 km, keep your eyes peeled for a signposted turn-off called Takapau Track. This marks the top of the ridge and the end of the line for mountain bikes. You can continue on foot to enjoy more kauri forest.

Turn around and enjoy the rolling downhill back to the car park.

Another good 20-km ride is the Mohau Ridge Track. This discreetly signposted 4WD track turns off Waiare Road exactly 5 km north of the Puketi Recreation Area. The Mohau Ridge Track weaves through mostly native bush all the way to Takapuwahia Trig. At 444 m, this trig is one of the highest points for miles around.

Track conditions   100% 4WD track

Notes   Don't forget your camera—the kauri are quite impressive. The Manginangina Kauri Walk, not far from the carpark, takes 15 minutes and offers excellent interpretation boards—definitely worth getting off your bike for. We walked it at night, which was pretty cool!

Take the DOC pamphlet on Puketi and Omahuta Forests.

8 Waitangi Forest

Waitangi, Paihia

Grade 2, 1–3 hours, 20 km   ★ ★

You wouldn't travel to the Bay of Islands for its mountain biking, but if you happened to be there with a bike, this is the place to go.

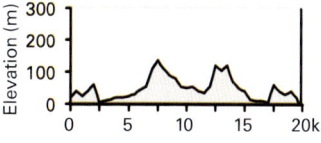

Landowners Endowed to the nation by Lord and Lady Bledisloe. Managed by Rayonier Forestry and the Waitangi National Trust.

Route description From Waitangi (near Paihia), ride north up past the golf course and down to the Wairoa Bay Picnic Area (a great spot for lunch and a swim after your ride). Just past the recreation area, turn left and cruise up Te Wairoa Road for 3 km. Turn left again at Rosella Rd and then, just before the top, turn right and climb up Lookout Road to check out Scoria Cone (Te Puke).

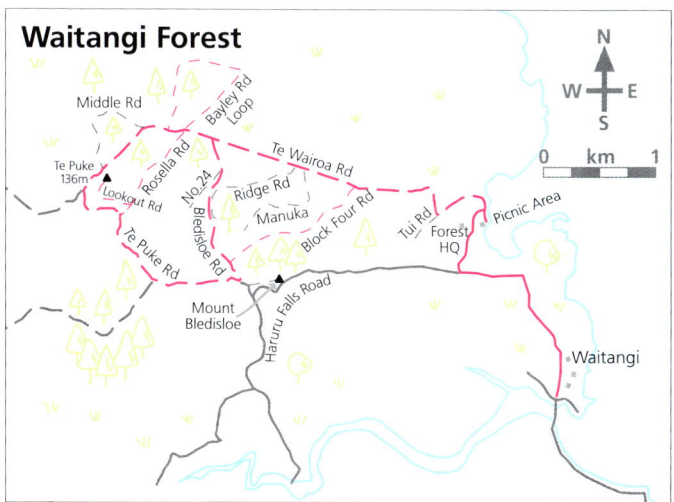

From the cone, freewheel back down Lookout Road and out to the main gravel road (Te Puke Road). If you're feeling tired, head left and take a short cut to Mt Bledisloe. Otherwise, turn right and ride round to Te Wairoa Road via Middle Road Loop and maybe Bayley Road Loop as well. When you reach Bledisloe Road, follow it up to the forest entrance near the top of the hill and down the other side a hundred metres or so to follow an obvious 150-metre-long track to Mt Bledisloe for some great views.

After taking in the views, backtrack along Bledisloe Road for a few hundred metres and take the first track on your right after passing the map board at the forest entrance. This is called Block Four Road and is a fun downhill that leads you back to Te Wairoa Road less than 2 km from the recreation area. Now follow your handlebars back home.

Track conditions 10% sealed road, 60% gravel road, 30% 4WD

Notes No smoking or dogs allowed in the forest—it is home to endangered kiwi. Watch out for logging trucks. Ridge Road is also a good downhill. Te Wairoa Road continues across the Waitangi Forest and leads to Kerikeri Inlet, but at times, that part of it may be closed for logging. DOC has a good pamphlet on the forest that includes a useful map.

9 Waoku Coach Road

INTERMEDIATE

52 km northwest of Dargaville

Grade 3, 2 hours, 40 km return   ★

An interesting place to visit for its scenery and history.

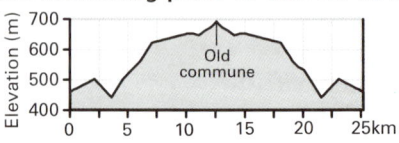

How to get there Head to Tutamoe, 12 km northeast of Donnellys Crossing.

Route description From Tutamoe School, ride north on Waoku Road. After 4 km, you'll pass a picnic area beside a large 'Walkways' sign. From here, the gravel road gradually turns into a muddy, but rideable, 4WD track. Within an hour, you will reach a gate bearing a 'Private Road...walking only' sign, which you should ignore—this is definitely a public road!

Continue up through the native bush and over the occasional stone culvert (built in the 1890s) to a signposted intersection. Turn left off the main track and ride past Honeymoon Hut and the old Honeymoon Commune site. Cross a clearing on a rideable 4WD track before entering the bush, where the track becomes a diabolical bogfest. Turn around here and head back the way you came.

Track conditions Gravel road and 4WD track

Notes Although climbing to a height of 700 m, the 100-year-old Waoku Coach Road never exceeds a grade of 1 in 12.

10 Kaiiwi Lakes

37 km northwest of Dargaville

Grade 2+, 1–2 hours, 4–13 km ★

This is a great holiday spot, and if anyone has been keeping the tracks clear of vegetation, the riding is good too.

How to get there Head north of Dargaville on Highway 12 for 24 km before turning left at the 'Kaiiwi Lakes' signpost. After another 10 km, turn right at Domain Road and head down to the motor camp.

Route description Ride from the motor camp back towards Lake Kaiiwi and take the first turn on your left down to the lake. Now simply follow the main track ahead to ride around the lake in a clockwise direction. When you hit Domain Road, turn left and look for a track on your left a few hundred metres along the road that crosses farmland. It will take you back around the lake in an anticlockwise direction. Route finding is more difficult in this direction.

To ride around Lake Taharoa (the big one) in an anticlockwise direction, cruise through the motor camp to the end of the gravel road. Squeeze through the gate and follow a 4WD track down to the lake. Now follow the walking track beside the lake. After a couple of kilometres, you'll spot an orange and white marker post on your right. Leave the lake and push your bike up a small hill through pines to farmland at the top. Continue following the track across farmland and out to the road. Turn left and ride 2 km back to Domain Road.

Track conditions A little bit of everything

Notes This is a popular area during the holidays, so be especially courteous to other users. The Kaiiwi Lakes to Maunganui Bluff Walkway provides a nice 30-minute ride across farmland down to the beach. The walkway starts on Kaiiwi Lakes Road, 2 km north of Domain Road. Follow the orange arrows to the coast.

11 Glenbervie Forest

INTERMEDIATE

10 km northeast of Whangarei

Grade 3, 2–10 hours, 10+km   ★ ★ ★

The single tracks in Glenbervie Forest have received a lot of TLC in the last few years, and several excellent new ones have been added. It is now the most popular riding area in Northland.

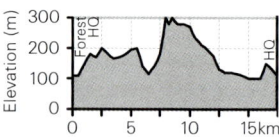

Landowners Rayonier Forestry. No permit required. Please respect all forestry operations.

How to get there   Head north through Tikipunga and out of town on Ngunguru Road for 3 km before turning left down Maruata Road at the 'Glenbervie Forest' sign. Two and a half kilometres down this road, you'll reach a signposted car park area on your left.

Route description Hop over the stile beside the car park and follow the fun Everready Track into the forest. Within a few minutes, it takes you to the MTB notice board beside the forest HQ. Have a look at the map for any new tracks or logging information. Then head off and explore or try the Single Tracks Loop that locals showed us in 2008.

Jonathan Kennett

Taunting the troll in Glenbervie Forest

Single Tracks Loop

Local mountain bikers have built a number of cool tracks, but they take a bit of hunting out. Best to go riding with the club if you can. If you can't, try this fun 1-hour loop. Ride up Mains Road and take the second left onto Marsden Road. Ride past the Tin Bum turn-off (overgrown) and take the next left down Flipper. It wasn't signposted in 2008 but is a hoot of a ride.

At the bottom of Flipper, turn right and ride up Burma Road for 10 minutes till you see a little bridge on your right—that's the start of FartEasy. Blast your way across to Mangakino Road, turn left and ride to Nursery Flat Road.

Turn right at Nursery Flat Road to get back to Main Road, then hang another right to get to Quarry Road. This leads to B'ware the Troll (signposted), which is a ripper of a downhill. It leads to Waitangi Road. Turn left, then take the next three right-hand turns to get to the top of Bluff Trail (signposted). This is also a cool downhill. We loved it so much that we rode up for another run, but the second time down Bluff Trail, try turning left onto Shoelace. This gives you the option of riding Frump back to the HQ. From the MTB notice board, take The Antidote back to the car park.

Brent Love peels off Bluff Trail onto Shoelace.

Notes Watch out for fast-moving forestry trucks. The forest was being logged in 2008—and may still be when you visit. Also, the car park may be shifted up the road (closer to town) in 2009. Check out Topomap Q06 Hukerenui for larger exploration trips.

12 Whanui Loop

15 km east of Whangarei

Grade 3, 2 hours, 17 km ★★

This is good old-fashioned fun on a bike. The single-track downhill is awesome, but you have to earn it.

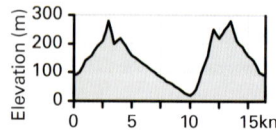

Landowners For access permission contact Hancock Forest Management Ltd, (09) 470 1300.

How to get there Head east from Mairtown, northern Whangarei, on Whareora Road (which becomes Pataua North Road), for 12.4 km and park at the Whanui Forest sign on your right.

Route description Hop over the gate and ride up Tuatua Road, climbing up through a farm and into a forestry area, then through a quarry. Stay on Tuatua Road until you reach a gate 5 km from the start. Turn hard right and head down into the bush on a superb, benched single track.

If you come across a slip near the top, just look for a new track to the right. Cross a couple of streams, jump a Taranaki gate and head out to a farm. Swing over the fence and turn right on the track marked 'Mussel Road' (but labelled 'Oyster Road' on the topomap—what is it with all these shellfish?). After a few minutes, cross a ford and grunt up the big hill.

Near the top, you reach a Y-intersection. Both forks take you back to Tuatua Road. Go left to get back to where you started.

Track conditions 70% gravel road, 30% sweet single track

Other users Logging vehicles

Notes Topomaps Q07 Whangarei and Q06 Hukerenui show the details.

13 Western Hills

Whangarei

Grade 3+, 1–2 hours, various lengths ★

This council-owned area of native bush and exotic forest borders the western edge of Whangarei. It has a few short technical tracks, mostly clay based, that are fun when dry. They're also popular with walkers and runners. Try this short ride for a starter.

Route description Head out of Whangarei on Western Hills Drive, then turn left up Whau Valley Road. Go to the dam and just as the reservoir comes into view veer left, across some grass, to a gate where a narrow track begins. After 20 minutes climbing, you'll reach another gate on a ridge top, by a pylon. Cross the gate and turn right. Follow the main track for 5 minutes as it veers right twice more and eventually reaches a well-defended trig, the highest point in these hills.

After checking out the view, backtrack 50 metres and turn right. Soon you'll come to a right-hand bend with two 4WD tracks heading off to the left—take the first left. Follow this track as it undulates and comes to a sudden stop. On your right, there is a single track, which forks almost immediately—head left onto Frank Holman Track. In fairly quick succession, you'll have to veer right, then left, then left again. At the bottom, cross the paddock and hop over a stile onto Russell Road. Go right and then turn right again onto the main road to get back to town.

Track conditions Mostly single track

14 Parihaka Loop

Whangarei

Grade 2+, 1–3 hours, 12 km ★ ★

In 2007, this forest was logged, destroying several mountain bike tracks in the process. The council is now leaving the area to regenerate and has plans to develop it into a major mountain bike attraction some time in the future. Best to get an update from the council, unless you feel like exploring.

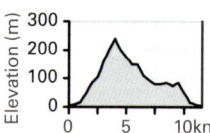

Route description Ride east out of Whangarei on Riverside Drive for 1 km before turning left at the 'Parihaka Memorial' sign and climbing up to the memorial 3 km away. After enjoying the view, head back down the sealed road for 100 metres and hop over the gate on your left onto a red-earth 4WD track. Follow this main track for a few hundred metres and explore the newly built single tracks off on your right. Hopefully the new tracks will be signposted soon.

Track conditions a mixture of sealed road, 4WD track and single track

Other users Forestry vehicles and horse-trekking tourists

Notes Contact the Whangarei District Council on (09) 430 4200 for up-to-date information on tracks.

Grant Tavinor

Lance crests a roller on Resurrection, Parihaka.

15 Mt Tiger

Onerahi, 5 km east of Whangarei

Grades 3–4, various times and distances   ★

Mt Tiger is an area of native and exotic bush riddled with forestry roads and secret single tracks open to the public. The tracks are deliberately hard to find to make it difficult for motorbikers to rip them up.

Route description From the Onerahi shopping centre, ride to the end of Cartwright Road (1.4 km) and hop over a steel gate. You're now on the walkway, and it starts steeply. Head up and explore, or better still, go riding with the Parahaki MTB Club.

Topomap Q07 Whangarei only shows a few of the tracks in this forest, but you'd find it useful if you were lost. The Waikaraka Walkway (marked on the topomap) is officially being promoted as open to bikes, so try it first to get a feel for Mt Tiger.

Notes For your own safety, stay away from the areas that are being actively logged. Forestry trucks and falling pine trees don't slow down for mountain bikers.

16 Waimahanga Track

5 km east of Whangarei

Grade 1, 30 minutes, 3 km return   ★

This is the ideal track for complete beginners

How to get there Head out to the end of Waimahanga Road.

Route description From the end of Waimahanga Road, follow the signposted track around to George Point Footbridge, and on to Cockburn Street. Return the same way. The track follows an old railway line through the mangroves between Sherwood Rise and Onerahi.

Track conditions gravelled single track

Notes The track is marked on the council pamphlet 'Walking Tracks in Whangarei'.

The area is a favourite with walkers and runners; please be considerate.

Auckland

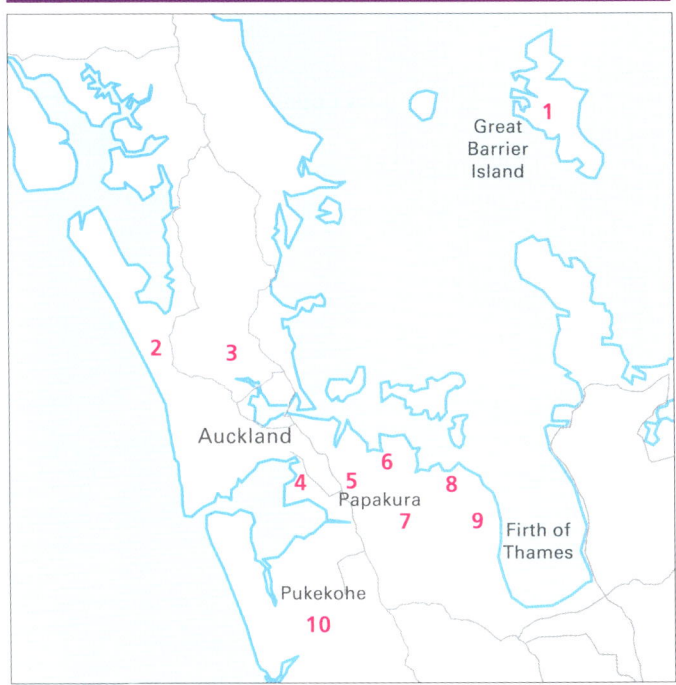

1 Great Barrier Island
2 Woodhill Forest
3 Riverhead Forest
4 Mangere Coastal Walkway
5 Totara Park MTB Track
6 Whitford Forest
7 Hunua Ranges
8 Tapapakanga Regional Park
9 Waharau Regional Park
10 Puni MTB Park

AUCKLAND HIGHLIGHTS

Woodhill Forest is the most popular riding area in Auckland, offering over 100 km of wicked single track. In dry weather, however, it can become a sandpit; that's when Riverhead's and Hunua's purpose-built tracks give it a run for its money. Mangere Coastal Walkway is great for beginners, and Great Barrier Island makes for a great fat-tyred holiday.

1 Great Barrier Island

80 km northeast of Auckland (as the sea gull flies)
Grade 3, 3–6 hours, 52 km ★ ★

There are 180 km of gravel roads and tracks on Great Barrier Island. The 54-km loop described here covers the best of them.

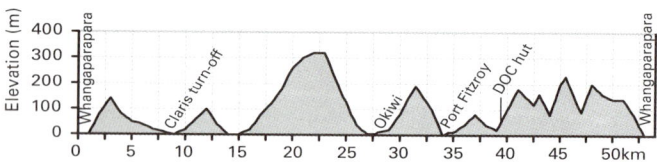

How to get there From Auckland, take the Subritzky Ferry, www.subritzky.co.nz, cost: $30 per person in 2008. Bikes are free.

Route description Hop off the ferry at Whangaparapara. Ride into the island over the Whangaparapara Road. Veer left past the Claris turn-off, onto the Kaitoke-Awana Road. Two kilometres beyond Awana Bay, climb over the Fitzroy-Harataonga Road. A third of the way up this hill, the Overton Road turn-off offers the option to visit Harataonga Bay, 2.5 km away.

Back on the main loop, keep following the Fitzroy-Harataonga Road to Port Fitzroy, ignoring a couple of right-hand turn-offs.

From Port Fitzroy, head south past the DOC headquarters to the road-end gate, where a 4WD track begins. By now, you've covered about 35 km of gravel roads—the best is yet to come. Follow the 4WD track through regenerating kauri forest, tackling several stream crossings and a few moderate climbs along the way. This is a tough section if wet. After 12 km, you'll come out at the top of the Whangaparapara Road, 3 fast km from Whangaparapara.

Track conditions 75% gravel road, 25% 4WD track

Notes Spend at least two days on the island to take advantage of the great beaches, bush walks and hot pools. There are plenty of options for camping as well as a backpackers' hostel at Whangaparapara and the DOC Kaiarara Hut.

There are general stores at Port Fitzroy, Claris, Whangaparapara and Tryphena and a bike shop at Tryphena. Refer to Infomap Great Barrier Island.

2 Woodhill Forest

40 km northwest of Auckland

Grades 1–6, 1 or 2 days, up to 120 km ★★★

This is the most popular riding area near Auckland city. There are more tracks than you could possibly ride in a day, and everyone is catered for, from beginners to complete adrenalin junkies. Because it is a sandy area, the tracks are best ridden after rain. In the height of summer, it becomes a sand trap, and many local riders head for Riverhead instead.

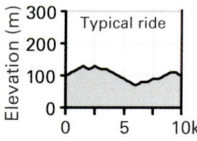

Landowners Managed by Bike Parks Ltd. Permit required with a range of fees, from free for under 11 years of age up to $69 for an annual pass. A one-day pass cost $6 in 2008 and comes with a free park map. Check www.bikepark.co.nz for fee changes.

How to get there Drive west from Auckland on Highway 16 for 37 km. Turn left at the Woodhill Forest road sign and drive a further 2 km to a large car park (it's well signposted). The main entry gate is open from 7am to 7pm daily (except Wednesdays when it stays open till 10pm).

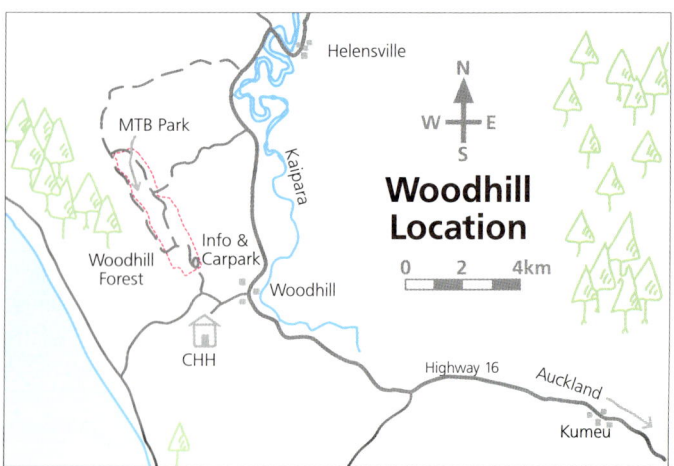

James Madigan

Luke McCombie gets a bird's-eye view of Woodhill's biggest jump.

Jonathan Kennett

Woodhill's slippery delight.

Route description At the huge car park, you will find a staffed information centre, toilets, a cafe, wash stands, and a bike shop with bikes to hire.

The map you are given when you register has all the tracks marked on it. Shown on the map are six main signposted courses to follow, ranging from 6 km to 25 km in length. There are also dozens of extra tracks to explore, but because 99.9% of riders stick to the main tracks, the others are covered in pine needles and can be hard to follow. It's interesting that, even on a day when the car park is totally packed, the back part of the park feels almost empty! Most people don't venture very far.

Our strategy was to cruise around asking locals what their favourite tracks were and then go and ride them. This worked a treat and helped us discover some real classics like Big Mumma, Cookie, SPCA and Slippery's Delight.

Although the easy tracks are by far the most popular, it is the difficult wooden structures that make Woodhill unique. We really enjoy some of these, but a word of caution: ride to your ability. The jumps and structures here have led to a world of hurt. If in doubt, take the bypass.

Track conditions 5% forestry road, 95% single track

Notes Because Woodhill Forest is sandy, it's one of Auckland's best wet-weather riding areas, although the wooden obstacles are slippery when wet.

There is a flash new jumps area next to the car park that hardly anyone rides because it's too difficult. Don't forget to clean the sand out of your drive train after your ride. For more info, check out www.bikepark.co.nz

3 Riverhead Forest

10 km west of Albany

Various grades, 1–4 hours, up to 50 km ★ ★

In the middle of summer, when Woodhill becomes sandy, Riverhead is the place to go. There are over 30 single tracks to explore and dozens of forestry roads.

Landowners Rayonier Forests Ltd. No permit required.

How to get there The track network is complicated and still evolving, so you'll need a map. Drop in to FreeRide'n' at 318 Main Rd, Huapai (it's only 3 km south of the forest). It shows the best access points to Riverhead Forest.

Route description Riverhead Forest is a large pine forest criss-crossed by gravel roads and tracks. Over the past few years, logging operations have closed some of the old favourites, but new tracks are being built by the West Coast Riders Club. A ride with them or the Auckland Mountain Bike Club is the best intro to this forest.

High-school racers at Riverhead.

The forest is plenty large enough to get lost in for a few hours, so get into the exploring spirit of things. The terrain consists of rolling hills up to 200 m high. Most riders cycle up forestry roads to a high point and then blast back down on single tracks.

For a first time ride, start from the Waitemata Motorcycle Club building on Barlow Road, and head up to Patterson Road from where you can choose between three tracks that head back down to the club buildings. The Number 13 track (signposted) is a good aperitif.

Be warned: after heavy rain, Riverhead is a bogfest! Head for Woodhill instead.

Track conditions 45% gravel rd, 25% 4WD track, 30% single track

Other users Forestry trucks, motorbikes and war-game soldiers. The forest is closed during motor sports events.

Notes   It's not a good idea to park too close to access gates. If there's a forest fire, your car could be totalled by a fire engine in a hurry.

There is a Dual Slalom Track on Ararimu Valley Road, 500 metres down on the right.

4 Mangere Coastal Walkway

BEGINNER

20 km south of Auckland City

Grade 1, up to 2 hours, up to 14 km return   ★ ★

An ideal place to teach your kids how to ride a bike or just go for an easy cruise.

How to get there From Auckland City, head south through Onehunga, over Mangere Bridge on Highway 20, and turn off to Mangere Domain. Drive 1 km west of Mangere Domain and all the way down Ambury Road to the Ambury Farm Park information centre.

Route description From the car park by the information centre, you can ride across the farmland by following the blue posts. It's also a shortcut to the Coastal Walkway, but you can ride from the car park to the coast on the main farm road just as easily.

Jonathan Kennett

The southern end of the Mangere Coastal Walkway.

The blue posts (and the main farm track) lead to the Mangere Coastal Walkway, which is a wide smooth gravelled path. The walkway skirts south around the coast to the Mangere Lagoon. You can ride all the way round the lagoon on your left or go straight ahead for a shortcut. The lagoon track is a lovely ride.

From the lagoon, the track continues past the waste water treatment plant—obviously not so nice. There are a few turns to make, but they are all signposted, and apart from a few steps, the track is still easy. You can continue all the way to the Oruarangi Creek Picnic area (3 km from the lagoon). Most people turn back here, but the track does continue for another 1 km if you cross the bridge. The track ends at a quieter part of the coast.

Turn around whenever you feel like it and cruise back to Ambury Farm Park.

Notes We were surprised how few people were using the track on a nice weekend day. It's a great little ride. Remember to give way to other track users.

5 Totara Park MTB Track

2 km east of Manukau City

Grade 3, 1 hour, 6 km   ★

This is one of the newest rides in the book. In fact, at the time of writing, it hadn't even been built!

How to get there   Drive or ride east of Manukau City on Redoubt Road. Totara Park is well signposted on your right.

Route description   In 2008, the Manukau City Council was planning a 6-km mountain bike track. Jonathan helped with the design and walked the proposed route. It promises to be a flowing grade-3 track and will hopefully be open by 2010.

From the car park, the track will drop down to a main 'hub' and then climb up to the far side of the park. Then the fun really begins. The track will flow across the hill and down into the main gully. Then you have to climb back up to the car park.

Notes   Google 'Mountain Biking in Manukau' for an update. In 2008, the only track mentioned, the bridle track, was not worth riding (that's why they are building a mountain bike track).

6 Whitford Forest

40 km southeast of Auckland City

Various grades, 1–4 hours, 1–20 km   ★ ★

A series of purpose built trails weave through this privately owned forest. They have been designed and refined over the last ten years, making Whitford Forest a popular destination for local mountain bikers.

Landowners   Privately owned and managed by Rayonier Forests Ltd. Entry by permit only.

How to get there   First up, head to the Howick Information Centre to buy a forest permit. Then drive to Whitford and turn northeast on the Whitford-Maraetai Road for 6 km. Park at the top of the hill.

Route description   Most people head for the single tracks near the entrance before exploring further afield. Hop over the gate, ride for 20 metres and turn left down Keanu Track (a 300-metre-long bus stop). At the bottom, follow the road to your left for a few hundred metres, turn left again at the next fork and stop just down the road to check out the map board.

There are several grade 2–4 tracks around this small area. Most are named after relatives of the main track builder in the area, Peter Clouston, but the best is named after himself! It's the jumps and drop-offs that make this area so much fun, but they demand respect—especially after rain. Start with Joshua's Track and work your way up to Pete's Track.

More tracks have been built since 2005 and these are graded at the start.

Track conditions 100% purpose-built single track

Notes Watch out for the larger jumps in this area. Also beware of the archery club that is now close to the Breadhead Track.

7 Hunua Ranges

28 km southeast of Papakura

Various grades, 1–5 hours, up to 42 km   ★ ★ ★

The Hunua Ranges Regional Park has the best collection of free-to-ride tracks in the Auckland area.

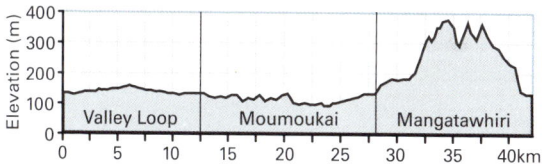

How to get there From Hunua township, follow Hunua Road southeast for about 7 km before turning left onto Moumoukai Road and driving over the hill to the Mangatawhiri Dam car park a further 7 km away. There is a map board, emergency phone and toilets at the car park.

Valley Loop Track/Family Trail

Grade 1+, 1–2 hours, 13-km loop with lots of detours possible
From the car park, ride back down the road, veer left at the first

intersection and slip round a large steel gate. Ride up the gravel road for a few hundred metres and veer left at the first main intersection to start the gravel road loop marked on the map. There is a tiny bit of single track near the end of the loop that needs to be walked (turn left when you hit the gravel road again). Otherwise this track is a piece of cake.

Moumoukai Farm Track and River Track

Grade 3+, 1.5–2.5 hours, 17-km loop

Most riders head straight for these tight and twisting mountain bike tracks. From the car park, follow the directions for the Valley Loop Track for about 2 km, then turn right at the 'River Track' signpost. After a short stretch of old gravel road, you'll pop into a tight 2-km single track constructed in 2005. When you pop back out onto a gravel road, head left back up the valley for a couple of hundred metres and look for a sign pointing to the Moumoukai Farm Track.

This single track twists through forest, fields and fords. Countless roots and ruts combine to ensure the trials and tribulations of everyday life are quickly forgotten. When you reach a 4WD track,

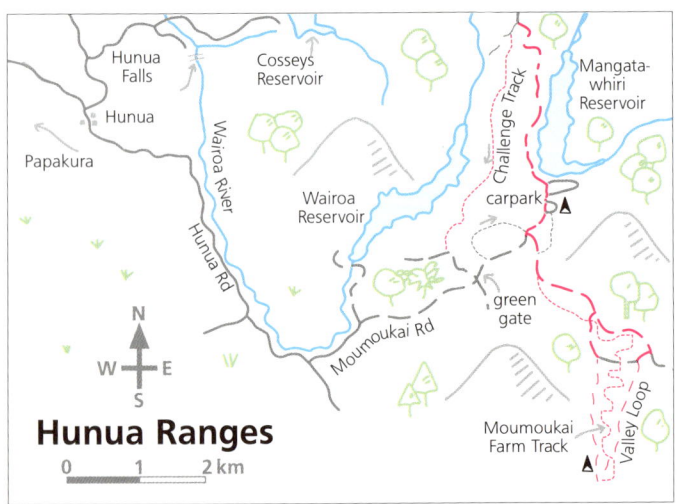

Hunua Falls
Cosseys Reservoir
Mangata- whiri Reservoir
Hunua
Wairoa River
Papakura
Challenge Track
Wairoa Reservoir
carpark
Hunua Rd
green gate
N
Moumoukai Rd
W — E
S

Hunua Ranges
Moumoukai Farm Track
Valley Loop
0   1   2 km

Sabrina Wilson tests the waters at Hunua.   Nick Lambert

turn left, then after 50 metres, right onto more single track. After a while, you'll reach a T-intersection where you need to turn hard left and climb beside a fence (don't go down to the 4WD track to the right). Then, after another 10–15 minutes, you'll merge with a grassy 4WD track (don't turn hard left—look for the trail marker hidden in the grass ahead).

A few hundred twists later, you'll hit a gravel road. Turn right, then left onto another deviant single track after a few hundred metres. At the very bottom, follow the Valley Loop Track back to the car park. Sweet!

Mangatawhiri Challenge Track

Grade 4+, 1.5–3 hours, scenic 15-km loop

From the car park, ride north up the main gravel road, climbing high above the reservoir. After about 5 km, at the top of a large hill, turn left onto a 4WD track, which soon becomes a single track and traverses the main ridge. Great views and gnarly little hills. At the next four intersections, turn left. Don't miss the cool 1.5-km section of single track halfway down the main gravel road back to the car park (it's signposted).

This track has many steep, slick sections of moss-covered clay — not recommended when wet. Even in the dry, expect some walking.

Track conditions gravel roads and single track

Notes Track building is likely to continue, so keep an eye on the map board at the car park or check www.aucklandmtb.co.nz Please keep well left on all park roads.

8 Tapapakanga Regional Park

70 km southeast of Auckland City

Grade 3, 1 hour, 7-km loop ★

To be perfectly frank, this little trip ranks at the bottom end of the fun scale and only just made it in to the book. But it's worth doing if you're in the park.

How to get there From Clevedon, 15 km from Papakura, drive northeast to Kawakawa Bay and then south on Kawakawa-Orere Road. Turn right again onto Orere-Matingarahi Road and then veer left onto Deery Road 28 twisty km from Clevedon. After a few hundred metres, turn left again at the large carved poles (pou pou) and drive down to the car park by the beach.

Route description There are usually maps at the car park. The 7-km-long mountain bike route starts here and is marked by yellow posts. It follows a mixture of gravel road, 4WD track and pasture up to a trig station and back via a different route.

Notes You can do the loop in either direction. Anticlockwise might be a bit more rideable, but either way involves short steep hills.

9 Waharau Regional Park

West of the Firth of Thames

Grades 3–4, 1–3 hours, up to 18 km   ★ ★

These old tracks provide a good range of opportunities. As long as you don't mind a little 'foot cycling', you'll be rewarded with awesome views and lengthy downhills. There are three loops to choose from.

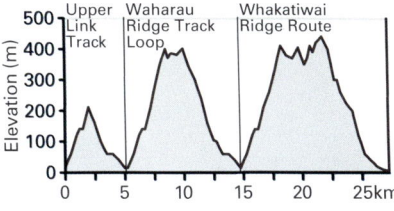

How to get there From Clevedon, 15 km east of Papakura, drive east to Kawakawa Bay and then south towards Kaiaua. About 40 km from Clevedon (and beside the Firth of Thames), turn right at the Waharau Regional Park signpost and drive up to the second car park.

Route description The ARC's 'Southern Parks' pamphlet, available at the car park, includes a map of the trails.

Upper Link Track

Grade 3, 1–2 hours, 4.5 km

From the map board, head left (not straight ahead) over a fence, then follow the yellow markers up a steep track to the spur on your right. Some walking may be required. After 2 km, turn left and follow a steep single track down to another fork where you should turn left again. From here, there are a couple of gates to hop over en route back to the car park.

Waharau Ridge Track Loop

Grade 4-, 1.5–2.5 hours, 11 km

Ride the first 2 km of the Upper Link Track and then continue climbing up to the ridge, following the red markers. Three kilometres from the car park, there is a fantastic lookout platform right beside the track. This is only 600 metres from the ridge. There's a fair bit of walking in the second half of this climb, especially when wet. Once on the main ridge, it's a 100% rideable vehicle track—turn left and enjoy. Keep an eye out for the left-hander off the ridge that will loop you back down to the start—it's pretty obvious if you're not moving too fast.

Whakatiwai Ridge Route

Grade 4, 2–3 hours, 18 km

From the map board, follow the Waharau Ridge Track Loop for 6 km, then carry straight on along the ridge. The old logging track gets rougher further along but is mostly rideable. Turn left at the 'Whakatiwai and Coast Rd 2 hrs' signpost for a long downhill, which spits you out at a non-signposted spot on the main coast road. Turn left to return to the car park 4.5 km away.

Other users Hunters and lots of walkers in summer

Notes These tracks haven't been built with cycling in mind, so ride cautiously and expect to push your bike occasionally. The views and native forest make it all worthwhile.

10 Puni MTB Park

EASY

4.5km southwest of Pukekohe

Grade 2+, 30 minutes, 6-km loop ★ ★

A small pine forest absolutely packed with fun single track.

How to get there Drive southwest out of Pukekohe on West Street, Puni Road and Waiuku Road. After 4 km, turn left onto Attewell Road. Less than a kilometre away on your right is the Puni Rugby Club. Park there.

Route description Ride up past the left side of the Rugby Club to the grassy slope and then veer right onto a 4WD track to climb to the top of the forest. After 1 minute, you will reach the start of the single track (signposted) ready to zigzag your way back and forth through the pine forest. At the bottom, the track exits the forest and climbs up to a BMX track quite close to the rugby club. Make sure you avoid the 'bear trap' jump near the end.

Notes This is about the smallest mountain bike park in the country. The track builders have done well to get so much out of it, and they have plans to build more. For more info, check out www.franklinmtb.org.nz

Waikato

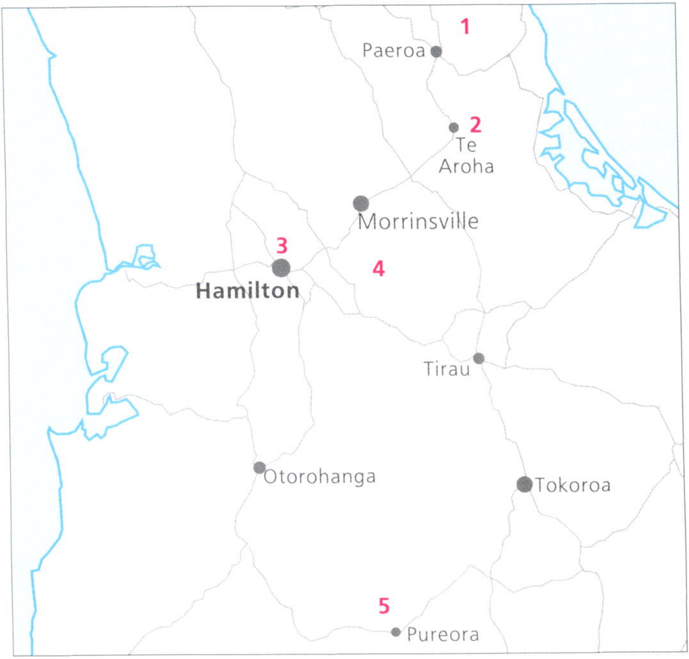

Paeroa **1**

2
Te
Aroha

Morrinsville

3
Hamilton **4**

Tirau

Otorohanga

Tokoroa

5
Pureroa

1 Wires Road
2 Te Aroha
3 Pukete Mountain Bike Track
4 Te Miro MTB Park
5 Pureroa Forest

WAIKATO HIGHLIGHTS

It's pretty slim pickings in the Waikato, but the small town of Te Aroha, with hot pools and a well-established mountain bike track, is a worthwhile destination. The best purpose-built tracks are at Te Miro MTB Park, an area with a constantly morphing track network.

1 Wires Road

INTERMEDIATE

90 km northeast of Hamilton

Grade 3, 2–3 hours, 20–30 km ★ ★

Rough 4WD tracks provide plenty of exploration potential on the Coromandel Range.

How to get there About 9 km north of Paeroa, turn right onto Maratoto Road. After 7 km, turn left onto Wires Road and park at the ford 500 metres down the road.

Route description From here, the gravel road soon becomes a rough 4WD track and climbs onto the Coromandel Range. There are a few tracks to explore up here before heading back down the same way.

This is a popular off-road vehicle area, but it is sometimes closed due to bad weather; best ridden when bone dry.

Track conditions Mostly 4WD tracks

Notes The Wentworth Track on the eastern side of the range is not open to bikes. Check out Topomap T12 Thames. DOC has a pamphlet on this area, titled 'Maratoto and the Wentworth Valley'.

Ann Williams on Wires Road.

2 Te Aroha

Te Aroha, 40 km northeast of Hamilton

Grades 2–3+, 1–2.5 hours, up to 11 km   ★ ★ ★

A fine ride for fit groups of varying experience levels, this fun track starts at the entrance to the Te Aroha Domain, right where the hot springs are.

Route description   From the hot springs, head out of the domain, right up Boundary Street and follow your handlebar stem to the new town water tank. From the water tank, the track is signposted all the way round and has a few optional 'hard' loops, which add a couple of challenging kilometres to the main track. Watch out for other users when coasting back down the last section of dual-use track.

The blue route markers are reflective, so this also makes a good night ride. A lot of effort has gone into making the tracks enjoyable all year round, but they're still a grade harder when wet.

Track conditions   99% single track

Notes   Te Aroha has an interesting history on display at the museum in the domain. There is a free trail map, available from the information centre or bike shop, but it isn't essential for the ride. The bike shop is Outdoor Adventure, located at 204 Whitaker St, phone (07) 884 4545. It has bikes for hire.

3 Pukete Mountain Bike Track

Hamilton

Grade 2, 20–40 mins, 2–5 km   ★

The Hamilton Mountain Bike Club has packed a bunch of nice grade-2 tracks into this small area—half park, half wasteland on the outskirts of town.

How to get there   Head north from the centre of Hamilton on State Highway 1 for 7–8 km, turn right onto Kapuni Road and right again after 100 metres onto Maui St. After 200 metres, look for a 'Pukete Farm Park, Hamilton Mountain Bike Club' sign on the left.

Route description   Ride through the paddock and around to the left until you see a gate and more mountain bike related signs. Follow the arrows and expect to get a little lost. Give yourself 30 minutes to blast around or longer if you repeat a few sections.

Notes   This area hosted the 2008 Cyclocross Champs.

4 Te Miro MTB Park

16 km south of Morrinsville

Grades 3–5, 1–3 hours, 5–20 km   ★★

Te Miro is a mixed bag. Some of the old classics like Gobblers Knob were closed a few years back because of logging but have now been reopened. However, logging is continuing, and other tracks are getting the axe.

How to get there   Pick up a map from Kaimai Cycles in Morrinsville or www.kaimaicycles.co.nz/temiro.html. From Morrinsville, drive southeast on Studholme Street. This becomes

Murray Drake

Dude! Where's my single track?

the Morrinsville-Walton Road and 1 km from town, at a railway line, veers right. About 10 km from town, veer right onto Chepmell Road and then, after another 700 metres, turn left onto Waterworks Road. This is a narrow windy road in places. After about 7 km, stop at a small parking area just above a lake.

Route description   From the car park, swing over the small gate and look for a track among pampas on your left. This takes you to the start of the PD Track only 100 metres away. The PD boys have built a long, mostly downhill track into the forest. It's good fun.

From the bottom of the PD Track, cross an old bridge and head left on a gravel road for 150 metres, then cut across an old skid site onto an old 4WD track. After 10 minutes, you will have climbed to the top of Gobblers Knob, one of the best tracks at Te Miro. It's 4 km long and mostly downhill. Follow the Joiner Link and Kaimeleon to return to the car park. This is a neat introductory loop, but there's lots more to explore.

Track conditions   10% forestry road, 20% 4WD, 70% single track
Notes   In 2008, tracks were being built in the native forest out the back. They are best ridden when bone dry.

5 Pureora Forest

69 km southeast of Te Kuiti

DOC has produced an excellent pamphlet titled 'Mountain Biking Pureora'. It includes a map showing 14 rides. Some are short dead ends not worth doing, but the three described below are good loop trips.

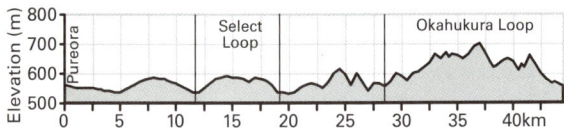

Bikers usually base themselves at Pureora Village, where there's a DOC information centre, cabins and a camping ground but no shops. It's a great place for a mountain biking holiday.

How to get there   Pureora is in the middle of nowhere. That's part of its charm. From Te Kuiti, head southeast on Highway 30 for just over 60 km. Just short of Barryville, turn right and drive 2.5 km to the DOC Forest Field Centre.

Select Loop Road

Grade 1+, 1 hour, 29 km from Pureora   ★

Route description   You can drive to the start of this 7-km loop, but that spoils half the fun of the ride. Instead, from the information centre, pedal northeast out to Highway 30 and turn left. After 2 km, turn right at the Pureora Forest sign (Waitaramoa Road). Follow this road for about 6 km and you will arrive at the start of Select Loop Road (signposted).

The loop is best done in a clockwise direction, so ride another 100 metres then turn right onto the other end of Select Loop Rd (not signposted). Head past the pines (cleared in 2008) and into dense native forest. Just stay on the main track (an old gravel road) and you will do an easy loop back round to the start. You can't go wrong. This area is being ecologically restored, so the ride is likely to become an ornithologist's utopia.

Okahukura Loop
Grade 3, 2 hours, 14–34 km ★ ★

How to get there This ride starts 10 km up the road from Select Loop Road. It's an old forestry road, too rough for your average 2WD, but makes for a good ride.

Route description From Highway 30 (just north of the Pureora Field Centre), head north up Waitaramoa Road, past Select Loop Road and on to Okahukura Road (signposted). Exactly 15 km from the highway, you'll reach a large clearing with a signpost —'Mountain Bike Loop'.

Lush regenerating forest on Okahukura Loop.

Head left at the signpost, across a small bridge and up into the forest. The track is quite mellow for the first 5 km, then becomes more interesting round the back with a few ruts and bogs. Route finding is easy–just stay on the main track all the way back to the start.

Waione Tram Track
Grade 4+, 3–6 hours, 26 km ★ ★

Route description This is the toughest of the three loops in Pureora Forest and the only ride in the book we haven't been able to complete, because the rivers were up. DOC staff told us it should only be attempted in summer. The track is not marked on the topomaps, so you need the DOC pamphlet.

The trip starts from the remote Piropiro Flats, south of Pureora Village. It's a long 80-km dog-leg of a drive to get there from Pureora! From the picnic area, ride south on Totara Stream Road and veer right to tackle the steep Panhandle, which is a clay quad bike track. A series of ups and downs takes you to the start of the loop. Follow the map on the pamphlet carefully. Getting lost in here would be serious.

Notes   The Pureora camping ground is 500 metres down the road from the information centre and in 2008 cost $7 per night per adult. The cabins need to be booked and cost $24 per night for a 2- to 3-bunk cabin and $48 per night for a 6-bunk cabin.

There's also an old-fashioned DOC camping area at Piropiro Flats. For more info, contact DOC in Pureora on phone (07) 878 1080.

STOP PRESS! Central North Island Rail Trail

The Dept of Conservation is planning a major rail trail project that will connect Ongarue (just north of Taumarunui) and Pureora, a distance of 60km. It will follow an old bush tramway into the vast Pureora Forest. In addition to new 'cookhouse' accommodation and camp sites, several loop tracks will be developed.

The total extent of new track for biking will eventually exceed 100km and will connect to the existing Pureora mountain bike tracks accessed from Piropiro Flats. Planning is well advanced and it is anticipated the track upgrade work will start in 2009. The first stages will involve drainage and earthworks along the route, which will be developed in sections; followed by a programme of upgrading the track surfaces, where required.

Check with DOC in Hamilton for an update.

Bay of Plenty

1	Stony Bay	**8**	Te Rawhiti MTB Park
2	Whitianga MTB Park	**9**	Tauranga Bridge
3	Whangamata Forest	**10**	Te Waiti Hut
4	Thompsons Track	**11**	Military Track
5	Oropi Grove	**12**	Pakihi Track
6	Summerhill Recreation Farm	**13**	Old Motu Coach Road
7	TECT All Terrain Park	**14**	Otipi Road

BAY OF PLENTY HIGHLIGHTS

There's a huge diversity of mountain biking in the Bay of Plenty—rides for everyone to love, and hate. The most exciting trails are at the new Te Rawhiti MTB Park, just out of Whakatane. Tauranga has two good riding areas with purpose-built tracks: Oropi Grove and Summerhill. But for old-school back-country style rides, Opotiki is the real hot spot.

1 Stony Bay

Top of the Coromandel Peninsula

Grade 4, 1–2 hours, 7 km 👎

It's hard to be grumpy in such a beautiful part of the world, unless you're 'riding' a really poxy track.

How to get there Drive 50 km north from Coromandel township to Stony Bay. The last 7 km is 'Unmaintained Road'.

Route description From Stony Bay, a steep, semi-rideable 4WD track hauls its way over a huge hill to Fletchers Bay.

It's well signposted and has been designated for mountain biking, with the aim of keeping cyclists off the walking track, which is infinitely more enjoyable (and safer) to ride but illegal.

After a 3-km hike up a rough, slippery stock route, you dive just as steeply down towards Fletchers Bay. Be warned—this track is slippery when wet and is often covered in cow pats.

Notes There are DOC camping areas at both ends of the track. As the DOC signs state, this track is unsuitable for cycle touring.

Surprisingly, hundreds of people 'bike and hike' this horrible excuse for a mountain bike track every year during a popular event called the Colville Connection. Why? Because the riding to and from the road ends is so good that it justifies a little torture in the middle. But as a stand-alone ride? Forget it!

2 Whitianga MTB Park

3.5 km from Whitianga

Grades 3–5, 1–2 hours, up to 10 km   ★ ★

This is a small MTB park, packed with single tracks containing enough variety to suit most riders.

How to get there Pick up a map from The Bike Man at 16 Coghill Street in Whitianga. Head out of town on Joan Gaskill Drive, turn left onto Highway 25, then right onto Moewai Road. Park at the small but signposted parking area.

Route description From the parking area, cross the road and enter the park at the signposted gate. There are several signs there, just in front of all the wooden structures. Follow the track across to the forested hill. There are about 6 km of track to explore, starting with Tank Entry. More tracks were being built in 2008.

Notes See www.whitiangabikeclub.co.nz for more details.

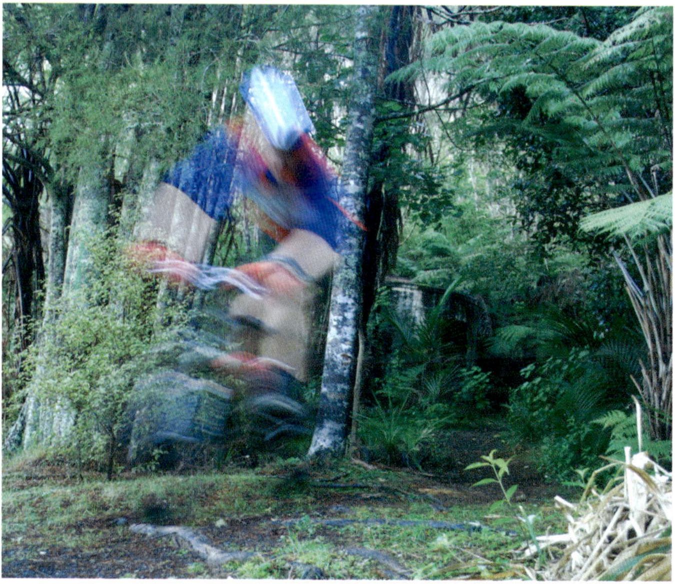

Floating through Whitianga.

3 **Whangamata Forest**

Whangamata

Grades 3–4, 1–4 hours, 5–50 km ★

This pine forest has a mixture of forestry and single tracks.

Landowners You need a permit (minimum of $10 for one month) and map to ride in this Rayonier NZ Ltd forest. Drop in to the information centre in Whangamata (phone 09 865 8340).

How to get there Ride northwest out of Whangamata along Highway 25 to the Carter Holt Harvey Tairua Forest HQ.

Route description The single tracks are hard to find, but most are tagged with small mountain bike markers at the start. Here's a recommended loop: Cycle via tracks 7, 4 and 2 to Otuwheti Road. There is a lookout about 50 metres west of the top of track number 2. Then sweat your way up Middle Ridge. Drop down Manuka Road and head back along Otuwheti Road.

  You'll definitely need the map to follow this route.

Track conditions A mixture of forestry roads and single tracks

4 **Thompsons Track**

30 km northeast of Tauranga

Grade 3, 2–3 hours, 20 km one way ★ ★

To be honest, many people don't enjoy this steep and muddy ride. But, in dry conditions, some love it for its remote scenery.

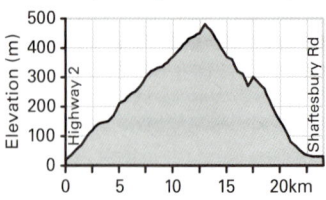

How to get there Turn off Highway 2 down Thompsons Track Road, about 30 km west of Tauranga. We recommend parking at the highway and riding up to the road end 5.5 km away. It's a good gravel road ride.

Route description You can cycle right over the Kaimai Range to Shaftesbury or just to the top and back. It takes 1–2 hours to the top from the tarseal and about 40 minutes down the other side, which is very rocky. There are a few big bogs on the eastern side, including one real bike gobbler early on.

At the top, it's worth taking a hard left turn and checking out the views from the trig 200 metres away.

Notes Refer to Topomap T14 Morrinsville. If you're only riding this track one way, it's easier west to east. Thompsons Track, is also used by 4WD vehicles, which have wrecked parts of it.

5 Oropi Grove

5 km southwest of Tauranga

Grades 2–5, 1–2 hours, up to 15 km   ★ ★ ★

This popular park is full of single tracks, jumps and stunts.

Route description From Highway 29 on the southern edge of Tauranga, follow Oropi Road for 3 km to the well signposted car park.

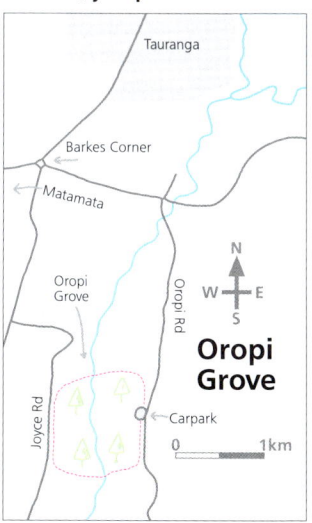

Check out the map board at the car park to plan your trip, then head into the forest on the single track to the left, behind the map board (that's 'Entry Track').

For your first ride, you should at least aim to get across to Joyce Road (the far side of the park and back). This area is not huge, so you can't get lost for long.

Track conditions 5% gravel road, 95% single track

Notes There are Oropi Grove MTB Park maps available at Tauranga bike shops. There's a toilet and washdown pad adjacent to the car park. These tracks are best ridden when dry.

6 Summerhill Recreation Farm

11 km southeast of Tauranga

Grades 2–4, 1–3 hours, up to 20 km ★ ★ ★

Part of this unusual farm has been developed for recreational mountain biking. The farm is owned by philanthropist and adventurer David Blackley and managed by mountain bike pioneer Karl Young.

How to get there From the southern outskirts of Tauranga, head east on Welcome Bay Road for several kilometres. Turn right on Reid Road and after another 3 km you'll reach a car parking area with toilets, showers and an information kiosk.

Route description At the information kiosk, register, give your donation, check out the info board and pick up a map. Ride through the kiosk and veer left to follow the track of your choice. The tracks are well signposted and cover areas of pasture and forest (exotic and native) on single track and 4WD track. Most are grade 3–4 tracks, but there is also an easy trail in the avocado grove, and more difficult tracks are planned for other areas.

This unique farm is an ideal location for social mountain biking. Expansive views, specimen forests, Mongolian gers and great single track combine to make Summerhill a truly unique experience.

Track conditions 10% 4WD farm track, 90% single track

Notes Please leave farm gates as you find them. To camp on the farm, or for general info, email info@summerhillfarm.co.nz or phone (07) 542-1838. Entry is by gold coin donation.

7 TECT All Terrain Park

Between Tauranga and Rotorua

This is an interesting project. Tauranga City and Western Bay District councils have bought over 1650 hectares of forestry land for a park to provide for motorised and non-motorised recreation as well as outdoor education and conservation activities.

The Park is being developed with a keen eye toward sustainability, so expect to see green building design, solar power, and sustainable tracks and trails built to international standards. Park manager Ric Balfour is looking forward to working with local mountain bikers to develop some world-class riding with plans for xc trails, 4x, downhill, free-riding and kids learning area. There are plans for a park opening in 2009. For an update see www.westernbay.govt.nz/Projects/AllTerrainPark

8 Te Rawhiti MTB Park

INTERMEDIATE   ADVANCED

11 km southeast of Whakatane

Grades 3–4, 1–3 hours, up to 15 km   ★ ★ ★

The tracks here have been well designed and built and are definitely worth trying out.

How to get there   This is an active logging area, so you need a permit to ride here. Pick up a permit and map for $5 from the Whakatane Information Centre, the Ohope Beach Holiday Park or any of the bike shops in Whakatane. These places should all be able to give you directions to the car park off Burma Road.

Route description   From the car park, throw your bike over the access gate and ride up the main forestry road. Head up the hill and onto the Ground Effect Grinder (test out Rex's Rat

Jonathan Kennett

Rex's Rat Run

Run en route). You will now have two choices of downhill. Mal's Mayhem is a purpose-built track with some awesome berms on the way down, then turn left and hook onto the Bobcat Exit Track. Alternatively, for a more old-school ride, take Works Whoops. Either way you'll have a blast.

There are more tracks being built, and more forest being logged, so expect major changes. The Whakatane Mountain Bike Club do a great job, so the new tracks will be guaranteed fun.

Burma Road—Riders who aren't into steep hills or narrow tracks could well enjoy riding Burma Road. It heads from the car park across a bridge on the right and through farmland to a gravel road a few kilometres away. This is an ideal easy ride for those wanting to keep fit.

Notes This is a production forest. If logging is happening, consult with the foreman before entering the park. If you're into racing, don't miss the Ohope Ordeal in late March.

9 Tauranga Bridge

ADVANCED

27 km south of Opotiki

Grade 4, 1 hour, 6.5-km loop ★

This interesting ride is high in historic and scenic values.

How to get there From Opotiki, drive south on Highway 2 for 27 km. Look out for a large parking area on the right-hand side of the road.

Route description From the car park, follow a wide zigzag track down to the historic Tauranga Bridge, 200 metres away. Cross the large bridge and ride up a signposted single track on the southern side of a side valley. After 3 kilometres, ford the stream and ride back down the valley on the other side. This track has some narrow sections with large drop-offs to avoid.

Just as the side valley approaches the main Waioeka River, you'll have to drop down to the stream and wade across it again. The bridge is then only 100 metres away.

Notes In 2008, this track was only 90% rideable. DOC has plans to maintain it, so it might be much easier when you get there. For an update, call DOC in Opotiki on (07) 315 1001.

A rare sighting of the lesser-known Swamp Thing.

10 Te Waiti Hut

16 km southeast of Opotiki

Grade 3+, 2–3 hours, 21 km return   ★ ★

This is a scenic single track ride through native bush.

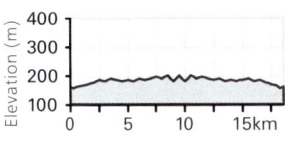

How to get there Head south from Opotiki on St Johns Street. Just past the edge of town, turn left onto Otara Road and drive/ride for another 14 km to a single-lane bridge.

Route description Don't cross the bridge. Instead carry straight ahead and cross a ford. About 10 minutes on from the ford, you will reach a point where the narrow road drops down to Bushaven Lodge and the track is signposted to the right. Veer right and, from here, you will be riding on a narrow bush track.

There are some long, steep drops off the side of this track and, when we went through in 2008, the track needed cutting back so we had to take it easy. After almost an hour, you'll drop down to Te Waiti Stream. The hut is only 500 metres further on in a

Jonathan Kennett

Quiet earth riding in Te Waiti Valley.

large clearing, but be aware that this stream becomes uncrossable after heavy rain.

Most local riders just turn round and head back from the hut. If you're keen, you can bash further up valley for a few kilometres to Stag Flat (grid ref. 976 265), but it's hardly worth it. The ride back from the hut is ever so slighty downhill and a lot of fun.

Notes Bushaven Lodge, mentioned in the last edition, is now closed. This trip is marked on Topomap X16 Motu, but you don't really need it. Navigation is easy.

11 Military Track

20 km east of Opotiki

Grade 4+, 3–5 hours, 20 km   ★ ★ ★

ADVANCED

This old-school ride was used for the national series in 2008 and got a lot of good feedback because it is one wild adventure. Even navigation is challenging.

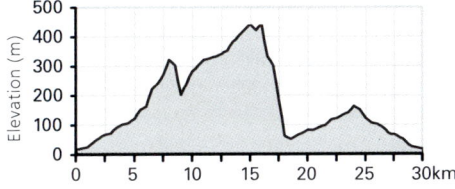

How to get there Drive east out of Opotiki for 11 km. Turn right onto Motu Road and drive for another 3 km before turning right again onto Gaskill Road. Locals sometimes park just along this road by the small church. Once you've gone 600 metres down Gaskill Road, just after a bridge, turn left to stay on Gaskill Road. Then after 1 km, turn right onto Block Access Road. This is a forestry road and despite slips was being kept open in 2008 for logging.

Route description The race was a big loop that started at a large flat clearing 5 km up Block Access Road. From the clearing, head left and climb up a forest road for 10 minutes. Turn right at 'Valley Stn Rd' and climb less steeply up an old forestry road. After another 15 minutes, you'll reach a fork where a toy koala

Paul rips down the Third Sister.

Jonathan Kennett

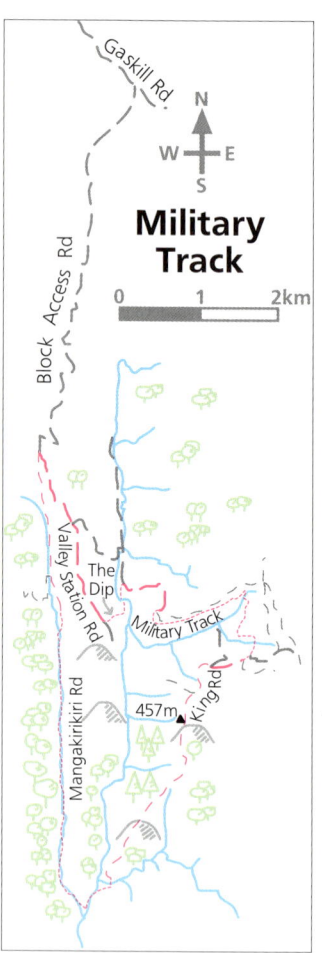

bear is tied to a tree. At this point, you should veer left and ride down 'The Dip' to a stream 5 minutes away.

Cross the stream and climb up a single track for 5 minutes to reach a large forestry road. Turn right and cruise along this main road for almost 10 minutes before veering right—at the signposted 'Military Track'.

Military Track was built in the 1860s and is now perfect for mountain biking, with one exception: a storm in 2008 blew some trees down near the start, which are difficult to clamber over.

After cruising along Military Track for about 40 minutes, you will reach a T-intersection with a 'King Road' signpost. Turn right and head along a bulldozed track. After 5 minutes, ignore a left turn—go straight. This road becomes a steep downhill track that ends with 'The Three Sisters'. This is the only grade 5 part of the ride. Take care.

At the river terrace, turn right and ride down valley, crossing the Mangatakaho/Taipouri Stream six times. After the sixth crossing, ride up to a farm fence on the right bank and follow it down valley 100 metres before heading right through a gate.

From the gate, you will be following a track called Mangakirikiri Road up valley for almost 5 km back to the large clearing you started from. There are 30 stream crossings in this section.

Track conditions 20% forest road, 30% 4WD, 50% single track

Notes This ride will leave you with a bucket of water in your bottom bracket and pedal bearings. Topomaps X15 and X16 only show some of the tracks. Take a compass or GPS for safety.

12 Pakihi Track–closed

In 2007, a big storm closed the Pakihi Track, dropping a load of trees and opening up some large slips. The damage is so bad that the track is now dangerous to walk, let alone ride a bike along. DOC plans to reopen it as a tramping route in 2009, but it doesn't sound like the Pakihi will ever be fully rideable again.

13 Old Motu Coach Road

Matawai to Opotiki

Grade 2, 4–8 hours, up to 77 km ★ ★

Motu Road is one of the roughest, most scenic public roads in the North Island. The road is usually closed to motorised vehicles after storms because of slips and flooded fords.

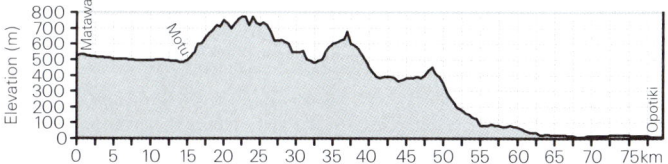

How to get there Matawai (550 m), the starting point on this ride, lies halfway between Gisborne and Opotiki on Highway 2. From there, head north to Motu township, 14 km away. Matawai has the last dairy, hotel and restaurant for 70 km. Stock up well.

Route description From the tiny Motu township, a narrow gravel road climbs into the hills and forest. There are awesome views for many kilometres during the ride along the ridge and then plenty of downhill en route to the Bay of Plenty. There are also many small grassy areas for resting or camping along the way. In places, the road crosses slopes so precarious that you are left wondering how much longer it will remain open.

About 70 km from Matawai, you'll reach the Tirohanga Beach Motorcamp and Store. It's then an easy 7 km to the bustling township of Opotiki.

Track conditions 40% sealed road, 60% gravel road

Notes To eliminate transport complications, many people simply ride part way up from Opotiki before heading back the same way. The top of the Pakihi Track is a good turn-around spot.

If it has been raining a lot, it's worth making a detour to check out Motu Falls, near Motu township. Take any good road map.

14 Otipi Road

INTERMEDIATE

33 km southeast of Opotiki

Grade 3, 4–5 hours, 60 km return   ★ ★

This is a scenic back-country ride, requiring fitness and some outdoor savvy. It follows a road that was built in 1952 when the Motu River was proposed as a hydro dam site. The dam never happened, and the road is now a great adventure ride.

How to get there From Opotiki, drive east for 10 km before turning right onto the Motu Road. After another 23 km, you will reach Toatoa at the 'Takaputahi Rd' sign. Park here.

Route description From Toatoa, ride east on Petipeti Road for 10 km. This is a rough and scenic road. Just after breaking out of a particularly narrow gorge, you'll reach a large bridge (on your left) with a DOC parking area (straight ahead) and the start of the Otipi Road (across a ford on your right).

Cross the ford and follow the old road up into the forest. There are several major slips to negotiate on the way, but generally the road is a grade-3 ride. Views from the top are worth the climb, and although some people carry on down to the Motu River, many prefer to turn around at this point. This is a there-and-back ride.

Track conditions Narrow gravel road, rough 4WD track and single track

Notes There's no longer a hut by the Motu River—just a campsite. The trip is shown on Topomap X16 Motu.

Rotorua and Taupo

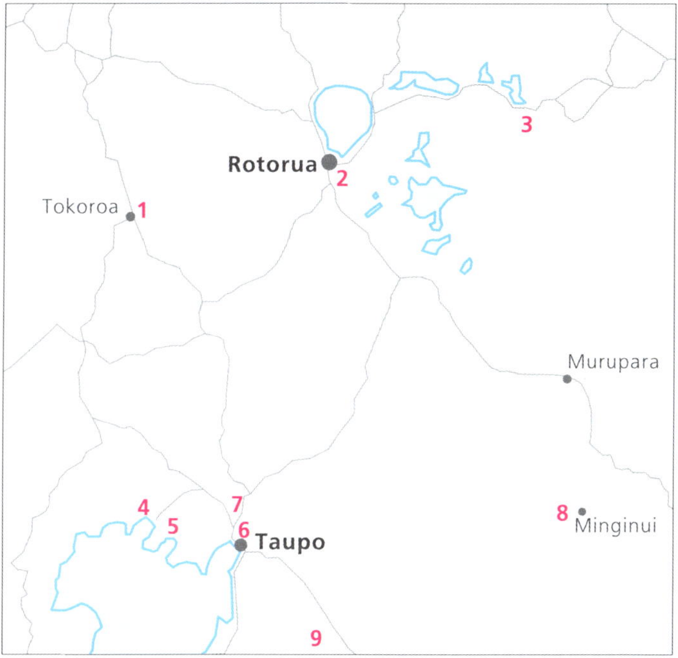

Rotorua

Tokoroa **1**

2

3

Murupara

4 **7**

5 **6** Taupo

8 Minginui

9

1 Cougar Park
2 Whakarewarewa
3 Lake Rotoma Forest
4 Kawakawa Bay
5 W2K
6 Waikato River Tracks
7 Wairakei MTB Tracks
8 Whirinaki Forest
9 Te Iringa

ROTORUA AND TAUPO HIGHLIGHTS

Most of the rides in this chapter are exceptional. First mention has to go to Rotorua's Whakarewarewa Forest—one of the biggest and best track networks in the country. That's why Rotorua has more bike shops per capita than anywhere else in New Zealand. But in some regards, Taupo, with its excellent new W2K track and well-established Waikato River Trails, is jostling for top spot. Meanwhile, out in Whirinaki Forest, DOC is working hard to build the longest, most scenic biking tracks in the North Island. It's all good.

1 Cougar Park

Tokoroa

Grades 2–5, 1–4 hours, up to 35 km ★ ★

For a quiet alternative to Rotorua, Cougar Park is a good choice.

How to get there Start by picking up a park map from the info centre on State Highway 1 in Tokoroa. From there, head southeast on the highway for 500 metres, turn left onto Mossop Road and left again after another 500 metres. Cougar Park is at the end of the road near the cricket ground.

Route description Head across the right-hand side of the field, over the bridge and then to the left of the ridge to get warmed up on a gentle contour track. Use the map to make a ride of whatever length tickles your fancy. In 2008, new track signs were put up in the forest and the map was redrawn.

Notes The Tokoroa club has a 25-year lease on this new area, so it's bound to get better and better as time goes by.

2 Whakarewarewa

3 km southeast of Rotorua

Grades 1–6, 1 hour to 2 days, up to 100 km ★ ★ ★ ★

Described as the 'Disneyland of mountain biking', Whaka-rewarewa contains some of the best purpose-built mountain bike trails in New Zealand.

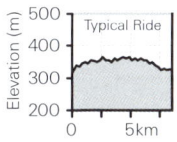

How to get there Head out of Rotorua towards Taupo for 3 km. One kilometre past the '100 kph' sign, turn left at the 'Cycle Trails' sign and ride 200 metres down Waipa Mill Road to the car park on the left. Alternatively, follow the cycle track from town to Long Mile Road.

Route description Pick up a $5 trail map from the forest Visitor Centre on Long Mile Road, or the MTB car park or any bike shop in town.

The excellent trail map shows all the forestry roads and mountain bike tracks. Every track is signposted at the start and finish and graded from 1 to 6 on the signposts and the trail map. The sheer

Redwoods by night—magic!

number of possibilities can be bewildering, so here are some suggestions for starting off.

For the easiest possible ride, stick to the forestry roads. You can just cruise along, side by side and head out for 20 minutes or 2 hours. No stress—just a good bit of exercise.

Next up are the fun grade-2 single tracks close to the Waipa Mill Road car park. Head out on the Tahi Trail, blast around The Dipper and fly home on the second part of the Tahi Trail. If you enjoyed that, head back and try the grade-3 Challenge Trail that links onto the grade-4 Rock Drop.

For experienced riders, the real drawcards at Whakarewarewa are the newer, and longer, 'outback trails'. The trail map shows four great 'outback' loops, ranging from 2 to 4 hours, on mostly grade 3 and 4 tracks. They are all worth doing. If for some silly reason you only have one day to ride in Rotorua, we recommend the following 30-km loop.

From the car park, cut straight to the chase by riding the gravel roads to the bottom of the A-Trail, a single-track treat that flows on to the similarly scenic Tickler. This ends at a rest area with a map board and water fountain. From there, follow Direct Rd and Frontal Lobotomy up to Billy T, one of the best intermediate downhills in the forest, surpassed by only one ... the single-track perfection of Split Enz. From the bottom of Billy T, ride Moerangi Road and Loop Road across to the start of Split Enz. There is a good rest spot halfway down, which has great views over Whakarewarewa. The downhill leads straight onto Pondy and the Chinese Takeaways. Finish off with Be Rude Not 2 and Mad If You Don't.

There's lots more to explore, and additional tracks are being built as we write.

Track conditions 70–80% single track, 20–30% forestry roads

Notes Walkers are not allowed on the mountain bike tracks and vice versa, so it's best not to wander off the marked routes. Most difficult sections of tracks are marked with 'XXX' signs. There is a map board and wash-down stand at the car park. Thanks to the Rotorua Mountain Bike Club, there's also a toilet

Jonathan Kennett

Whakarewarewa... a mountain bike mecca. Amen.

a couple of hundred metres into the forest from the car park. New map boards have been put at several key intersections around the forest.

Southstar Adventures provide a shuttling service. It costs $10 per trip to shuttle the main downhill tracks. Check out www.southstaradventures.com

3 Lake Rotoma Forest

40 km east of Rotorua

Grade 3, 1–2 hours, 13 km ★ ★

This ride is an honest mix of heaven and hell. There's some magnificent native forest, but the track tends to get overgrown from time to time. If it hasn't been maintained recently, you'll soon know, so go prepared to do your own track clearing or turn around and head elsewhere.

How to get there The track entrance is difficult to spot, especially if you're in a car. Park at the lakeside picnic area at Lake Rotoma

Time warp on the timeless Rotoma track.

(40 km east of Rotorua), and then ride east on Highway 30 over the hill for 2.4 km before looking out for an obscure opening in the bush on your right.

Route description Ride down into the forest. Within 10 minutes, you will cross Waikanapiti Stream and a few hundred metres later reach a fork in the track—this is the start/end of the loop. Continue along the main track for a good 20 minutes. During a short downhill stretch along a waist-deep rut, you'll reach a fork. Go right and ride down to a clearing by Waikanapiti Stream—a great spot for a rest because from there it's climb time.

This next section is very scenic, but it is steep, and many riders will need to walk it, especially if it's wet. It's about a half-hour ascent. As soon as you enter a clearing with some pines ahead, you've reached the top. Turn right and head back into native forest for a curly downhill. When you rejoin the main track, turn left and pedal back to the highway.

Track conditions 30% 4WD track, 70% single track

4 Kawakawa Bay

Kinloch, Lake Taupo

Grade 4, 3–4 hours, 14 km return   ★ ★ ★

This old walking track provides excellent technical riding for experienced riders. The scenery is fantastic.

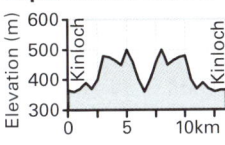

How to get there To drive or ride, that is the question. The W2K track mentioned below is an excellent warm-up for this ride. Alternatively, drive 20 km from Taupo to Kinloch.

A third option is to take a water taxi from Taupo to Kawakawa Bay and ride back.

Route description From the shop at Kinloch, head west along the lake front, on a minor track for a few hundred metres. Just after going over a small bridge, head left to ride on the sand beside the shore for 200 metres. This will take you to an obvious signposted start of the Kawakawa Track.

The track itself is generally sweet native bush single track, but you should expect to spend about 10% of the time walking, double that if it's wet. There is one particularly awesome vista from the top of the last climb. It takes about 1–2 hours to get to Kawakawa Bay, where there's a secluded beach and toilet. It's a dead-end track but actually rides better on the way out. Enjoy!

Track conditions 100% single track

Notes Remember to expect walkers around any blind corner.

5 W2K

15 km west of Taupo

Grade 2+, 2 hours one way, 14 km ★ ★ ★ ★

The beautiful Whakaipo Bay to Kinloch single track is the latest feather in Bike Taupo's helmet and it's a stunner at that.

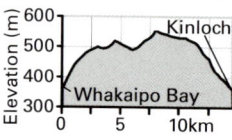

How to get there Ride or drive north out of Taupo on Highway 1 and within 1 km turn left at the large 'Acacia Bay' sign. After 8 km, you'll reach the small Acacia Bay suburb and should turn right up Mapara Road. After a further 6 km, at the bottom of a downhill, watch out for a small turn-off on your left that is signposted 'Whakaipo Bay Recreation Reserve'.

Route description The W2K track starts from the western end of the bay and is well signposted. Hop over a large stile and check out the signboard. Once you pick up the first marker post, you can't get lost. This is an ideal intermediate track through native bush with occasional views out over the lake.

After a brilliant 6-km downhill, you'll roll out to a street in Kinloch. Following the marker posts, cross the street and enter the final bit of track down to the bay. There is a neat new boardwalk that takes you towards the lake. Head right at the lake and then follow the marker posts slightly away from the lake to get around the marina. The track ends near the toilets and shops in the 'centre' of town.

Your choices are now; (a) retrace your tracks for a double dose

Simon Kennett

Thomas test-riding W2K.

of sweet single track, (b) carry on and ride the technical track to Kawakawa Bay (see above), or (c) head back via the road.

Track conditions 100% single track

Notes There are toilets and a picnic area in all three bays, and a shop in Kinloch. See www.biketaupo.org.nz for a map of this ride. Work was ongoing in 2008. Bike Taupo are building a long loop out around the Peninsula. Some of it is already rideable and it starts from near the highest point on the W2K Track.

6 Waikato River Tracks

EASY

Taupo

Grade 2+, 2–3 hours, 23 km Aratiatia return ★ ★ ★

There are several great tracks to ride on either side of the Waikato River. The most popular is the Rotary Ride, which goes from Taupo to Huka Falls. From Huka Falls, riders can go to Aratiatia Dam or cross the river and head back down stream. There is also a good track from Huka Falls to the Wairakei MTB tracks.

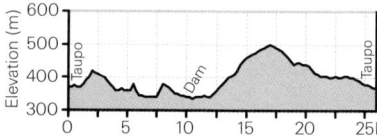

How to get there Pick up the 'Bike Taupo' map for $2 from the Taupo Info Centre, one of the local bike shops or the Helistar Hub Cafe (beside Highway 1, near Huka Falls).

Route description Start with the Rotary Ride. Head northeast of downtown Taupo on Spa Road for a few minutes and turn left onto County Ave—there is a cycle path beside the road. From the car park at the end, you can just make out a Rotary Ride logo post straight ahead. From here, the Rotary Ride is 4 km of varied single track to Huka Falls.

After checking out the falls, backtrack 100 metres to take the Aratiatia Dam track. It starts with a short, sharp uphill and then mellows out as it follows the true right side of the river on a good quality track all the way down to Aratiatia Dam. Time things just right, and you'll be there to watch the impressive water flow when the dam gates open: 10am, 12noon, 2pm and also 4pm from October to March. The gates close 30 minutes after opening.

From Aratiatia Dam, backtrack to Huka Falls. From Huka Falls, you can return to Taupo on the Redwoods Track. Cross the falls bridge and turn left to enter a single track at the end of the car park. The track leads you back to the road. Just across the road you'll find the start of the 2.5 km-long Redwoods Track, which pops out onto Huka Falls Rd again about 2 km from town. Turn right, climb back to State Highway 1, then hang a left to blitz back to the nearest cafe. There is a concrete cycle path running beside the highway.

The other popular choice from Huka Falls is to cross the bridge and head right on a single track that offers two ways to climb to the Helistar Hub Cafe. From there, you can ride through a tunnel track to Wairakei Forest Tracks shown on the other side of the 'Bike Taupo' map and described below.

Track conditions 90% single track, 10% sealed road

Notes There are toilets at Huka Falls and Aratiatia Dam. For the most up-to-date information on these tracks, check out www.biketaupo.org.nz

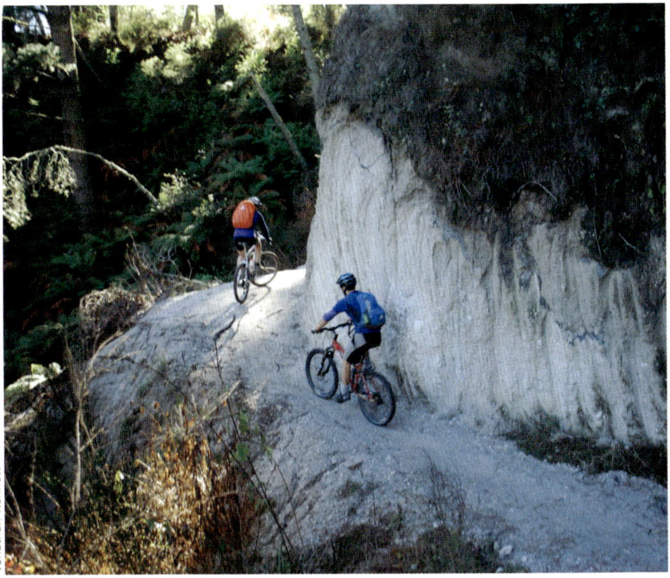

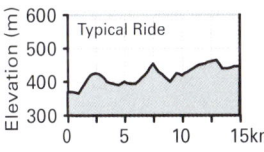

Spinning along the Rotary Ride.

7 Wairakei MTB Tracks

Also known as Craters of the Moon

5 km north of Taupo

Grades 1–3, 1–4 hours, 5–25+ km ★ ★ ★

These sweet purpose-built single tracks weave through mature pine forest at one of New Zealand's oldest MTB areas.

Land managers Wairakei Tourist Park–no permits required.

This area is popular with Taupo riders as it's close to town and provides lots of curly loop tracks to test your skills on. It's good for any rider and any length of time.

Pick up a map from the Taupo Information Centre, the Helistar Hub Cafe or one of the local bike shops.

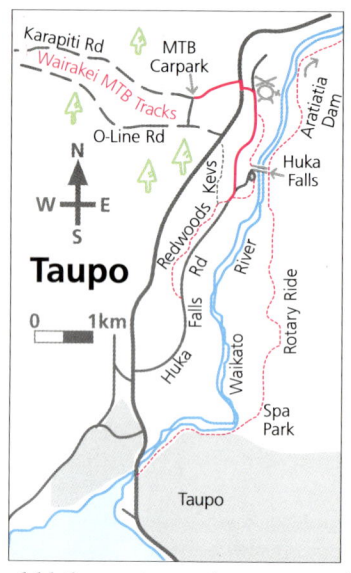

How to get there   You can drive or ride to these tracks from Taupo township. If driving, head north on Highway 1 for 5.5 km and turn left into Karapiti Road. After another couple of hundred metres, turn left onto Powerline Road, where there's a car park and map board. If riding, use the Waikato River Tracks map to take the Rotary Ride, or the Redwoods Track (described in Waikato River Tracks above) to the Helistar Hub Cafe beside Highway 1.

Route description   Presuming you rode to the Hub Cafe, now look for the makeshift fence of old bikes a stones throw away. That's where the Tunnel Track starts, and it leads underneath the highway and across to the main track system.

The first track is Inward Goods, and this leads to the Tourist Trap, which is an excellent starter. This will pop you out at the main mountain bikers' car park.

From the car park, ride through the tunnel and generally uphill on the Lake Hire Link, the Tank Stand and then the Ground Effect Grinder. Phew! Now you have earned a rest, and, more importantly, a long downhill. Fly down the Buzzard and Missing Link, pedal up the Incline and roll the Coaster back to the car park.

Track conditions   90% single track, 10% 4WD and gravel road

Other users   Walkers, equestrians, forestry vehicles. Steer clear of the designated horse riding tracks.

Notes   In 2008, some of the more remote tracks like The Dipper were so covered in pine needles they were hard to follow.

Jonathan Kennett

Beats YouTube any day.

The neighbouring 'Craters of the Moon' is a geothermally active area open to walkers only. From time to time, parts of the forest will be out of bounds due to logging.

8 Whirinaki Forest

EASY

90 km southeast of Rotorua

Grade 2, 1.5–4 hrs, up to 16 km   ★ ★ ★

This new DOC track was built in 2006 especially for mountain bikers. The Rotorua-esque single track links a few old forestry roads and runs through some of the finest native forest you'll see anywhere in New Zealand.

How to get there Whirinaki Forest lies adjacent to Minginui, 90 km from Rotorua via Murupara (on Highway 38). As you approach Minginui, veer right to stay on Minginui Road, right again onto Old Tewaiti Road, cross the river and turn left onto Fort Road (there's a car park/picnic area at the end).

Route description There are short and long loop options, with information panels along the way. The loops are best ridden

Simon Kennett

Whirinaki's famous tree-trunk bridge.

in an anticlockwise direction. From the car park, follow the MTB signs, climbing gently into the forest. After several minutes, turn right to begin the first loop. This becomes '104 Track', which comes out to Okurapoto Road. Turn left to complete the short loop or right for the longer ride back via the sweet Tangitu Track.

Notes Pick up the DOC pamphlet for this ride from the visitor centre in Murupara, phone (07) 366 1080.

STOP PRESS As this book was going to print, DOC was working on a new MTB/tramping track in Whirinaki Forest. The track is being built in three stages, and stage 1 (12 km to Moerangi Hut) has just been completed. DOC estimates that there will be another 20 km of track built by the end of 2009, which will take this new track to the Okahu Road End. The route passes through mature and regenerating native forest with tramping huts along the way. Awesome! To discover more, head out there, or contact the Rangitaiki Visitor Centre, phone (07) 366 1080.

9 Te Iringa

EXPERT

43 km southeast of Taupo

Grade 5, 1–2 days, 38 km return ★ ★ ★

This arduous bike 'n' hike mission is a true classic for lovers of the outdoors with good fitness and bike handling skills.

How to get there Turn right off Highway 5 (Napier-Taupo Road) 27 km southeast from of Taupo, and drive down Taharua Road. After 9.5 km, turn right on to Clements Mill Road. Stop at the car park 5 km down this road.

Route description The semi-rideable track climbs 330 m from the car park to a clearing where the old Te Iringa Hut used to be, then skirts around Mt Te Iringa (1241 m) before dropping down to a swing bridge just downstream from the junction of Tikitiki Stream and Kaipo River.

Cross the swing bridge and turn left to take the main track down the Kaipo Valley to Oamaru Hut (12 bunks) by the confluence of the Kaipo and Oamaru rivers.

This is a big day packed with technical riding, so we recommend staying at the hut overnight and soaking up the wilderness, rather than racing through. From here you have to head back the same way – all the other tracks are closed to bikes – this one is just open as a trial.

Track conditions 100% sweet technical single track!!!

Notes Take Topomap U19 Kaimanawa. The track through Poronui Station along the poled route to Taharua Road crosses private land and is not open to mountain bikers.

Murray Drake

Split Enz—our favourite trail in Whakarewarewa.

Tongariro

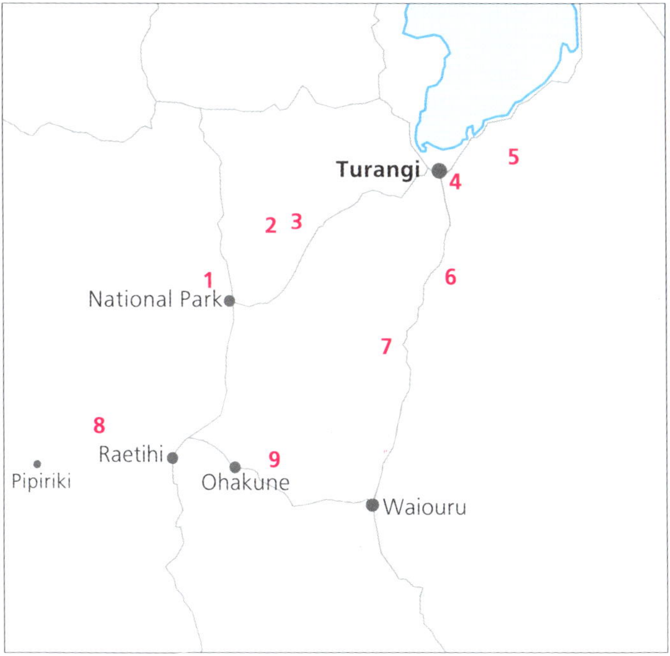

Turangi
5
4
2 3
1
National Park
6
7
8
Raetihi
9
Pipiriki
Ohakune
Waiouru

1 Fishers Track
2 42 Traverse
3 Tongariro Forest Loop
4 Tongariro Walkway
5 Kiko Road Loop
6 Tree Trunk Gorge
7 Tukino Mountain Road
8 Bridge to Nowhere
9 Rangataua Forest

TONGARIRO HIGHLIGHTS

The Tongariro region is home to three of New Zealand's greatest mountain biking adventures; the much loved 42 Traverse, the challenging Tongariro Forest Loop and the stunning Bridge to Nowhere. Tree Trunk Gorge is also a true classic, although quite a bit shorter than most adventure rides. Navigation skills and a first aid kit are essential for all these expeditions—we're talking reality mountain biking here!

1 Fishers Track

National Park

Grade 2, 3–5 hours, 50-km loop ★

Here's a scenic trip for fit cyclists in search of smooth riding.

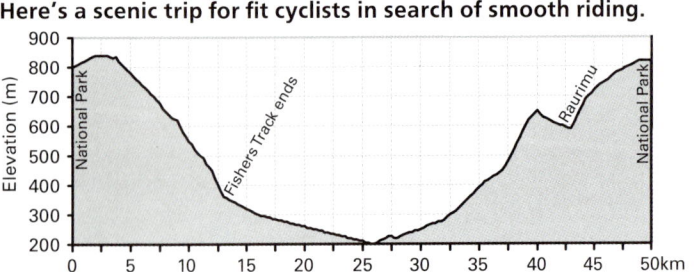

Landowners This ride is on public roads the whole way.

Route description From the northwestern corner of National Park township, cross the railway line and follow the 'Fishers Road' signpost. A gravel road soon turns into a 4WD track as it heads into the native forest.

After about 4 km, ignore a turn-off up a steep climb. For the next 6 km, the navigation is straightforward, views are excellent and it's all downhill. After about half an hour, veer right at the

'Public Rd' sign and keep coasting on down the hill.

   The track meets a gravel road, which eventually leads out to a three-way intersection by a farmhouse. Turn right here and ride 12 km down valley to a war memorial. This is a good spot for a rest because there's 650 m to climb between here and National Park.

Turn right and follow the 'Raurimu' signposts up to Raurimu, then turn right again at Highway 4 and continue climbing up to National Park. Beats going to the gym.

Track conditions 23% sealed road, 42% gravel road, 20% 4WD track, 15% single track

Notes Fishers Track is poxy when wet. Topomap S19 Raurimu or Terrainmap 6 Taranaki show the route.

2 **42 Traverse**

INTERMEDIATE

Tongariro Forest, 18 km northeast of National Park

Grade 3, 3–6 hours, 45 km ★ ★ ★ ★

This is one of the most popular adventure rides in the North Island. It involves brilliant biking on old logging tracks through remote native bush and has an overall descent of 570 m.

Landowners Department of Conservation

How to get there From National Park township, head northeast on Highway 47. After 18 km, you'll reach Kapoors Road on your left (signposted with a DOC route description board). This is the usual drop-off point for the ride as it's predominantly downhill riding from here.

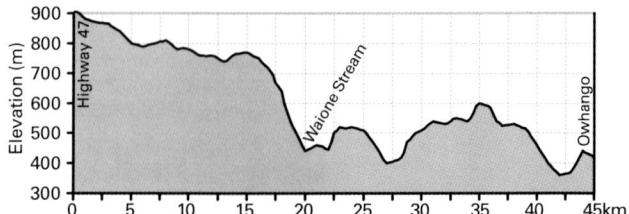

Route description DOC has signposted this track with dark
green roadside markers 10 metres before and after most major
intersections. However, don't count solely on the markers
for navigation—some have disappeared and when you're
spinning along quite fast, it can be hard to spot them.

After riding down Kapoors Road for 7 km, you'll reach a large
cleared area with a few motorbike jumps and another big DOC
sign. Turn right and head north on a 4WD track that follows
the main ridge past high point 831. After 1.5 km, there is a smaller
clearing on your left (Kiwi Clearing) with great views back to
Mt Ruapehu, on a fine day.

The next few kilometres are undulating, and there are a few
major turn-offs to ignore, until you get to an intersection at
grid reference 247 369. Miss this right turn and you will soon
be seriously lost (trust us, we've been there). In 2008, it had a
'Kiwi Zone' sign at it. After turning right, cruise past high point
793.

Now here's a hot tip. Just over 1 km down from 793, you might
notice a little track heading off on your right. This leads to a
fantastic lookout over Echo Canyon. The lookout is only 100 metres
off the main track, at grid reference 264 387, and offers the
best vista on the whole ride.

From the Echo Canyon lookout, the downhill is a universally
popular rip snorter all the way to Waione Stream. If it is wet,
just be wary of the odd slippery patch of clay.

When you reach Waione Stream, follow the main track right
and down valley for a few hundred metres. The track then hangs
another sharp right and climbs steeply away from the stream
for a couple of minutes then swings left and sidles down valley

again. Before long, you'll dive down steeply to meet the main ford across the Waione.

This is the halfway mark, but it's not all downhill from here; there are still a few good uphills to tackle.

The first significant turn-off on the right is called the Pony Club Track, and from here, you can look down into the head of the Whanganui River. Awesome! But don't take any of these enticing-looking turn-offs. Just stick to the  main track, which is called Dominion Road, and you will ride through lovely native bush and past Te Kaha and Waterfall Bridge before blasting down to the Whakapapa River bridge. This is where most people arrange to be picked up, although it is only a 10-minute ride up to Owhango if you're keen to finish the ride off in style. There is a picnic area, toilets and a swimming hole near the bridge and, up at Owhango, a pleasant pub and plenty of accommodation.

Track conditions 35% gravel road, 65% 4WD track

Notes This is an isolated area that has seen many bikers become totally lost. Take extra clothes, food and first aid and make sure someone responsible knows what you're up to. For safety, Topomap S19 Raurimu is essential, but it has some old tracks marked on it that don't exist anymore. The *Tongariro Forest Adventure Map* is now out of print. For this reason, a compass or GPS is recommended.

National Park BackPackers (phone (07) 892 2870 or email nat.park.backpackers@xtra.co.nz) offers a shuttle service.

Budget accommodation is available at Owhango and National Park, and there is a free camping area at the Owhango end of the track (1 km east of Whakapapa River).

The Overlander train can take you and your bike to National Park. After big storms, it's worth checking with the Whakapapa Visitors Centre (phone (07) 892 3729) that all the tracks are open. Some tracks are occasionally impassable due to flooding.

3 Tongariro Forest Loop

EXPERT

aka John McDonald Loop
20 km northest of National Park
Grade 5+, 5–8 hours, 40 km   ★ ★ ★

This is a fantastic trip for fit and skilled riders with lots of outdoors experience. Choose a dry day and take safety glasses, a long-sleeve top and long-fingered gloves as this is now a full-on jungle ride. Expect a toitoi thrashing, a freezing tramp down a mountain stream and difficult navigation. In return for these tribulations, you will be rewarded with awesome downhills, stunning scenery and an honest adventure.

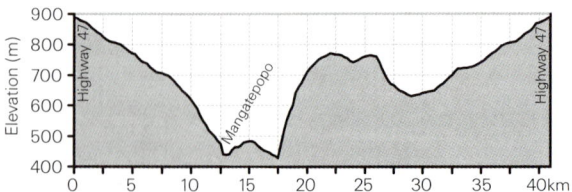

How to get there Start at the picnic area where John McDonald Road meets Highway 47, 4 km south of the Outdoor Pursuits Centre (OPC) turn-off.

Route description This ride used to be called John McDonald Loop, but that road was being logged in mid-2008, so we started from Taurewa, just 2 km south of the OPC road. All the old buildings at Taurewa are now part of OPC as well.

At Taurewa, park your car out of the way and carry your bike across a carpeted footbridge at grid reference 311 334.

Jonathan Kennett

Echo Canyon lookout.

Nip around the side of the lodge and ride down the obvious old forestry road (Pukehinau Road). You will pass John McDonald Road on your left, then 'Taurewa Intake' track on your right and then, after one more kilometre, at grid reference 295 357, you'll reach Danahars Track (not signposted).

Turn right down Danahars Track. The main track narrows to single track and delivers you to a flat area directly above the Mangatepopo Stream. At the northwest corner of the small clearing, a tiny track drops steeply down to the stream. There are ropes to help, but carrying a bike makes the job difficult all the same. Expect to take about 15 minutes to reach the bottom.

When you hit the stream, walk down valley for half an hour to connect with the old OPC-Owhango track where it fords the Mangatepopo Stream. You'll see the OPC end of the track on your right first, then you'll have to continue walking down the stream for another 200 metres to find an uber-steep quad bike track on the left bank. Grovel your way up this for 5 minutes, and you'll reap the reward of being able to return to your saddle.

At the next major intersection, turn right and tackle a steep downhill leading to a bridge (of sorts). Continue on the main

track and, after about 15 minutes, you'll sidle around the east side of a large knoll and meet up with the 42 Traverse track just above Waione Stream.

Head southwest above Waione Stream on the 42 Traverse– it's a 40-minute climb, all rideable (honest!), to the Echo Canyon lookout at grid reference 264 387. After a well-deserved rest, the riding flattens out as you continue along the 42 Traverse to the Pukehinau Track turn-off, on your left, at grid reference 253 360.

Now, blast down this forestry road for a fun 1 km, then keep a look out for a small track branching off on your left. This seems to be the sole domain of quad bikes these days and in 2008 was dangerously rutted at the top. After 50 metres how-ever, it transforms into technical riding bliss! It leads out to a desolate picnic area with toilets and back to Pukehinau Road where you started. Enjoy, if you dare!

Track conditions   35% gravel road, 35% 4WD track, 25% single track, 5% unrideable

Notes   Take the same gear as mentioned in the 42 Traverse write-up. A GPS really is a good idea. Topomaps S19 Raurimu and T19 Tongariro are essential, although not all the roads are marked on them accurately.

4 Tongariro Walkway

EASY

Turangi

Grade 2, 1–2 hours, up to 12 km   ★ ★

This scenic loop is suitable for all riders. However, it's heavily used by walkers and anglers — ride carefully, give way to other users and avoid it during the holiday season.

Route description   From the Turangi Information Centre, head east across the main highway and make your way down to the Tongariro River on Arohori Street. Ride through the park at the end of the street and you'll find the Tongariro Walk-way beside the river.

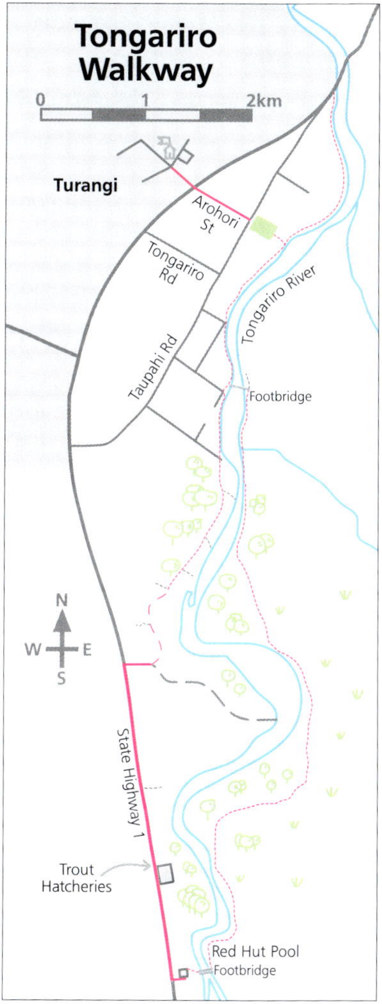

Turn right and follow the walkway up river for at least 5 minutes. New sections of track are being added along here, but before long you will have to head right out to the highway.

Ride south on Highway 1, and 4 km from Turangi, turn left at the 'Red Hut Pool' sign. Drop down to the river and cross the large swing bridge 100 metres away.

After crossing the bridge, follow the main track down river to Turangi. Don't be tempted to turn left down any of the anglers' tracks; they soon peter out at the river. The track rolls through a mixture of scrubby forest and farmland on its way down to another swing bridge at Major Jones Pool, just next to town (you passed it on the way up).

Re-cross the Tongariro River here and head back into Turangi via any one of the several obvious access tracks.

Tongariro Walkway

0   1   2km

Turangi

Arohori St

Tongariro Rd

Taupahi Rd

Tongariro River

Footbridge

N
W   E
S

State Highway 1

Trout Hatcheries

Red Hut Pool
Footbridge

Notes New sections of track continue to be built on the Turangi side of the river.

5 Kiko Road Loop

27 km northeast of Turangi

Grade 2+, 30–60 minutes, 4-km loop ★

A very short, but very fun, easy loop. Well worth it.

How to get there 10 km north of Turangi on Highway 1, turn right on to Kiko Road and make your way 17 km to the road end. Just stay on the main road and switch your lights on as logging trucks are the main users of this gravel road.

Route description This is a mostly flat, benched track, passing through a lush and varied forest that includes matai, miro, red/silver beech, kamahi and rimu.

Also keep an ear out for kaka flying overhead.

Notes The trip is so short, we recommend riding from Motuoapa.

6 Tree Trunk Gorge

22 km south of Turangi

Grade 2+, 2–4 hours, 19 km ★★★

This popular ride has beautiful native forest single track.

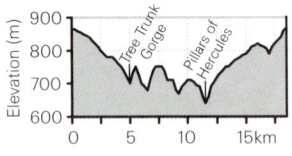

How to get there From Turangi, head south on Highway 1 for 22 km before turning left onto Tree Trunk Gorge Road (signposted). Park just out of sight of the main road.

Route description From the highway, coast 5 km down to the Tongariro River bridge and check out the gorge. Cross the bridge and carry on for 500 metres before turning left onto a track signposted 'Kaimanawa Rd 1 hr'. This is the start of the Tree Trunk Gorge track.

For almost 6 km, this track weaves through native forest, dealing out a steep little climb, a couple of picturesque river fords and two wooden bridges en route. At the first stream crossing, you'll need to look upstream 20 metres to find the ford. You'll be ready for a rest by the time you reach the picnic/camping area beside a gravel road.

Cycle out of the picnic area on the gravel road. After 50 metres, turn left onto another single track. At the end of that satisfying little trundle, hang a left to cross the new Pillars of Hercules bridge. Unfortunately, the new bridge is so high up that you can't really see the Pillars of Hercules any more.

Magic riding on Tree Trunk Gorge.

After crossing the bridge, follow the main 4WD track past several turn offs, for 4.5 km, out to Highway 1. Turn left at the highway to return to Tree Trunk Gorge Road.

Track conditions 45% sealed road, 25% 4WD track, 30% single track

Notes Be careful not to spook any walkers. If you are keen for the 'works burger', cajole someone into dropping you off at the top of the Tree Trunk Gorge Road, ride through to the Pillars bridge, then head right and cruise back to Turangi via Kaimanawa Road, the highway and the Tongariro Walkway.

7 Tukino Mountain Road

EASY

Middle of the Desert Road

Grade 2, 2–4 hours, up to 28 km return ★ ★

This ride involves just over 600 m of climbing (with the same amount of descending) and offers some great views of Mt Ruapehu.

How to get there From Turangi, head south on Highway 1 for 32 km. Turn right onto the Tukino ski field access road and park a few hundred metres from the highway.

Route description Follow the main 4WD track towards Mt Ruapehu. Just over halfway up, you'll pass DOC signs pointing

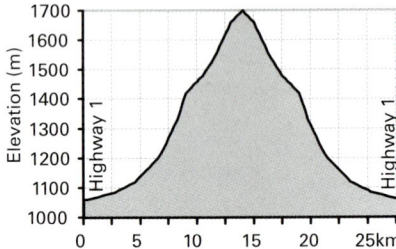

out where the round-the-mountain walking track heads off. Carry on past these signs up a steep section to the Telecom transceiver and then around the hill to tackle the last stretch up to the ski field.

From the ski field, head back the same way, but remember, those sandy/snowy patches will send you straight over the bars if you're not ready for them.

Clear your lungs and your soul with a winter workout.

8 Bridge to Nowhere

Whanganui National Park

Grade 4, 2–3 days, 135-km loop ★ ★ ★ ★

If you only have the chance to do one adventure ride this year, this is the North Island's best. There are several ways to tackle this ride. We really enjoyed the full round trip, so that's the way we've written it here.

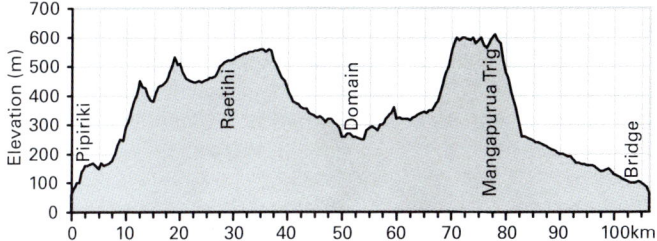

How to get there From Wanganui, take Highway 4 north and then drive 78 km up the Whanganui River Road to Pipiriki. If you are coming from Auckland, then aim to start and finish the ride at Raetihi.

Day One From Pipiriki, cycle 28 km up to Raetihi (2–3 hours). It's a quiet winding road, with great bush scenery in the first half, and then the mountain comes into view. We stayed the night at the Raetihi Holiday Park (good value).

Day Two This is a big day, so you really want to be away by 8am. First of all, there is a 40-km back-country road ride to the start of the track. The first half to Ruatiti Domain is mostly downhill—fast fun on a sealed road. Then the road narrows and breaks into gravel. From Raetihi, give yourself 2–3 hours to reach the signposted start of 'Mangapurua Road'.

The history of this road is mind-boggling. After the First World War, returned servicemen were given a portion of the Mangapurua Valley to farm. The Government assisted by building the impossible road to the Bridge to Nowhere. It didn't last long, and neither did most of the settlers.

All going well, it should take you about 4–5 hours to ride the next 38 km along the Mangapurua Track to the Bridge to Nowhere. From the start of the track, head left through a gate and cruise up a well-graded 4-km climb. Look over your shoulder at the second gate—the views are stunning on a clear day. This is the one big climb of the day, but it's a piece of cake really. After an hour, you'll reach a letterbox and see a 'National Park' sign ahead. The track is a paper road, so it's ok to continue riding.

Jonathan Kennett

The Mangapurua drifts by under the Bridge to Nowhere.

About 2 km from the letterbox, you will reach a Y-intersection and must go left. Continue rolling along the ridge, and you'll soon reach a signposted walking track on your left that goes up to the Mangapurua Trig. Note that the bush has flourished, and there are no longer any views from the trig.

Prepare for a technical downhill into the valley. Quad bikes have done some serious damage, so if the track is wet, you are likely to get bogged down in places. Otherwise, it's a real hoot. Make sure you veer right at the 'Stafford' sign. Half an hour after that sign, you will reach a large clearing in the valley that is a good place for a rest and regroup.

The track follows the valley gently downhill all the way to the bridge; so gently, it's almost flat. There are many narrow swing bridges, a few bluffs and several large clearings en route.

The bridge itself, quite aptly, appears out of nowhere. It was opened in 1936 and overgrown by 1948. DOC has recently restored it, and it now looks weirdly new.

There is a lookout track 100 metres on from the bridge and then toilets a few hundred metres further on. The steep ride down to Mangapurua Landing and the Whanganui River takes about 15 minutes. There is a shelter 200 metres before the landing (not a bad place to camp if need be).

From the landing, we caught a jetboat down to the Bridge to Nowhere Lodge and stayed the night

Heading towards Pipiriki.

before canoeing down to Pipiriki. It meant we could travel without camping gear and enjoy a big dinner and breakfast at the lodge. The paddle down the river takes about 5 hours from the lodge if you allow plenty of time for photos. Much of the river is like⁻ a long narrow lake with hardly any flow at all, but there are several grade II rapids to negotiate.

The two most obvious alternatives are a) save time by getting a jetboat all the way down the river or b) save money by camping out and having canoes bought up to the landing so you can paddle all the way to Pipiriki (7 hours).

Track conditions 27% sealed road, 27% gravel road, 8% 4WD track, 15% single track, 23% river

Notes Remember to leave gates as you find them. To organise transport and accommodation, contact Bridge To Nowhere: email info@bridgetonowhere.co.nz, phone toll free 0800 480 308. Check out their website, www.bridgetonowhere.co.nz for ideas on all the different options. The jetboat, lodging and meals and canoeing option altogether costs about $250 per person in 2008. The best map to take is Whanganui Parkmap 273-05.

9 Rangataua Forest

Ohakune

INTERMEDIATE

Grade 3-, 1–2 hours, 10–20 km ★

A pleasant ride, in dry conditions, on old native forestry roads.

Route description From Ohakune Railway Station, ride east on Dreadnought Road to Rangataua Village 5 km away. A couple of hundred metres after passing through Rangataua, you cross Mangaehuehu Stream and the railway line at the same spot. Continue following a 4WD track beside the railway line for 5 km, then turn left and climb up Rangataua Road (which starts near Karioi railway station–a good place to start the dirt riding if dry feet are a priority and you don't mind an extra 15 minutes of road riding).

You can climb up this old gravel road for about 10 km. It is well graded and passes some fantastic forest. After several kilometres, the track veers right and the surface becomes a mixture of grass and bare earth, eventually petering out in dense forest. It took us an hour and a half cruising to reach a small grass turn-around area (beyond which the bike was a hindrance due to a bolognese of tree roots).

On the way up, you might have noticed Middle Track (5 km from the railway line) heading back down to the railway line on your left. If it's been dry for a while, try that on your return for a bit of single track adventure. Avoid the other tracks; they've gone to custard.

The East

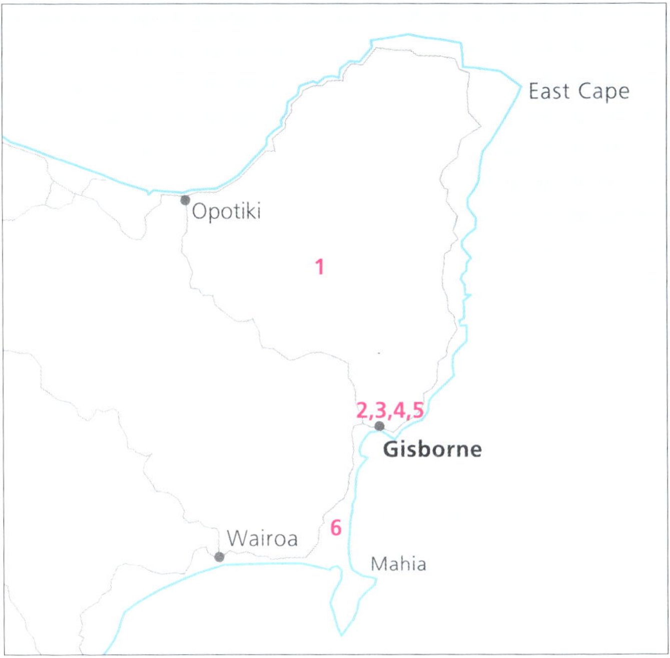

East Cape

Opotiki

1

2,3,4,5

Gisborne

6

Wairoa

Mahia

1 Tarndale
2 Fox St MTB Tracks
3 Cave Road
4 Legbreak Loop
5 Razorback
6 Old Mahanga Road

THE EAST HIGHLIGHTS

There are only a few purpose-built trails on offer in The East, at Fox Street, Gisborne, but there are plans to open up new areas. Otherwise, all the riding is on old gravel roads and forestry roads—nothing particularly epic, but they still provide some challenges and a chance to get out there.

1 Tarndale

65 km northwest of Gisborne

Grade 3-, 3–4 hours, 45-km loop   ★

This is a very old-school ride, featuring remote forestry roads and a slip so humungeous it will stagger the mind.

How to get there Head northwest out of Gisborne on Highway 2 for 35 km. Three kilometres past Te Karaka, turn right and drive to Whatatutu. From there, take Mangatu Road for 14 km and park at the start of Tarndale Road.

Route description Eight kilometres along Tarndale Road, you'll pass the top of the largest slip in the southern hemisphere. This slip feeds into the Waipaoa River, making it as heavily silted as the Yangtze in China.

The old Tarndale settlement is 5 km past the slip. Another 13 km on, veer right and descend into the forest. At the bottom, follow the Weraroa Road and then the Armstrong Road to complete this clockwise loop.

Track conditions a mixture of gravel road and 4WD track

Notes The slip may become unrideable, and even unwalkable, in future.

2 Fox St MTB Tracks

Gisborne

Grade 3, 1–2 hours, 1–10 km   ★ ★

This small reserve on the edge of town is riddled with purpose-built single track.

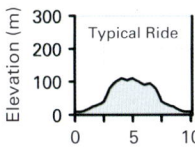

How to get there   The park is well signposted near the end of Fox Street. Refer to a Gisborne street map. There is not much parking at the road end, but it is only 5 minutes ride from town.

Route description   First timers should try to memorise the map board at the entrance (or take a digital photo). Then ride to the top by heading up the grass bank and taking the Village Trail to the left, followed by Norm's Track and finally the Ground Effect Trail (both signposted). That will take 15–30 minutes.

Take in the views of the city and coastline before descending the Ground Effect Trail and swinging onto Annette's Trail. A couple of minutes later, you will see a track heading into the forest on your left. This is the best track in the park. It's unnamed, but we called it 'Maximus Single Track' because it's so long.

Dropping onto the start of 'Maximus Single Track'.

At the bottom, you'll probably want to ride back up just to do that one again, only faster.

Track conditions 10% 4WD track, 90% single track

Notes In early 2008, the map at the park entrance was quite faded. Hopefully it will be replaced by the time you get there.

3 Cave Road

Gisborne

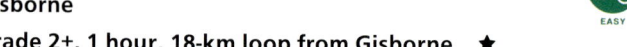

Grade 2+, 1 hour, 18-km loop from Gisborne ★

If you've done all the other local rides and are still looking for something new, try this satisfying little loop.

Route directions Head north from Gisborne on Riverside Road for 7.5 km. Turn left on the gravel Cave Road. Follow this road for 2 km to the end, veering left at the Stewart farm gate/cattle stop. Carry on up the farm track, through two or three gates and past a house on your right. You are now on an unformed legal road. Follow the fluoro orange arrows sprayed on fences and gates. Pop over the hill and ride down the dirt track to Matokitoki Valley Road, which leads back to town.

Notes Please leave gates as you find them.

4 Legbreak Loop

Gisborne

Grades 3–4, 4–5 hours, 40 km ★ ★

For experienced riders, this is the best back-country mountain bike ride near Gisborne. The uphill is physically demanding, and the downhill slots in some challenging technical tidbits.

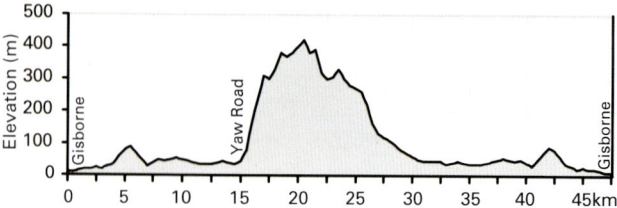

Landowners This ride passes through Waimanu Forest, owned by Hikurangi Forest Farms, phone (06) 867 9799. Visit their Gisborne office on the corner of Gladstone Rd and Derby St for a permit and maps. Access is on weekends and holidays only, and the forest is sometimes closed because of fire risk.

Route description From Gisborne, head north on Riverside Road for 13.5 km. At the end of the road, hop over the 'Waikereru Road' gate and follow a farm track for 200 metres before veering right and hopping over the 'Waimanu Plantation' gate. After a few minutes, you will cross a ford and almost immediately turn left onto 'Yaw Road'. Now settle in for a long climb.

Follow the main road right up onto the main ridge (don't turn onto Circuit Rd). Near the top, you will reach a four-way intersection (where 'Peak Rd' is signposted to the right). Go straight ahead onto Legbreak Road. It undulates along the top for a kilometre or two before dropping down, down, down, into the valley of countless fords, some of which are dangerously slippery.

Turn right at each of the two major forks and you'll return to the bottom of Yaw Road. Cruise out the way you rode in.

Track conditions 80% sealed and gravel road, 20% 4WD track

Notes Refer to our Waimanu Forest map (next page).

5 Razorback

INTERMEDIATE

Gisborne

Grade 3+, 4–6 hours, 55-km loop from Gisborne ★

This is a great training loop. After a 1-hour warm-up on the road, you traverse Waimanu Forest and then warm back down on the road to Gisborne.

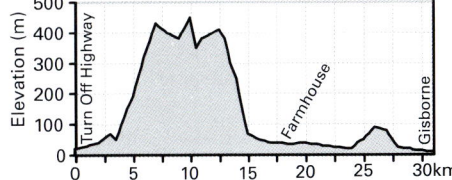

Landowners Waimanu Forest is owned by Hikurangi Forest Farms. Pop into their Gisborne office on the corner of Gladstone Rd and

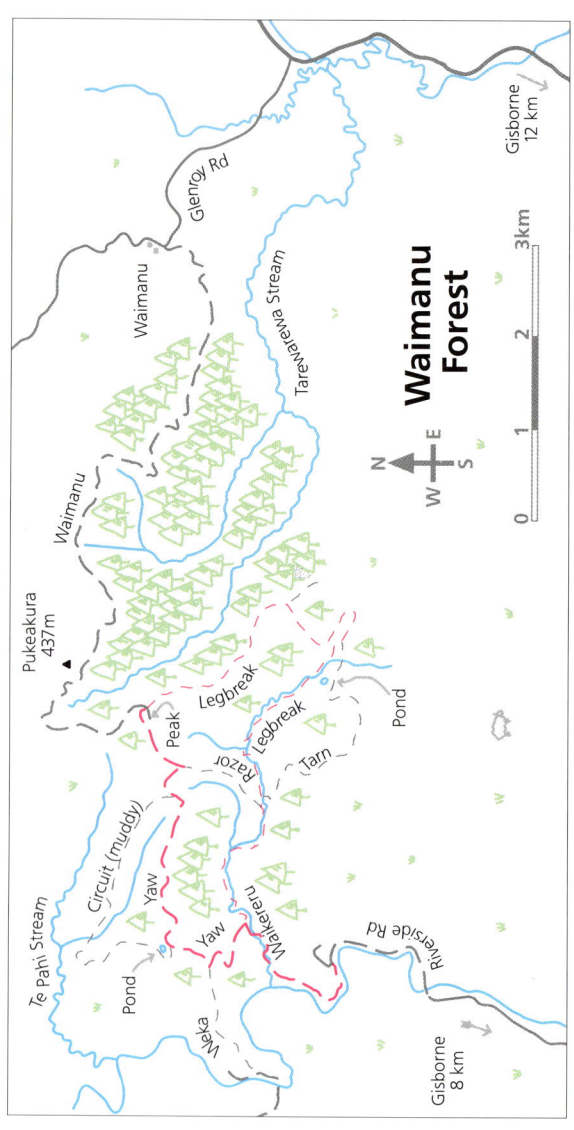

Waimanu Forest

Derby St for a permit and maps. Access to the forest is on weekends and holidays only. This forest is sometimes closed in summer due to the risk of fire. You also need to contact Mr Lane to cross his farm at the end of Glenroy Road, ph (06) 862 2865.

Route desciption From Gisborne, ride northeast on Highway 35 for 22 km before turning left onto Glenroy Road. After another 3 km, hop over a gate on your left at the 'Waimanu Rd' sign and follow the main gravel road up through the forest for 10 km. When you reach a four-way intersection, you can either veer left for a long gentle downhill on Legbreak Road or turn hard right to ride down Razor Road, then Bing Road, then Yaw Road. Both options lead to Waikereru Road, which becomes Riverside Road. This leads back to Gisborne 13 km away.

Track conditions 55% sealed rd, 25% gravel rd, 20% 4WD track

Notes Refer to our Waimanu Forest map.

6 Old Mahanga Road

40 km south of Gisborne

Grade 2, 2–4 hours, 26 km one way ★★

This pleasant old road offers expansive views of the Pacific and a peaceful escape from the rat race.

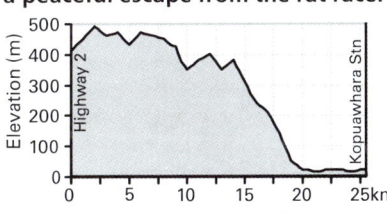

Landowners This is mostly on a legal road, but it is important to ask for permission from Te Au Station owners Malcolm and June Rough, phone (06) 837 5751.

The Roughs offer modern accommodation with flawless sea views (www.quarters.co.nz).

The road also passes through Crown forest. To check on logging activities call Juken Nissho Ltd on (06) 869 1180.

Route description From the lookout at the summit of the Wharerata Range (40 km south of Gisborne on Highway 2), ride north for 700 metres to Paritu Road and head east on a

Simon Kennett

Back-country riding on the Old Mahanga Road.

major gravel road. For much of the way, the route follows the border between farmland on your left and forest on your right. As you head south, the track becomes rougher.

Along the way, you'll see the 'Railway Rd' and 'Top Circuit Rd' turn-offs—ignore them. Shortly after the 'Top Circuit Rd' intersection, you'll pass a house on the left. At the next fork, go left onto the dirt road that leads up the hill. After about an hour's riding, you'll reach a point (just after gaining your first good views inland) where the route is blocked by a fence with no gate. Jump over the fence, take the left fork towards the pine trees and continue along the farm track.

The track hugs the hillside overlooking the Pacific Ocean, with views of the Mahia Peninsula. Please leave all gates as you find them. At the Te Au Station stockyards, watch out for dogs. From here, it's back onto gravel roads. From Kopuawhara Railway Station, it's a further 14 km to Nuhaka on Highway 2.

Track conditions 70% gravel road, 30% 4WD track

Notes Take a good road map and Topomap Y19 Wharerata. There was a landslide on the road in 2008. Unless it has been repaired you will have to scramble around it.

Hawke's Bay

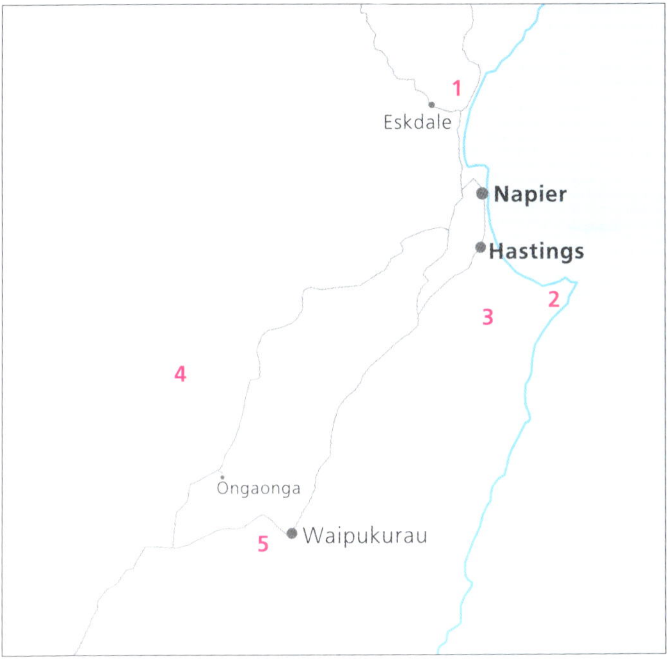

Eskdale

1

● **Napier**

●**Hastings**

3

2

4

Ōngaonga

5 ●Waipukurau

1 Eskdale MTB Park
2 Cape Kidnappers
3 Te Mata Peak
4 Yeoman Track
5 Pukeora MTB Park

HAWKE'S BAY HIGHLIGHTS

The mountain bike scene is humming in the Hawke's Bay, with 99% of the action happening in Eskdale MTB Park, a pine forest with a massive network of tracks. You need a permit to ride there, as at the new Pukeora MTB Park, and will receive a map when you sign up. Cape Kidnappers and Yeoman Track are also worth checking out for their scenic values alone.

1 Eskdale MTB Park

19 km northwest of Napier

Grades 2–6, 1–10 hours, over 60 km of tracks ★ ★ ★

This is the premier spot to ride on the east of the North Island. It's also the reason why the Hawke's Bay MTB Club is the largest in the country, with over 1850 members. There are more than 60 named trails, averaging 1 km in length, and all are signposted.

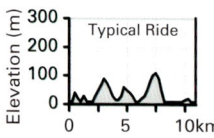

Landowners Pan Pac Forests. You must have a permit to access this privately-owned production forest. Either join the Hawke's Bay MTB Club or buy a three-week permit for $5 from a local bike shop, the Bayview 4 Square or the Napier Information Centre. You can also check out maps of the mountain bike parks (which include Aropaoanui DH Park and Pukeora MTB Park) and join the club at www.hawkesbaymtb.co.nz

How to get there Head north from Napier on Highway 2, then left on Highway 5 to get to Esk Valley. Turn right onto Waipunga Rd 18.5 km from Napier, at the 'Eskdale Mountain Bike Park' sign. There is a signposted car parking area 500 metres up the road.

Jonathan Kennett

Paul tries out some of the funky structures at Eskdale.

From your car, swing your bike over the gate and ride up Burden Rd for 300 metres until you reach the forest. The Hawke's Bay MTB Club has posted a large map board here.

Route description For an easy 7-km ride, start with Barley, Pace and Lower Magog before heading back on Merv's and Burden Rd and finishing off with Blink.

For an average difficulty ride, try the following 1-hour loop. Blast along Barley, link up to Twoman, heading for Upper Magog, through and down to Luge and then left into Lower Magog, right down the Drop, left around into Boulder, through all of Boulder onto Burden Road. (Check it all out on the map.) Cross Burden Rd to connect with Merv's, turn right along Merv's, fly past the gravel pile and left onto Burden Rd again, right into Pace (just before the cattle stop), out of Pace, bunny hop the cattle stop and right into Barley to finish this seamless 10 km of single track.

For a harder 2- to 3-hour ride, head out to Ridgeline via Twoman. Then pedal on to the 120-m high trig via Fenceline and Ledge, taking in the views over Napier. From there, fly down the popular Dam Canyon, across Zip and return via Dingo Valley, Blackberry Nip, Lower Pond, Forrest Gump and Eskdrive down to Burden Road. Whew! Finish off by doing part of Lower Magog, Boulder, Pace and Barley.

After those three options, you will have scratched the surface of Eskdale. Return another day to explore further.

Eskdale tops—looking out over Hawke Bay.

Track conditions 70% single track, stitched together with new and old forestry roads

Notes There is a new car parking area at the east end of the forest. It's off Highway 2 and Tait Road. Only a couple of hundred metres from this car park is the cool new Trials Arena, which you can easily spend an hour or two playing at. If you are exploring, keep well clear of the Pan Pac mill, off the closed trails near the Gun Club and out of the closed forest area out the back.

2 Cape Kidnappers

EASY

Clifton, 22 km southeast of Napier

Grade 2, 2–4 hours, 12 km return   ★ ★

During low tide, you can cycle from Clifton along the beach past a small gannet colony towards Cape Kidnappers. But first, contact the Napier info centre for tide times, on (06) 834 1911.

Route description Park at the DOC sign and ride through the motor camp and onto the beach. After half an hour, you will pass a minor gannet colony (be careful not to scare them). Five minutes later, you'll reach a track leading away from the beach to a DOC shelter. This track is for walking only, so you will have to leave your bike if you want to go up to the main gannet

Time and tide wait for no cyclist!

colony 20-minutes walk away. It's well worth the break from the bike.

Track conditions   100% beach

Notes Because of the tide, you can't spend more than 4 hours on this trip. Trust us, if you don't return on time you will get wet! To hire a bike for $22, contact Gannets by Bike on 027 412 8666. The gannets are usually only at Cape Kidnappers from November to March.

3 Te Mata Peak

Havelock North

Grade 4-, 1–2 hours, 12-km loop   ★

Biking on the established tracks in this area was banned years ago, so the local PD workers have built a special-use mountain bike track. Their supervisor designed it after watching a Red Bull event full of jumps on TV. The result? NZ's humpiest, track. At speed, it would be suicidal. We took it slowly and kind of enjoyed it.

Route description Head south out of Havelock North on Te Mata Peak Road. Ride to the top (399 m).

The start of the mountain bike track is well signposted 200 metres from the top of Te Mata Peak. Three-quarters of the way down, navigation becomes tricky, but the track becomes easier. After crossing a fence and entering the pine forest, head left, down to the Redwoods. Then aim for the farm track on the other side of the main valley. It will lead you down valley to a road on the edge of Havelock North. Follow your handlebars back into town.

Track conditions 70% sealed rd, 15% farm track, 15% single track

Notes This area is lightly farmed. Watch out for stock.

4 Yeoman Track

EASY

Ruahine Range, 50 km northwest of Waipukurau

Grade 2+, 2–3 hours, 17-km loop   ★ ★

This ride has a fine mix of logging roads and vintage single track through exotic and native forest.

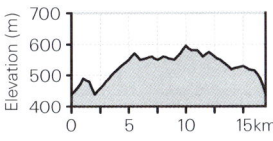

How to get there Turn down Wakarara Road (3 km north of Ongaonga on Highway 50). Follow it to the road end at the Makaroro River ford—half an hour's drive away.

Route description From the road end, head straight across the ford and up the overgrown 4WD track for a few hundred metres before taking the first right-hand turn. Carry on along this gravel road through exotic forest for several kilometres. About 10 minutes after passing the Leatherwood Road turn-off, you'll cross a creek and pedal up a small climb to a major intersection. Turn left onto Ellis Road—this is mostly downhill to Ellis Hut, 5 minutes away. Veer left 150 metres past the hut, onto a grassy track leading into native bush. There is a sign pointing to Yeoman Track.

Because Yeoman Track is an overgrown logging road, it generally has a reasonable gradient, but there are one or two steep, slippery pitches. When you rejoin the main gravel road, head down hill for almost 2 km and you'll reach the river again.

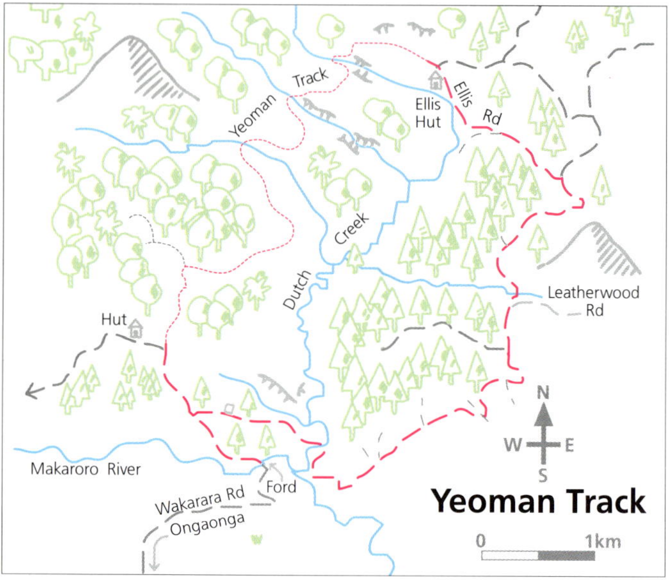

Yeoman Track

Track

Yeoman

Ellis Hut

Ellis Rd

Creek

Dutch

Leatherwood Rd

Hut

Makaroro River

Wakarara Rd

Ongaonga

Ford

N
W E
S

0   1km

Riverbed option: After you exit Yeoman Track, take the gravel road past Craig's Hut to the Makaroro River. If the river is low, you can ride down it back to the road end ford.

Track conditions 65% gravel rd, 5% 4WD track, 30% single track

Notes This ride includes 6 km of walking track, which is popular on summer weekends. If you meet walkers, greet them early and pass slowly. Topomaps U21 Kereru and U22 Ongaonga show the route but are not essential.

5 Pukeora MTB Park

INTERMEDIATE ADVANCED

6 km west of Waipukurau

Grades 3–4, 2 hours, up to 12 km   ★ ★

This mountain bike park through pine forest was opened in 2008 and is a smaller version of Eskdale.

Landowners You need to buy a permit, which comes with a map, to ride in this private forest (a 2-week permit cost $5 in

Simon Kennett

Bernie at the end of the Yeoman Track.

2008). You can get both from the Hatuma Cafe on your way out of Waipukurau.

How to get there From Waipukurau, drive west on Highway 2 for 6 km. Stop at the car park on the corner of the highway and Pukeora Scenic Road.

Route description From the car park, head east to cross a bridge and climb a gentle single track beside Pukeora Scenic Road. After 10 minutes, you'll start the 'Main Loop Trail', which is best taken in a clockwise direction. There are some fun berms and dippers that will keep you on your toes. We spent quite a while just riding the biggest dipper back and forth.

After completing the main loop, and exploring the extra few tracks, we recommend riding out on the track you started on. It flows better than the entry/exit trail that goes through the Paint Ball Area.

Notes The climbs are never more that 50 vertical metres. The tracks were still being worked on in late 2008. This park is another creation from the Hawke's Bay MTB Club.

Jonathan Kennett

Picking up speed at Pukeora Hill.

Taranaki

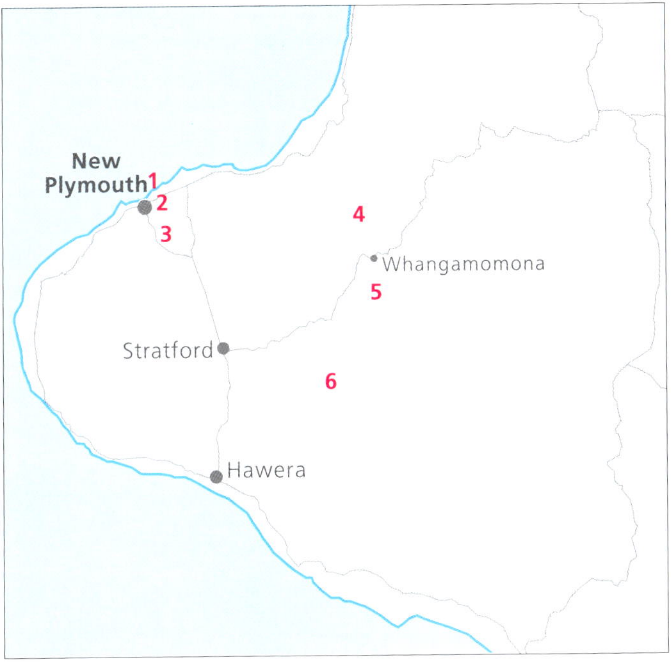

New Plymouth **1**
2
3
4
• Whangamomona
5
Stratford
6
Hawera

1 New Plymouth Walkways
2 Colson Forest
3 Mangamahoe Forest
4 Moki-Rerekapa
5 Bridge to Somewhere
6 Waitiri Track

TARANAKI HIGHLIGHTS

Taranaki is dominated by national parks and farmland but has some great riding in the dry. There is ongoing track building at Mangamahoe Forest near New Plymouth, where most locals ride. Out in the boonies, the Moki and Rerekapa tracks provide an excellent technical single-track adventure—but be warned! In the wet, we've literally had to drag our mud-laden bikes along the tracks.

1 New Plymouth Walkways

New Plymouth

Grade 2, 1–2 hours, 12 km ★★

This is an interesting urban ride with a few different options for variety. Pick up a free map from the New Plymouth Information Centre, down by the waterfront.

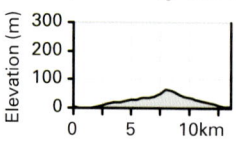

Route description From downtown New Plymouth, head to the Coastal Walkway and turn right. Follow the Coastal Walkway till you reach Te Henui Stream.

Now follow the Te Henui Walkway up stream for 4–5 kilometres, until it runs out at houses. Then follow your nose west through the suburbs on Junction Street, Tarahua Road, left onto Carrington Street, then right onto Huatoki Street until you hit Huatoki Stream, which has another walkway starting on your right.

Murray Drake

Real mountain bikers scorn the paved pathways.

Follow the Huatoki Stream track back to town as far as Vivian Street. The last 100 metres of walkway has a 'No Biking' symbol, so cruise the streets back to the coast.

Track conditions 25% sealed road, 75% single track (including some concreted sections and a few flights of steps)

Notes These tracks are very popular with walkers and runners—take it easy and slow down when overtaking. You may want a New Plymouth street map to navigate the bits between the walkways.

If you're looking for a slightly longer ride, take the Coastal Walkway right out to the mouth of the Waiwhakaiho River and back (good for another 20 minutes riding). There are plans to put a cycle bridge across the Waiwhakaiho River.

2 Colson Forest

New Plymouth landfill

ADVANCED

Grade 4, 15 minutes, a couple of kilometres 👎

This smelly little pine forest is the worst ride in the country.

Route description Close your eyes and imagine grovelling along a muddy track, through a scrappy pine forest, with an undergrowth of wind-blown rubbish from a landfill just within smelling distance. It's a nightmare! To be fair, at least no one is promoting this as a good ride.

Colson Forest is a small area next to the New Plymouth rubbish tip. Locals have been building tracks and jumps here for years; we guess it's a sign of how desperate a few riders must be for some track options close to town.

Track conditions 100% single track punctuated with countless double jumps

Notes Better to head 10 kilometres south of New Plymouth to the Mangamahoe Forest mountain bike park where the local club is building a lot of new tracks.

3 Mangamahoe Forest

10 km south of New Plymouth

Grades 2–5+, 1–3 hours, up to 20 km ★★

This has been the premier mountain biking destination in New Plymouth for several years now. There are dozens of purpose-built single tracks and more being built in 2008.

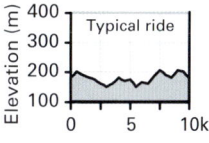

Landowners New Plymouth City Council—no permission needed for casual use.

How to get there Head south 10 km out of New Plymouth on State Highway 3 till you see the Lake Mangamahoe turn-off, then carry on 800 metres to the next left turn-off (Plantation Rd). Turn left and, 200 metres later, stop at the obvious row of angle parks by a gate. The gravel road beyond the gate denotes the western border for mountain bikers—everything between it and the Waiwhakaiho River is open to cyclists.

Route description Start by riding back up the road towards the highway for 200 metres. Head left just before the highway and ride 50 metres to another gate. An entry-level single track starts on the other side of the gate to your left and takes you to the gravel road near your car. Then ride down the main gravel road for about 3 km to get a feel for the area. You will reach an area that was logged and replanted in 2008, but before the new trees went in, the locals built a few kilometres of track.

After exploring the new tracks, head back to the car park and start exploring the tracks that go left/east towards the river. The Dress Circle track is a great intro. Closer to the car park are some downhill tracks with a few extreme jumps to watch out for. The steeper tracks are on slick clay and best avoided when wet.

The New Plymouth Mountain Bike Club has built almost a dozen squiggly tracks of varying difficulty through the forest. Once you have scoped out the main tracks, just explore for as long as you like.

Jonathan Kennett

Single-speeding Mangamahoe.

Our map provides a snapshot of how things stood in 2008. There is also a map board at the entrance worth checking. Fast growing vegetation and logging will change the picture over time.

Track conditions   30% old gravel road, 15% 4WD track, 55% single track

Notes   Mangamahoe Forest is riddled with an invasive weed called African Club Moss. The spores are viable for up to two years. Please clean your bike before riding elsewhere.

4 Moki-Rerekapa

ADVANCED

85 km east of Stratford

Grade 4, 5–10 hours, 45-km loop   ★ ★ ★

After a week of fine weather, this is one of the best adventure rides in New Zealand and certainly the best in Taranaki.

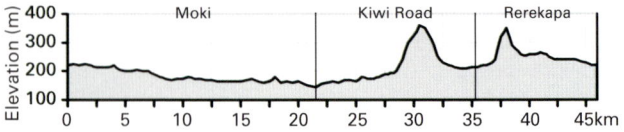

How to get there   Head 21 km north of Whangamomona on Highway 43, through the 'Hobbit Hole' to Moki Road on your left. Head down Moki, then Mangapapa Road for 8 km to park at the small DOC camping area.

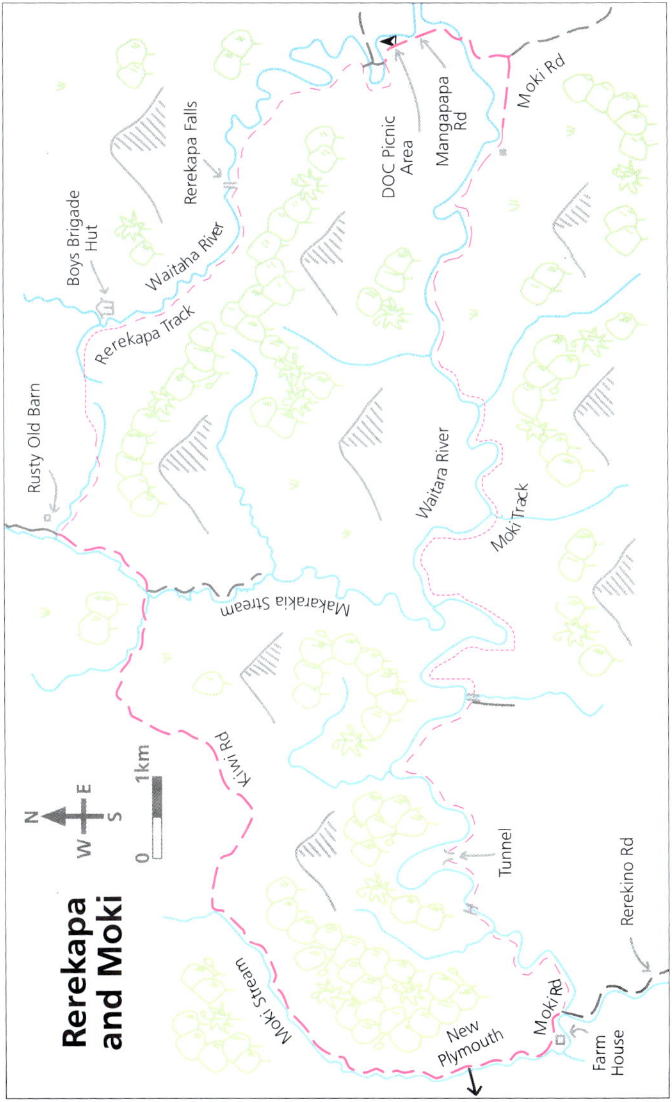

Rerekapa
and Moki

N
W — E
S

0 — 1km

Moki Stream

Kiwi Rd

Makarakia Stream

Rerekapa Track

Waitaha River

Rerekapa Falls

Boys Brigade Hut

Rusty Old Barn

DOC Picnic Area

Mangapapa Rd

Moki Rd

Waitara River

Moki Track

Tunnel

Rerekino Rd

Moki Rd

Farm House

New Plymouth

Route description   From the camping area, nip back to Moki Road and follow it west. It soon becomes a farm track. After passing a farm shed, keep your eyes peeled for a fork, at which you veer right. Your route follows the Waitara River down valley.

After about 40 minutes of farm track, you'll come across an old tin hut and the start of the single track. If the vegetation has been cut back recently, there's about 2 hours of uninterrupted, tight and technical riding.

The last of five swing bridges marks the return to farmland at the far end. Turn right to stay with the river. After 30 minutes, you'll reach a concrete bridge, and the farm track becomes an old gravel road. Turn right soon after you hit the fresh gravel of Kiwi Road. It's 12 km of gravel road with a bit of a climb till you reach the start of the Rerekapa Track—signposted on the right.

Be sure to follow the orange triangle markers, which cross to the left side of the valley after less than a kilometre. The track then sidles up the side of the hills. After the very slippery stile, the track narrows and the surface improves but continues uphill. Once you reach the Boys' Brigade Hut at the top, riding becomes a bit easier.

Soon you'll reach more farm track, which leads down valley till you hit Mangapapa Road again (turn right) 5 minutes north of the DOC camping area.

Track conditions   5% sealed road, 20% gravel road, 50% 4WD track, 20% semi-rideable single track, 5% unrideable

Notes   At both ends of the Moki and Rerekapa tracks are sections of somewhat unpleasant farm track on a papa mud base. In summer, the mud sets to a lumpy concrete and is harmless to ride across. In winter, it's hopeless. If it's wet, go elsewhere. The Forgotten World Highway is a mighty fine road ride with some gravel.

Refer to topomaps R18 Ohura and R19 Whangamomona.

5 Bridge to Somewhere

65 km northeast of Stratford

Grade 3+, 1 day, 85-km loop ★ ★

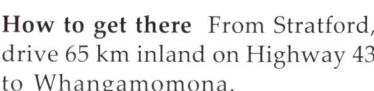

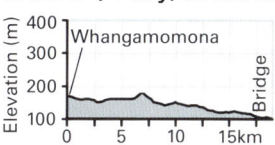

How to get there From Stratford, drive 65 km inland on Highway 43 to Whangamomona.

Route description From the pub, ride down Whangamomona Road. After 2 km the gravel road becomes a grassy 4WD track. The route follows the old road to the Bridge to Somewhere, about 20 km away. There are countless bogs and washed out bridges—it's best ridden in dry weather.

The bridge crosses the Whangamomona River, and looks identical to the Bridge to Nowhere, except it still has some traffic crossing it most days.

The ride to the bridge takes 2–4 hours. You can return the same way, which is what most people do, or tackle the full loop as described below.

From the Bridge to Somewhere, ride 26 km southwest on Upper Mangaehu Road to Makahu, turn north on Brewer Road for 2 km and then follow Jury Road for 24 km to reach Highway 43. Complete the loop by turning right and riding 13 km over Whangamomona Saddle to Whangamomona.

A long stretch of Jury Road is quite unusual—the local farmer has fenced it off, claiming it as part of his farm. Don't be put off. Now covered in grass, with overhanging trees, this section makes for a very picturesque ride.

The tunnel to somewhere.

Simon Kennett

Track conditions 10% sealed road, 30% gravel road, 60% 4WD track

Notes Remember to leave gates as you find them. The Whangamomona camping ground is $5 per night. If doing the full loop, take topomaps R19 Whangamomona and R20 Matemateaonga.

6 Waitiri Track

EASY

36 km southeast of Stratford

Grade 2, 2–3 hours, 18 km return   ★

Unless you live locally, this is a lo-o-ong drive for a fairly average sort of ride.

How to get there This little track starts 25 km east of Eltham (1 km before the hamlet of Omoana).

Route description The ride starts at a white letterbox next to a blue '3345' marker. Head through the gate, veer left and follow the track north, along the scrub-covered ridge. There are no great climbs or drops until you reach the northern end. Veer left at all three Y-intersections on the grassy-clay farm/forest road.

At the end of the cool 1-km single-track section, head through the gate, follow the fence for 500 metres, then go through another gate and carry on for another kilometre until you pop through the curved cutting. It's all downhill from here to the next valley floor, so turn around and head back before dropping too far.

Notes Refer to Topomap Q20 Stratford. Waitiri Track could be used as part of a 60-km training loop ride from Eltham or Stratford.

Manawatu

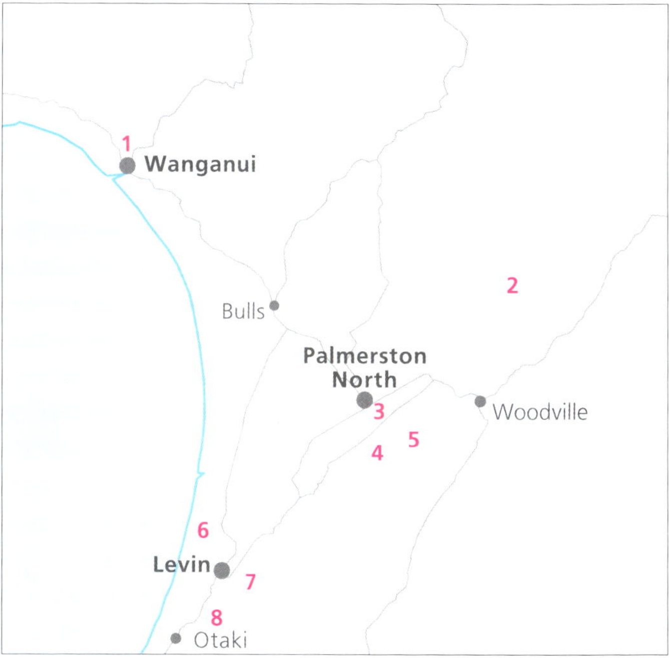
1
Wanganui
2
Bulls
Palmerston North
3
Woodville
5
4
6
Levin
7
8
Otaki

1	Steelform Hylton Park	5	North Range Road
2	Takapari Road	6	Waitarere Forest
3	Riverside Bridle Track	7	Kohitere Forest
4	Kahuterawa Loop	8	Mt Thompson

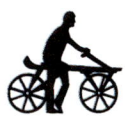

MANAWATU HIGHLIGHTS

The Manawatu is a region dominated by farmland and inaccessible mountains. The real gem here is Kahuterawa Forest, which has been further developed for mountain biking since the council bought a large parcel of land there in 2007. Hylton Park and Kohitere Forest also have purpose-built tracks, while Takapari Road and Mt Thompson give riders a chance to sample some rarified mountain air.

1 Steelform Hylton Park

Wanganui

Grades 3–4, 1–2 hours, up to 10 km   ★ ★

It takes 10 minutes to climb to the top of this humble little forest, and there are several great tracks to ride back down on. Feel the flow.

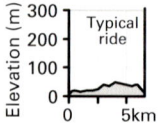

How to get there From downtown Wanganui, head to Somme Parade on the western bank of the Whanganui River and ride upstream 5 km to Brunswick Road. From the corner dairy, it's only 600 metres to the old fertiliser works on your left and the gravel road entrance to Hylton Park on your right.

Route description The Wanganui MTB Club has built several kilometres of fun single tracks in the park. Hop over the gate and blitz up the gravel road to a flat area with jumps. There are single tracks sprouting off both sides of this road, as well as the sides of the jumps area. We followed red arrows up to the top of the park and explored tracks back down. Once just wasn't enough, so we repeated the exercise on different

Jonathan Kennett

The sweet flow of Hylton Park.

tracks. They were all well-designed with good flow and options for repeating specific sections.

Give yourself at least an hour to explore this maze of grade 3–4 tracks. The area isn't large enough to get lost in for more than a few minutes.

Track conditions 10% gravel road, 15% 4WD track, 75% single track

Notes If you're not used to getting big air, watch out for the double jumps.

2 Takapari Road

INTERMEDIATE

50 km northeast of Palmerston North

Grade 3, 3–7 hours, 32 km return ★ ★

A simple and scenic back-country ride up onto the spine of the Ruahine Range and back.

How to get there Takapari Road is about 50 km northeast of Palmerston North, and just east of the Pohangina River. Turn right onto Takapari Road just past Pohangina Scenic Reserve.

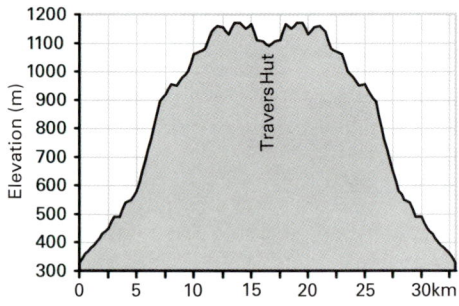

Route description
Head up the road to a locked gate and throw your bike over. The road then deteriorates (i.e., improves) to a 4WD track as it climbs to Delaware Ridge at 800 m elevation. It then winds steeply into the Ruahines, and although you may sweat buckets on the way up, take warm clothes as you will cool off fast on the exposed tops.

Once you reach the main Ruahine ridge, turn south; and ride on to Travers Hut or beyond. Head back the way you came.

Notes It's shown on Topomap T23 Kimbolton. According to the log book at Travers Hut, this ride was once conquered by three fringe cyclists riding a Raleigh 20 and two ancient 28" Triumph bicycles.

Above the tree line on Takapari Road.

3 Riverside Bridle Track

Palmerston North

Grade 1+, 1–2 hours, 10 km one way ★

This is a pleasant riverside track for riders of all levels.

How to get there The track runs from Te Matai Road, south-west to Maxwells Line. You can also access it along the way at several streets including Centennial Drive (beside Fitzherbert Bridge) near the halfway mark.

Route description Head northeast out of Palmerston North on Highway 3 for 1 km before turning right onto Te Matai Road. After 500 metres, veer right and head down Riverside Drive for another 500 metres. You will reach the start of the Bridle Track on your right.

The Bridle Track meanders its way down valley beside the Manawatu River, passing a couple of golf courses and ducking under Fitzherbert Bridge. This is the halfway mark.

From the bridge, cruise through Fitzherbert Park and then back streets to Maxwells Line, at the southern edge of Palmerston North. There is a new MTB skills park near the riverside end of Maxwells Line, suitable for average to expert riders.

Notes This track is popular with walkers and runners and is really only suitable for a slow cruise.

4 Kahuterawa Loop

18 km south of Palmerston North

Grade 3, 1–2 hours, 11-km loop ★ ★ ★

This is, and has been for decades, the main mountain biking area for Palmerston North riders.

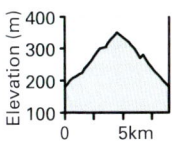

Landowners The local council has purchased the pine forest—no permission required, but please respect the land.

How to get there From Palmerston North, head southwest out of town, past the

Kahuterawa is also a popular racing area.

university on Tennant Drive for 3 km, until you hit Old West Road (State Highway 57). Turn left, and then straight away right, onto Kahuterawa Road. Head down this road until you are 4 km past Kahuterawa Reserve—there's a car park on the right, 100 metres before the road ends at an old wooden bridge.

Route description Ride across the bridge and veer right. The track climbs steadily for about half an hour as an uphill-only track and then tops out at a four-way intersection.

At the intersection, turn left through the gate into pine forest. Orange arrows painted on trees and standard race track markers show the route of a XC race course. The local club has extended the track network with single track crossing and eventually rejoining a 4WD track that leads back to the old wooden bridge.

There are a number of alternative routes that all lead back to that same 4WD track—if you lose the marked route, you should be able to pick it up again quickly.

Track conditions 50% 4WD track, 50% single track

Notes This area is best avoided when wet. Keep an eye out for other riders when crossing tracks. There is a big swimming hole just in sight upstream from the old bridge. At the time of writing, it appeared likely that the council would soon develop signs and maps for this area. Sounds all good to us!

5 North Range Road

BEGINNER

17 km southeast of Palmerston North

Grade 1+, 2–4 hours, 25 km ★

On a fine day, this is an easy ride through a spectacular wind farm.

How to get there Start from the summit of the Pahiatua Track, which connects Palmerston North to Pahiatua, 17 km southeast of Palmerston North. There is a signpost at the summit: 'North Range Road—No Exit'.

Route description Follow North Range Road as it traverses the northern tip of the Tararua Range. The gravel road climbs gently for most of the first 5 km, then there is a drop and another climb before the road heads on to the wind farm. All the rough sections were smoothed out when the road was upgraded for the wind farm.

After traversing the range, either head back the way you came or make a round trip of it by descending steeply to Hall Block Road. Turn right at Ballance Gorge Road and ride back to the Pahiatua Track.

Track conditions 100% gravel road

Notes Pack a windproof parka—you'll be riding right through New Zealand's largest wind farm, and it's there for a reason. Refer to any good map of the area.

6 **Waitarere Forest**

13 km northwest of Levin

Grade 2, 30–60 minutes, 4–12 km ★

A once popular race destination, Waitarere Forest is now seldom visited. Most of the single tracks have faded away, leaving mostly flat forestry roads to explore.

How to get there Turn off Highway 1, 7 km north of Levin at the 'Waitarere' sign and cruise 6 km down to the township.

Route description At the old garage building, you can head right into the North Block and explore forestry roads or left to the South Block, where (in 2006) there were a few single tracks left as well as forestry roads. Both blocks are well signposted at the gated entrances.

To get your bearings, head straight out to the coast along Waiterere Coast Road and then turn left and ride along the beach for several hundred metres. Keep an eye out for an old shipwreck half-buried in the sand dunes. Walk inland past the wreck and you'll strike single track within a couple of minutes. Head south until you run out of single track and then head back on the forestry roads that lie just a little further inland.

Notes Waitarere Forest is owned by Rayonier NZ Ltd—no permission needed. Watch out for logging trucks. The single tracks are firmer after recent rain. The beach is not suitable for riding during high tide.

7 **Kohitere Forest**

Levin

Grades 2–4, 1–4 hours, 5–20 km ★ ★

This is Levin's main riding area, and locals have been building tracks here for years.

Landowners Rayonier NZ Ltd—check the signboard at the forest entrance for access restrictions, or ask at Southend Cycles, 117 Oxford Street, Levin, phone (06) 368 5459.

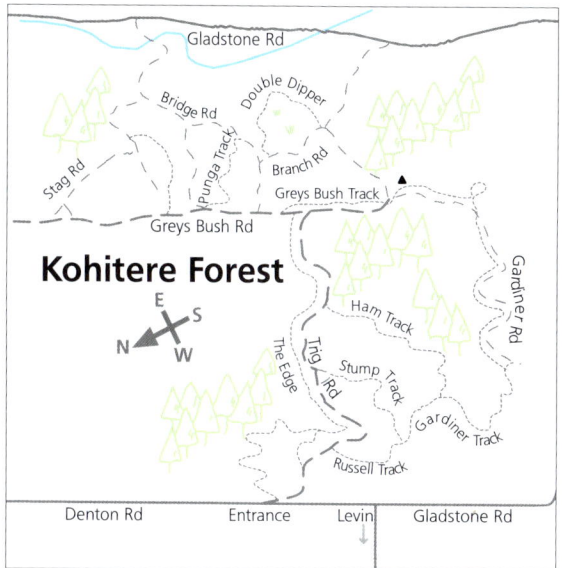

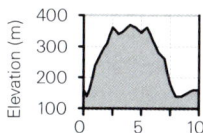

How to get there From the Levin Post Office, head east on Queen Street East for 3.9 km to Denton Road on your left. Head north for 300 metres to a gate and signboard.

Route description Generally you'll want to ride up the gravelly Trig Road and down one of the following single tracks:

The Edge: this popular, grade-3 single track is narrow, rutted and steep in places; definitely on the edge.

Russell Track: a very cool, twisty, grade-3 track; our favourite track in the forest.

Gardiners Road Track: a long, grade-3 downhill that starts on a logging road then cuts through rank grass beside a deer fence.

Ham Track: this less used grade-4 track is steep and rutted. Put your seat down and treat that front brake with respect.

Track conditions Some gravel road and lots of purpose-built single track on a clay base that denies traction when wet.

Notes This forest was about to be logged as we went to print. The locals are hopeful that the tracks will be re-opened by the end of 2008. Our map may be out of date already!

8 **Mount Thompson**

11 km northeast of Otaki

Grade 4+, 3–4 hours, 26 km for the full loop ★ ★

ADVANCED

A grunty granny-gear climb, followed by a chunky rock-garden type descent scares most people away from the 711 m Mount Thompson. Any experienced rider will love it.

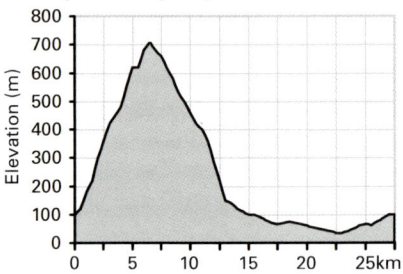

How to get there Access is via the Waikawa Stream picnic area on North Manakau Road (8 km north of Otaki).

Route description If your bike has a good granny gear and is a full-suspension machine, the ride up to the top and down the other side to Waitohu Stream is primo. By the time you're halfway up the climb, you're into lush native bush. Once down at Waitohu Valley Road, you've got a 12-km road ride back to the picnic area.

On a fine day, there are stunning views from the top of Mount Thompson.

Notes Topomap S25 Levin gives a pretty good idea of the route, but be warned that Rayonier NZ Ltd have done some roading work to log the forest, so the map's track data is out of date.

Wairarapa

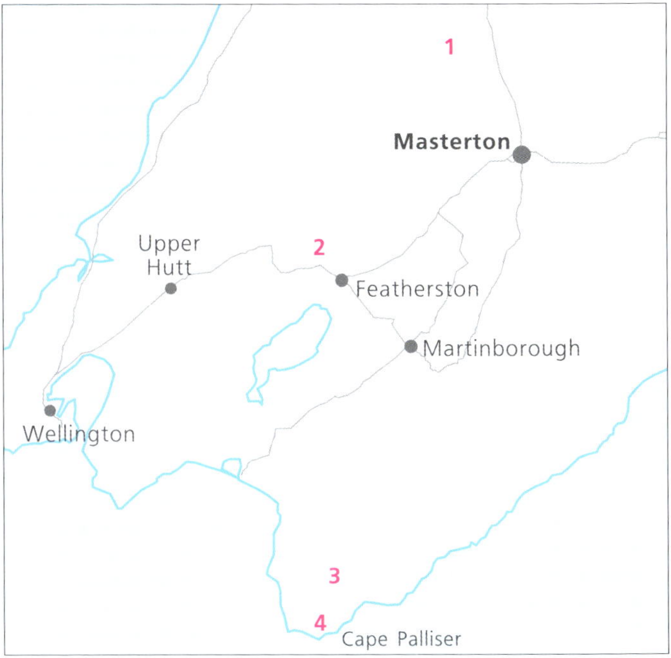

Masterton

Upper
Hutt

Featherston

Martinborough

Wellington

Cape Palliser

1 Kiriwhakapapa Tram Track
2 Rimutaka Pylon Track
3 Aorangi Crossing
4 Cape Palliser

WAIRARAPA HIGHLIGHTS

There isn't much mountain biking action to be found in the Wairarapa, but both the Aorangi Crossing and Cape Palliser are old-school classics. They can be combined to make a 2 to 3-day mission—a rare opportunity in the lower North Island!

Also check out the fantastic Rimutaka Rail Trail (in the Wellington chapter), which links the Wairarapa with the Hutt Valley.

1 Kiriwhakapapa Tram Track

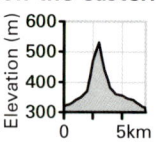

ADVANCED

22 km northwest of Masterton

Grade 4, 2–3 hours, 15 km return ★ ★

This hard-core ride covers 7.5 km of semi-rideable single track on the eastern side of the Tararua Range.

How to get there Drive 14 km north of Masterton on Highway 2 before turning left onto Kiriwhakapapa Road and driving another 8 km to the road end.

Route description From the Kiriwhakapapa road-end picnic area, head up the old tram track (stay left; do not cross the main valley bridges). Unrideable sections become more frequent as the track climbs over a 200 m saddle and descends steeply to the Mikimiki Valley on the other side.

Cruise down the valley onto a grassy 4WD track, out to the Mikimiki road end about 6 km from Highway 2.

Once you reach the large map board, have a breather and then turn around and follow your tyre prints back.

Track conditions 20% 4WD track, 80% single track

Notes There are many slippery sections that are unrideable when wet; this ride is best done at the end of summer after a prolonged dry spell.

2 Rimutaka Pylon Track

Featherston

Grade 4, 1–2 hours, 16 km return   ★

This is the nastiest climb in the lower North Island. It's long, extremely steep and technical. Endorphin addicts love it.

Route description From Featherston, ride south on Highway 2 for 3 km. Nip across the highway onto a 4WD track on your right just before the double bridges over Abbots Stream. From there, follow the main pylon road, which veers to the right and climbs from 100 m up to almost 800 m in less than 5 km. Phew!

There is a funny little hut tucked in beside the road in beech forest not far beyond the top of the climb. That's the best spot to aim for before turning around and heading back. But beware! The downhill is far too fast to be safe. Bleed the speed.

Notes Unfortunately the farmer at the Upper Hutt end of this track no longer lets people through, that's why it is a 'there-and-back' trip now.

3 Aorangi Crossing

Martinborough, Southern Wairarapa

Grade 4, 1–2 days, 24–104 km   ★ ★ ★

The full loop is a gung-ho combination of mountain biking and cycle touring, with plenty of great scenery thrown in for good measure. This is a classic from way back.

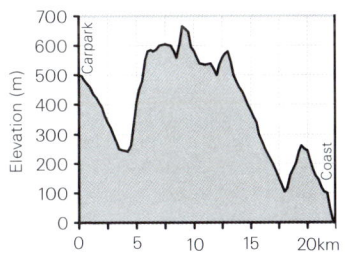

How to get there From Wellington ride/drive/train to Featherston and then head southeast along Highway 53 to Martinborough, 17 km away. Another alternative is to catch the train to Upper Hutt and cycle via the Rimutaka Rail Trail (see Wellington chapter).

Simon blasts through to Sutherlands Hut on the Aorangi Crossing.

Route description   Head southwest from Martinborough on Jellicoe Street. Turn left after 2 km, then right after another 7 km; both intersections are signposted 'Haurangi Forest Park'. Blink and you won't realise you've passed through Ruakokoputuna. After 25 gravelly kilometres, you'll pass through a gate and climb 4 km to a small car parking area and a 'Sutherland Track' and 'Haurangi Forest Park' sign.

From the car park, descend on a fast 4WD track to the first of several stream crossings. After 1.5 km in the valley, you'll come to a left-hand fork at the base of a humongous hill. Sutherlands Hut is another 200 metres down the valley.

The main obstacle of the ride starts from this fork—a teeth-gritting granny-gear climb. It's at least an hour to the top, often involving walking, sometimes defying gravity, up a super-steep 4WD track. From the top (just above a large slip), the track generally undulates along the ridge west towards the sea for about 9 km before dropping steeply to Hurupi Stream. It then climbs straight up on the other side to a gate beside a park boundary map.

From here, take the 1 km diversion to the Putangirua Pinnacles. Some of these gigantic alluvial towers are capped with castaway islands of bush. This is where Peter Jackson shot one of his first films, *Brain Dead.*

Return to the gate beside the park boundary map board and descend through farmland on the obvious 4WD track to the Palliser Bay coast. Just ignore the minor turn-offs and follow the orange markers around the last paddock. From the coast road, return via either Cape Palliser or the roads to Martinborough.

Track conditions 60% sealed road, 20% gravel road, 20% 4WD track

Notes There is a pub and motor camp at Lake Ferry. This is a hunting area, so wear all your fluoro gear. The Aorangi Range catches the full brunt of southerly storms, so go prepared. Topomap S28 Palliser and/or Terrainmap 8 Wellington are essential.

4 Cape Palliser

Martinborough

Grade 3-, 2 days, 145-km loop ★ ★

A little bit of rough stuff, lots of good scenery and quiet back-country roads make this the quintessential fat-tyre touring trip.

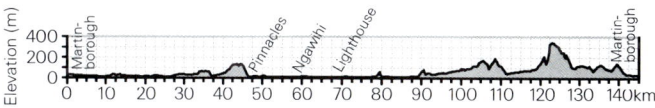

Landowners There is a section of private land that you need to cross to get around Cape Palliser. Phone Haami Te Whaiti, (06) 307 8230 for permission to go through.

Route description From Martinborough, ride south via Pirinoa (which has a dairy) to the coast about 45 km away. Five hundred metres after reaching the coast, you'll pass the Aorangi Forest Park entrance and a DOC camping area. If you have a spare

Dave Mitchell

Bulldozers form a guard of honour along the shoreline at Ngawihi.

hour or two, check out the Putangirua Pinnacles, New Zealand's answer to the Grand Canyon.

Continue round the coast to the tearooms at Ngawihi, which offer good views of this little fishing village. It's only 6 km from here to the Cape Palliser lighthouse from where a 4WD track continues along the coast, passing a large seal colony en route.

About 6 km on from the lighthouse, you'll have to walk a short sandy stretch before dropping down to the DOC hut at Te Rakauwhakamataku Point. There are good camping spots between the lighthouse and the hut, and also at White Rock. The hut, however, is the only spot with a reliable water supply and one of the few places sheltered from the wind.

From White Rock, follow the main road inland back to Martinborough, 55 km and a couple of huge hills away.

Track conditions 60% sealed road, 33% gravel road, 6% 4WD track, 1% unrideable sand

Notes Ngawihi has more bulldozers per head of population than anywhere else in the world! Be warned: this route is hellishly exposed to strong winds. You can take your bike on the train from Wellington to Featherston (for free) and start the ride from there. Take Terrainmap 8 Wellington.

Wellington

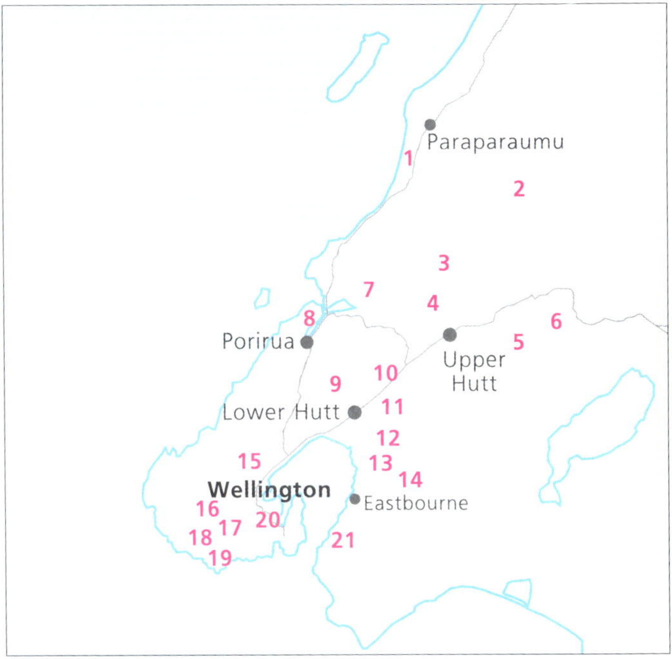
Paraparaumu
1
2
3
7
4
8
6
Porirua
5
Upper
Hutt
9
10
Lower Hutt
11
12
15
13
14
Wellington
Eastbourne
16
20
17
18
21
19

1 Queen Elizabeth Park
2 Waiotauru Valley
3 Karapoti Classic
4 Cannon Point
5 Mt Climie
6 Rimutaka Rail Trail
7 Battle Hill
8 Whitireia Park
9 Belmont Regional Park
10 Hutt River Trail
11 Eastern Hutt Hills
12 Wainuiomata MTB Park
13 Mt Lowry
14 Wainuiomata Rec. Area
15 Skyline Track
16 Makara Peak
17 Sanctuary Fenceline
18 Long Gully
19 Hawkins Hill
20 Mt Victoria
21 Pencarrow Head

WELLINGTON HIGHLIGHTS

For a decade now, the hills around Wellington have been alive with the sound of picks and shovels crafting fine single track. Most locals head to Makara Peak, the undisputed hub, but there are great tracks almost everywhere. The Karapoti Classic is a 'must do' for advanced riders. The Rimutaka Rail Trail is an excellent beginners' ride.

1 Queen Elizabeth Park

INTERMEDIATE

Kapiti Coast, 7 km south of Paraparaumu

Grade 3, 1–2 hours, 7-km loop   ★ ★

In 2008, there were three short walking tracks open to bikes in this iconic coastal park and plans to build easy bicycle tracks in the future.

How to get there If you are driving, head for the main entrance to the park at MacKays Crossing. This is 3.5 km north of Paekakariki or 7 km south of Paraparaumu. Alternatively, catch the commuter train to Paekakariki and ride 5 minutes to the park entrance at the northern end of this village. Bikes are carried for free on commuter trains on a first-come, first-served basis.

Route description From wherever you start your ride, it is easy to do a loop using the Inland Track and the Coastal Track, and there are plenty of connector tracks between the two if you're looking for a bit of variety. There are also lots of picnic areas, and the beach is as good as any you could wish for after a satisfying blast on a hot summer's day.

The two main tracks are well signposted. We recommend you head south to north on the Coastal Track and north to south on the Inland Track. The tracks are mostly 2 metres wide and well gravelled, although there are a few short steep sections that some riders walk up.

Lapping up some sun on the Inland Track at Queen Elizabeth Park.

One other track, which is ideal for beginners, is the 1.8-km long Whareroa Stream Track. It branches off the Inland Track and is clearly signposted.

Track conditions 5% sealed road, 95% gravelly single track

Notes This park is hugely popular for walking, horse riding and picnicking. Please be considerate of other users. For more information, including a map, check out www.gw.govt.nz/section404.cfm

2 Waiotauru Valley

22 km north of Upper Hutt

Grade 5, 5–10 hours, 45 km ★ ★ ★

EXPERT

This is one tough trip, but the scenery is great. If you're fit, and don't mind a few kilometres of tramping, you'll love it.

How to get there From Upper Hutt, head 3 km north on Highway 2, then turn left onto Akatarawa Road. The saddle is 22 km away.

Dave, Ditte and Mike in the Waiotauru.

Route description From the saddle of Akatarawa Road (455 m), take the 4WD track east into the Tararua Forest Park. Ignore several minor turn-offs along the way. After 9 km (1–2 hours), you'll pass the Renata tramping track on your right, as the 4WD track veers left and drops down to Waiotauru Hut 6 km away. Don't get too excited; it's a scuzzy old bulldozer shed.

The 4WD track continues past the hut to a crossing of Waiotauru River. From there, route finding is confusing because 4WD vehicles have created a small maze of tracks. Use the map and aim to climb up onto the original sidle track on the true right side of the river. Almost 4 km from the hut, the 4WD track turns right, but you should take a narrow single track down to a swing bridge at Waiotauru Forks. The turn-off was marked with a cairn in 2007.

Cross the bridge and follow the track marked on the map to the Otaki Forks road end. The first few kilometres are mostly unrideable, and there are some difficult slips to cross—teamwork will help. (Last time we did this ride, the river was so low that we left the track and took to the river for a couple of kilometres.)

From the scenic picnic area at Otaki Forks, it's 15 km on road to Otaki (most riders get picked up here or head back to Akatarawa Saddle via the Mangaone Walkway).

Notes In 1986, Paul planned to use this track for the first national mountain bike champs. Fortunately friends convinced him that it was too damn hard, so he settled on the easier Karapoti Classic instead. Take Topomap S26 Carterton and a compass/GPS.

3 Karapoti Classic

Akatarawa Forest, 10 km northwest of Upper Hutt

Grade 4+, 4–8 hours, 45-km loop ★ ★ ★

The famous Karapoti has seen more racers, over a longer period of time, than any other track in New Zealand. The course is physically, and in places technically, very demanding.

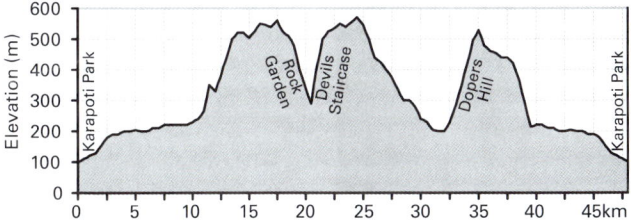

How to get there From Brown Owl (3 km north of Upper Hutt), head up Akatarawa Road for 6 km till you reach Karapoti Road. Turn left and follow Karapoti Road for 2 km to a large car park. We often catch the train to Upper Hutt and ride from there.

Route description From the car park, the road turns into a 4WD track that leads you through the Karapoti Gorge. About 6 km from the car park (and 2 km past a concrete bridge on your left), there is a 4WD track branching off on the right. This is the start of the main 32-km loop.

Take that track on the right and head northeast, always staying on the main track. After 4 hilly kilometres and a short sharp descent, the track appears to end at a stream. Follow the streambed to your right for 100 metres, and you'll pick up the track again.

Ride (if you can) uphill for about 2 km till you reach a T-intersection, then turn left towards Deadwood.

After 5 km of a roller-coaster 4WD track, you should spot a small clearing with a track on your left signposted the 'Rock Garden'.

This gnarly downhill has some intimidating drop-offs and lots of, you guessed it, rocks. At the very bottom, veer right for 30 metres and cross the stream. On the other side, a rutted boggy track leads to the Devils Staircase, the second major hill climb. Carry or push your bike up for about 1.5 km to a pleasant clearing at 520 m elevation.

Boggered on the Devils Staircase.

From there, an old gravel road undulates west past Titi (613 m) towards Paekakariki. Stay on the main track until you reach an intersection by a small stand of pine trees. Turn left at Whakatiki Road and ride on to the Pram Track (both signposted).

The downhill continues for 4 km before ending at a stream crossing. This is followed by a 1-km flat section (during which you must veer left). This takes you to Dopers Creek at the foot of the last major hill. After a steep climb to 547 m, it's all downhill-ish to the clearing at the top of Karapoti Road where you started the 32-km loop.

From the clearing, it's a cruisy 6 km back down the Karapoti Gorge to the car park.

Track conditions 30% gravel road, 55% 4WD track, 10% single track, 5% unrideable

Other users Motorbikes, forestry vehicles, hunters, horses

Notes Riders get lost in the Akatarawas every year, sometimes having to spend the night out. Start early and take warm clothing and plenty of food. Motorbikes can't hear you, so be cautious, especially in the Karapoti Gorge. You must take Topomap R26 Paraparaumu (or a guide) with you.

In 1986, the Karapoti Classic was New Zealand's inaugural national championship race. It now attracts well over a thousand riders every year. See www.karapoti.co.nz for more info. In any weekend throughout January and February, you will meet other mountain bikers training for the big race.

4 Cannon Point

INTERMEDIATE

aka Valley View Forest

Totara Park, Upper Hutt

Grade 3, 1–3 hours, approx 17 km ★ ★ ★

The Cannon Point Walkway and Karapoti Challenge loop combine to create an excellent introduction to the Akatarawa Forest.

How to get there Make your way to Tulsa Park, on Tulsa Grove in Totara Park (a suburb of Upper Hutt). Totara Park can be accessed via the Hutt River Trail.

Route description From Tulsa Park, ride up the Cannon Point Walkway for a few hundred metres and then turn left to continue your climb on a gentle old pylon road. After a couple of kilometres, veer right onto Valley View Road and keep climbing up to a major intersection by Cannon Point (345 m). Stay on Valley View Road for roughly another 1.5 km and then turn left onto Airstrip Drive (you are now on the course used for the Karapoti Challenge, the beginners' version of the Karapoti Classic, described above).

A few minutes later, turn right onto Woolshed Road—a major descent with some sketchy clay traps when wet. At the bottom, veer right to rejoin Valley View Road and climb back to the main ridge to complete the loop. Then drop back to Cannon Point and follow the walkway's many zigzags from there down to Tulsa Park.

Notes This is an area of mostly exotic forest in the southern Akatarawa Range. It contains a wide variety of logging roads (some overgrown) and offers commanding views from the tops.

Major intersections are signposted. Be aware that logging operations periodically close some areas during weekdays.

Refer to topomaps R26 and R27 or the map in the Greater Wellington Regional Council's free 'Akatarawa Forest' pamphlet.

5 Mt Climie

10 km northeast of Upper Hutt

Grade 3+, 1–3 hours, 12 km return   ★ ★

INTERMEDIATE

The top of Mt Climie is a cool place in fine weather or foul. After a hard hill climb through forest, you'll either be treated with fantastic views or an exhilarating storm experience.

How to get there Head north of Upper Hutt for 5 km on Highway 2, then turn right at the Te Marua dairy. This ride hits the dirt at Tunnel Gully Reserve, located at the end of Plateau Road. Go to the last car parking area.

Route description The 6-km 4WD road to the summit of Mt Climie (860 m) starts at the back of the car park. Most people take over an hour to struggle up in bottom gear.

The views of the Wairarapa, the Hutt Valley and the Rimutaka and Tararua ranges are spectacular. If the weather is good and your lungs permit, ride right to the last building and take the single track around it to get the best panorama.

Watch out for the loose off-camber corners on the way down. A few hundred metres from the bottom, you can turn left at the Maymorn sign and blast down the clay 'Big Dipper' track. Take the next left turn and then follow the 'Tunnel Gully' signs right back to the top car park via a long tunnel.

Notes Keep an eye open for walkers and service vehicles. If you want to explore other tracks in this area, check out the Greater Wellington regional council map of the Tunnel Gully area at www.gw.govt.nz/section628.cfm

6 Rimutaka Rail Trail

Between Upper Hutt and Featherston

Grade 1+, 2–4 hours, 18 km one way   ★ ★ ★ ★

This historic rail trail is the most interesting and scenic beginners' ride in the Wellington region. The gradient is generally gentle, and there are old bridges, tunnels and railway stations to keep the interest piqued.

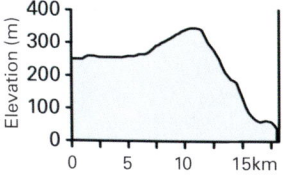

How to get there From the Upper Hutt railway station, follow Highway 2 north for 10 km before turning right onto the signposted Rimutaka Rail Trail.

Route description There is a car park at the first locked gate about 1 km up the road. Over the gate, a gravel road climbs gently to Rimutaka Summit 10 km away. You'll find a picnic area at the summit and the longest of four tunnels. If you haven't got a torch, just concentrate on the speck of light at the end of the

The Rail Trail is an ideal family trip.

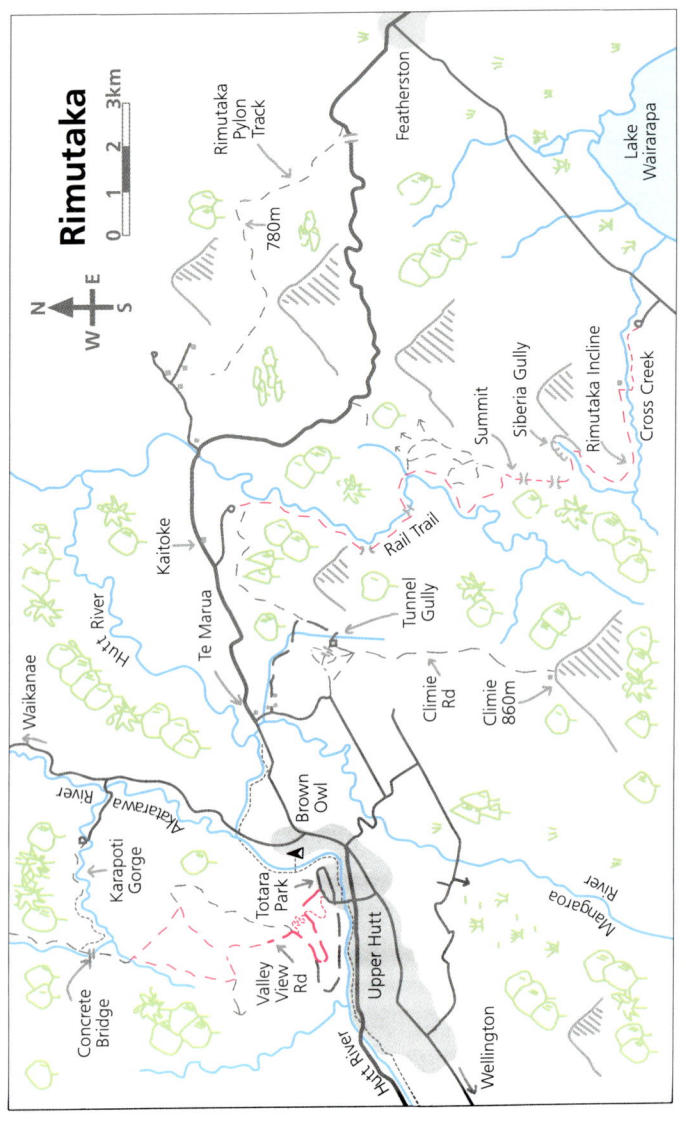

Ghost riders haunt the Rimutaka Rail Trail.

tunnel almost 600 metres away and keep your elbows out to act as feelers.

At Siberia Gully (1 km on from the summit tunnel), you'll encounter the most technical section of track. This gully is famous for its gale-force winds—in the 1890s, a 10-tonne locomotive was blown off the tracks here! From the other side of the gully, you can relax and coast 5 km down to Cross Creek.

When you reach Cross Creek shelter, ride over the footbridge on your right and cycle through manuka forest on weaving single track to another little shelter at a car parking area. From here, either backtrack or head down the gravel road to the Wairarapa plains. Turn left on the sealed road to ride to Featherston.

Track conditions 90% wide smooth rail trail, 10% single track

Notes This trail used to be the main railway line to the Wairarapa, hence the gentle gradient, tunnels and station shelters along the way. Most family groups just ride up to the summit tunnel and back. The last bit of single track on the Featherston side is grade 2+. A 2.5 km-long 4WD track called Station Road now connects the Rail Trail (from the Kaitoke end, next to Highway 2) with Tunnel Gully (see Mt Climie) and Maymorn Station.

7 Battle Hill

20 km northeast of Porirua

Grades 3–4, 2–4 hours, 4–14 km ★

This is far from Wellington's finest, but for somewhere a little different, it's nice enough, and it's a good place for a picnic.

How to get there Battle Hill Farm Forest Park is situated 6 km north of Pauatahanui on the Paekakariki Hill Road.

Route description There are two short tracks in this area; the best is the 10 km-long Transmission Gully loop. It's fully marked. Head straight past the ranger's house and woolshed to start climbing gradually up a gravel road. From the top of this small hill, you'll be looking down on Horokiwi Stream (aka Transmission Gully).

Cross the stream, head left and change into your granny gear to tackle a 400-m climb on a well-graded forestry track. There are brilliant views from the grassy knoll beside the top of the climb. From the top, ride straight down and follow the markers to return to Horokiwi Stream/Transmission Gully.

Experienced riders looking for an adventurous day trip can head through to Karapoti Road via Transmission Gully (Horokiwi Stream), Wainui Stream and Dopers Creek. Alternatively, ride through to Maungakotukutuku Road (southeast of Paraparaumu) via Transmission Gully (Horokiwi Stream), Wainui Stream and the pylon tracks past MacKay Trig.

Notes For more general information and maps, refer to www.gw.govt.nz/section398.cfm

8 Whitireia Park

Porirua

Grade 1+, 30–60 minutes, up to 9 km ★

An easy family trip with coastal scenery and good picnic spots. Ride it there and back or make a loop out of it.

How to get there Located next to Titahi Bay, 4 km north of Porirua, Whitireia Park overlooks Porirua Harbour.

Route description Turn right off Titahi Bay Road onto Onepoto Road and follow the track round the coast to a small sandy beach at Onehunga Bay, suitable for picnics and swimming. From here, you can return along the coast or head over the hill on a sealed road to Titahi Bay (2 km away).

Track conditions mostly single track if you take the there-and-back option

9 Belmont Regional Park

Hutt Valley

Grades 3–6, 2–4 hrs, 17 km ★ ★ ★ ★

Belmont Regional Park is a huge area with many great riding options. The route we've described below is a great first-time trip. After that, check out the other options listed below the notes. All tracks are best ridden when dry.

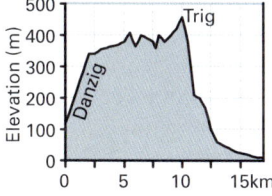

Landowners Greater Wellington Regional Council and DOC

How to get there The main entrance for biking is Stratton Street. Turn off Highway 2 near Lower Hutt at the 'Belmont Regional Park' sign and head up to Maungaraki. Stay on the main road until you reach Stratton Street. Then turn left and ride down to the very end of the road.

Route description From the end of Stratton Street, follow the 'Old Coach Road' sign. Within a few hundred metres, you'll pass a wool shed and have to squeeze through a gate. Ten metres later, veer right, and after another 10 metres, you'll pick up a single track on your left. This track, called DANZIG, was built by the Hutt Valley MTB Club. It climbs at an intermediate grade for 2 km.

At the top of DANZIG, turn left. Now follow the Old Coach Road and orange markers to Round Knob. All the main intersections are signposted. From Round Knob, ride to Cannons Head. There are several concrete bunkers there to shelter in on a breezy day.

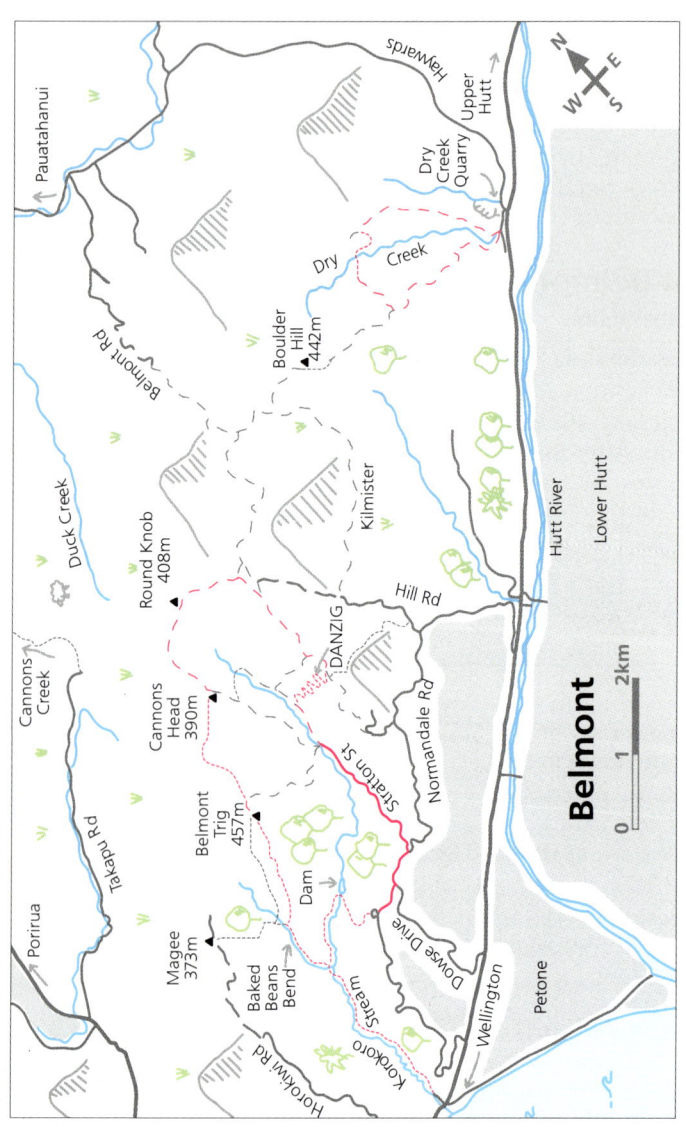

Grade 6 riding below Belmont Trig.

Now ride from Cannons Head to Belmont Trig. Some of this is untracked pasture and requires a little walking. The trig is the highest point in the ride. It's a spectacular spot—well worth the pilgrimage.

From Belmont Trig, follow the narrow track towards Wellington harbour. This is an awesome track—technical and scenic—but watch out for walkers; it's a popular area. On the way down, turn left at a 'Korokoro' sign. Then at the next intersection, turn right to ride out to Cornish Street via the Korokoro Track or left to ride up to Oakleigh Street (not far from Stratton Street).

Track conditions 35% 4WD track, 65% single track

Notes Pamphlets with detailed maps covering the area can be downloaded from www.gw.govt.nz/section399.cfm or there are map boards at the track entrances. Bikers are welcome on most tracks in the park as long as they don't skid. Much of Belmont Regional Park is closed during lambing. No dogs allowed on the farmland. Other popular rides in the park are listed below.

Trig Short Cut

If it's a really windy day, or you simply want to take the shortest route to Belmont Trig, ride into Stratton Street and stop at the first car park with a map board. The map shows a farm track starting 100 metres down the road. Its gradient is punishing up to the trig, but the ride down the other side (described above) is ample reward.

Dry Creek Loop

This is a grade 3, 1–2 hour loop. It starts from the regional park buildings, 200 metres south of the Haywards turn-off, just beside Highway 2. From the information board at the car park, follow orange markers up through farmland, into an area of regenerating native bush and then back down to the car park. Best ridden in a clockwise direction.

Boulder Hill

Grade 3, 2–3 hours, 13 km

Start by climbing up the gravel road 200 metres south of the Haywards turn-off, beside Highway 2. Follow the orange track markers to Boulder Hill (442 m). From the top, keep following the markers down to Belmont Road.

   From Belmont Road, the best routes out are either via the Kilmister Track to Hill Road or round to DANZIG via the Old Coach Road.

The Slide

This scary downhill track starts from the top of DANZIG. The first half down to the green hut is grade 5. The second half is grade 6. Ride only when dry.

10 Hutt River Trail

Upper Hutt to Petone

Grades 1–2+, 2–4 hours, up to 30 km ★ ★

This is an excellent 'family ride'. The trail follows 26 km of single tracks, 4WD tracks and sealed cycle paths from Te Marua (just north of Upper Hutt) to the harbour at Petone. There are plenty of picnic spots and swimming holes en route.

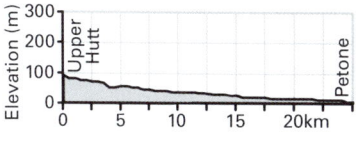

How to get there Catch the commuter train up the Hutt Valley to Upper Hutt. Bikes are now taken for free on the train (space is limited though). If you are going to drive, then start from Harcourt Park.

Route description If you caught the train, just ride through the shopping centre and out to the Hutt River. You will have to cross Highway 2. The river trail is obvious here, and stays on the eastern side of the river all the way down to within 400 metres of Wellington Harbour. Here the trail ducks under and then loops back to cross a large bridge. On the other side, hang left and follow the track round to McEwan Park, on the coast. You can ride all the way along the Petone Beach reserve.

Parts of the trail are right beside the river, while others follow along the top of the stop bank, giving great views.

The main route is well described in the Hutt River Trail pamphlet available from the Upper Hutt Information Centre or Greater Wellington Regional Council offices in Wellington. It's also shown on up-to-date street maps, and can be found online at www.gw.govt.nz/section401.cfm

Track conditions 98% flat easy riding, with a mixture of seal and gravel

Notes As well as walkers and runners, keep an eye out for the odd equestrian. Harcourt Park, near the northern end, is a highlight. The Hutt River Trail almost connects with the Rimutaka Rail Trail, via Tunnel Gully.

11 Eastern Hutt Hills

Hutt Valley

Grade 3, 2–5 hours, up to 22 km ★ ★

These old service roads provide a good training ride through the regenerating forest on the hills beside the Hutt Valley.

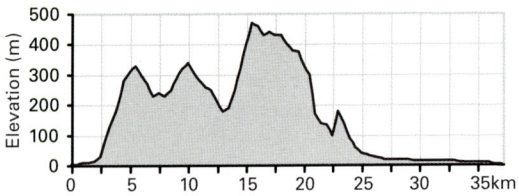

How to get there We usually make the trip a loop by riding from Petone up the Wainuiomata Hill, north along the hills to Stokes Valley and then back along the Hutt River Trail.

Route description From the top of the Wainuiomata Hill Road, head north on the gravelled 4WD track, through scrub and regenerating bush. After about 20 minutes, you'll see a transmitter on your left and come to a fork where you should veer down to the right. One minute later, veer up to the left and sidle around the ridge for a while.

Just after sidling below Fitzherbert (377 m)—the knob with a radio mast right out of a NASA garage sale—there is a four-way intersection. Take the middle track and 500 metres later veer right, following the main track. This drops 200 m elevation to reach a valley. Head south down the valley for 500 metres before turning east to climb steeply to a major ridge. At the top of the climb, carry on northeast along the tops. After 1 km, the main track heads right, but you should ride straight, onto a minor 4WD track beside a fence. After a few more kilometres, you'll reach a fork at a sharp right-hand bend.

Turn left and you'll soon reach a clearing with a hump at the end. Ride up the hump and you'll see a track heading down to the left. Follow it out to the top of Kingsley Street, Stokes Valley. Then it's simply a case of dropping down Kingsley Street and then popping across Eastern Hutt Road onto the Hutt River Trail (see above).

Track conditions 50% gravel road, 40% 4WD track, 10% single track

Notes If you backtrack from Fitzherbert for 5 minutes and turn right down the wide Summit Road firebreak, you should end up in Epuni, Lower Hutt. Watch out for killer ruts and water bars (there are good sidle track alternatives to the worst of these). Also, don't get

Oxygen debt in the eastern hills.

suckered into the steep side firebreaks, which often end in Rottweiler-infested backyards. It is worth taking along Topomap R27 Wellington, just in case you get really lost.

12 Wainuiomata MTB Park

INTERMEDIATE   ADVANCED

7 km southeast of Petone

Grades 3–4+, 1–2 hours, 8 km   ★ ★ ★

This new mountain bike park is developing fast. It already has five tracks through native forest that provide two good loops.

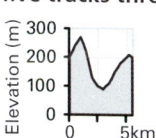

How to get there From Petone, head along the Esplanade to Gracefield and follow the 'Wainuiomata' signs up the Wainuiomata hill. Stop at the top of the hill.

Route description From the top of the Wainuiomata hill, head left through a large steel gate and go up the gravel 4WD road for 50 metres. Take the obvious right turn and ride into the bush on a cruisy single track.

After another 30 metres, this track splits in two. This is the top of Jungle Gym, which you will ride back up to complete a

loop. Head left at this fork and follow Labyrinth, which sidles through forest, climbing gently to a pylon.

From the pylon, a technical track called Spoonhill (grade 4+) follows the spur down to a park on the edge of Wainuiomata. If you find the start of the track too difficult, then part way down hang a left at the obvious intersection to take a new easy option.

At the park at the bottom of the track, head right and out to Waiu Street. At the end of Waiu Street, check out the map board and follow signs to the bottom of Jungle Gym, a 2-km, grade-3 climb back to the top of the Wainuiomata hill.

That's a 6-km loop. In 2008, there was only one other track: the Beeline, which was a steep downhill track going from near the top of Jungle Gym down to the end of Waiu Street.

Future plans include a grade-1 track for families that will circumnavigate the wetland near the end of Waiu Street.

Track conditions   100% single track

Notes   There are map boards at the top of the Wainuiomata Hill and at the end of Waiu Street. Most of the tracks have temporary signs.

13 Mt Lowry

7 km southeast of Petone

Grade 5, 2–3 hours, 5 km one way   ★ ★

EXPERT

Some old bush tracks have recently been opened for cyclists in the East Harbour Regional Park and provide slow, technically demanding riding that expert riders drool over.

How to get there   Follow the directions to the Wainuiomata MTB Park. This ride starts on the south side of the top of the Wainuiomata hill road.

Route description   From the Wainuiomata hill, head south on the Main Ridge Track all the way to Mt Lowry (373 m). From there, the track veers east and passes a couple of lookouts before descending in earnest to Wainuiomata. You have a choice of two tracks, the Zig-Zag Track or the Rata Ridge Track.

From the bottom of either track, it is a 20-minute ride back to the top of the Wainuiomata hill.

Notes Check out www.gw.govt.nz/section400.cfm for a map of the mountain bike and walking tracks in this park. Avoid when wet.

14 Wainuiomata Recreation Area

Grades 2–3, 1 hour, 5 km ★

Here's a good area for families looking for a short ride and an idyllic picnic spot.

Route description From Main Road in Wainuiomata, head up Moores Valley Road for just over a kilometre and then turn right. A few minutes ride up this road will bring you to a parking area and map board. All up there's about 5 km of track to explore here. Gums Loop is the easiest (at grade 1+), while Sledge Track is steep and has some scary water bars on the descent (making it about grade 3).

15 Skyline Track

Wellington

Grades 3–4, 5–8 hours, up to 36 km ★ ★ ★

The Skyline Track is Wellington's ultimate point-to-point ride. It traverses the hills bordering the western side of Wellington on a mixture of farm and single track.

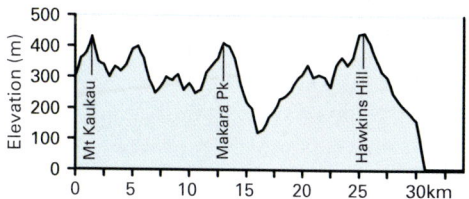

How to get there From Wellington Railway Station, catch the commuter train to Johnsonville. Bikes are now free on Wellington commuter trains. Then cycle up to Carmichael Street.

Route description In a nutshell, the Skyline Track starts from the Old Coach Road in Johnsonville and follows the Outer Green Belt southwest all the way to the south coast, near Island Bay. On the way, it traverses Mt Kaukau, Makara Peak, Wrights Hill and Hawkins Hill.

The Skyline Track can be tackled in several ways as there are numerous side tracks connecting it with various Wellington suburbs. It provides excellent routes to/from Makara Peak.

Here is a breakdown of the ride:

1. Johnsonville to Makara Peak (2–3 hours). From the end of Carmichael Street, in Johnsonville, take the Old Coach Road track to a signpost on the ridgeline (a few hundred metres away).

Follow the ridge south (to the left) to Mt Kaukau. Some short sections were unrideable in 2008, but we're working on these and hope to have it 100% rideable by the middle of 2009. On a fine day, the views from the lookout platform on top of Kaukau are magnificent. From the top, marker poles lead you south along grassy sheep tracks to a farm track above Chartwell. Veer right to carry on along the main ridge following marker poles to Makara Peak. The last kilometre to Makara Peak Mountain Bike Park is fun single track. This section ends at Makara Road.

2. Makara Peak to Wrights Hill (1–2 hours). Cross Makara Road and take the following single tracks to traverse Makara Peak: Varley's, Zac's, Ridgeline (or the main access road), SWIGG (or Lazy Fern). They lead you to the main car park on South Karori Road. Head out of the car park and turn right, then after 300 metres turn left up Hazlewood and then right into Fitzgerald Ave. At the end of Fitzgerald, follow the track on your left up a moderate 3-km climb (known as Salvation). When you reach a sealed road, you are almost at the top of Wrights Hill.

3. Wrights Hill to the Coast (2–3 hours). From Salvation, climb up the sealed road for 100 metres, then turn right onto a gravel road. The main gravel road leads you to the Karori Sanctuary Fenceline (see below). Head right and follow the fence for a few kilometres. After climbing solidly for about 10 minutes, you will see a narrow sealed road on your right. Hop onto it and

Simon's 69er on the Skyline Track. Jonathan Kennett

turn right to ride almost to the top of Hawkins Hill. Now follow the Hawkins Hill to Red Rocks description (see Hawkins Hill below) to reach the coast and Owhiro Bay.

Track conditions 10% sealed road, 55% 4WD track, 35% single track

Notes The section above Crofton Downs and Karori (from Kaukau to Montgomery Ave) is still being farmed, and over winter parts are so churned up by cows, they become unrideable. Dogs are not allowed on this part of the track. The Skyline Track is dual-use; be prepared to meet walkers and other cyclists around any corner. Most of the track is exposed to high winds.

16 Makara Peak

Karori, 8 km from downtown Wellington

Grades 2–5, 1–6 hours, up to 40 km ★★★★

The hub of Wellington's vast track network is the popular Makara Peak Mountain Bike Park. Eight kilometres of sweet single track leads to the 412-metre-high summit. After taking in the views, there are several great options to choose from for your homeward run, ranging from easy to extreme.

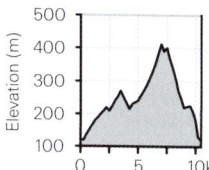

How to get there From the cenotaph near Parliament in downtown Wellington, follow the trolley bus cables up Bowen Street and all the way to the end of Karori Road, 7 km away. When you reach the bus turna-

round area, veer left and ride down South Karori Road for 800 metres to the main car park.

Alternatively, there are great options for riding to Makara Peak via Wrights Hill or the Skyline Walkway (see Skyline Walkway).

Route description The map opposite shows the single track that has been built by mountain bikers since 1998. The single track is connected by an 8-km network of 4WD pylon tracks. Track building is ongoing, so check out www.makarapeak.org.nz for up-to-date information.

Tracks built at the time this book went to print are:

Koru: grade 2 climb, 3 km, provides easy access from the car park to the Skills Area and Sally Alley.

Lazy Fern: grade 2 downhill, 2.5 km, provides an easy exit from the park to South Karori Road.

Sally Alley: grade 3, 2 km, sidle track that leads to Missing Link.

Magic Carpet: grade 2+, 600 metres, easy track leading to the Skills Area.

Livewires: grade 4, 1 km, technical descent from the Skills Area to the car park on South Karori Road.

SWIGG and Starfish: grade 3+, 1.5 km, fun descent to car park on South Karori Road, tricky in places.

Missing Link: grade 3, 2 km, popular track that sidles down into Nikau Valley and climbs out again to a pylon.

Aratihi: grade 3, 2 km, hill climb from Missing Link to the summit.

Ridgeline: grade 4+, 1.5 km, downhill from the top of Makara Peak, great views but exposed to the wind.

Ridgeline Extension: grade 3, 1 km, downhill connecting Ridgeline with SWIGG.

Zac's Track: grade 3+, 1 km, narrow two-way track with great views.

Varley's Track: grade 3, 1 km, two-way track with lots of switchbacks.

Rimu Trail: grade 2+, 1 km, two-way track between Allington Road and St Albans Ave. There is a connector to the Ridgeline Extension.

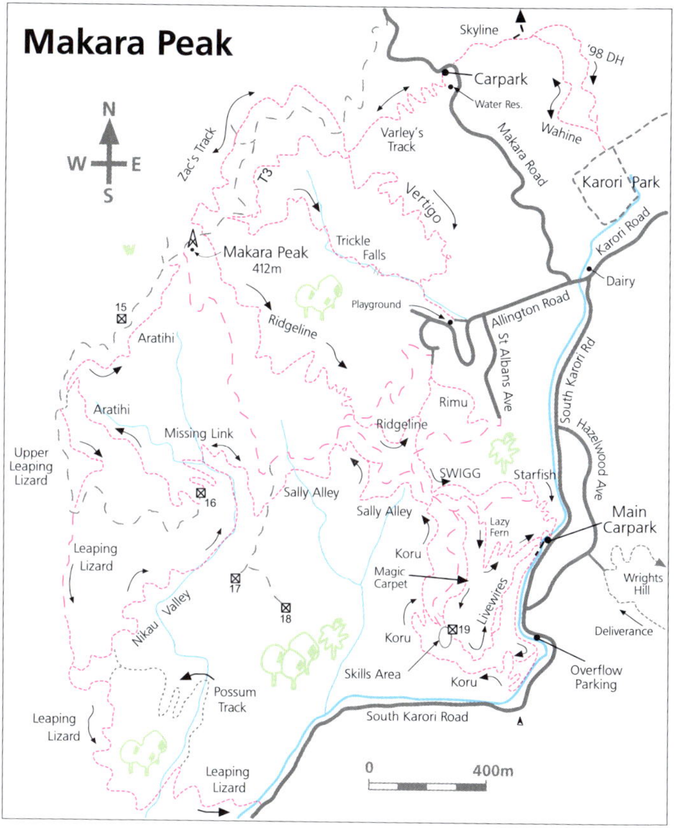

Makara Peak

Skyline

'98 DH

Carpark

Water Res.

Wahine

Varley's Track

Makara Road

Zac's Track

T3

Vertigo

Karori Park

Karori Road

Trickle Falls

Makara Peak
412m

Playground

Dairy

Allington Road

15

Ridgeline

St Albans Ave

Aratihi

South Karori Rd

Aratihi

Rimu

Hazelwood Ave

Missing Link

Ridgeline

Upper Leaping Lizard

16

Sally Alley

SWIGG

Starfish

Main Carpark

Sally Alley

Lazy Fern

Leaping Lizard

17

Koru

Magic Carpet

Livewires

Wrights Hill

18

Deliverance

Nikau Valley

Koru

19

Overflow Parking

Possum Track

Skills Area

Koru

Leaping Lizard

South Karori Road

Leaping Lizard

0   400m

Vertigo: grade 5, 1.3 km descent to the bottom of Trickle Falls, steep and gnarly with a few tricky obstacles to keep it interesting, ride only in dry weather.

T3 (Technical Torture Trail): grade 5, 1 km, two-way track with lots of challenges.

Trickle Falls: grade 5+, 2 km downhill track, the hardest track in the park; not suited to hard tails, ride only when dry.

Leaping Lizard: grade 3+, 2 km downhill in the southern end of the park.

Possum Track: grade 4-, 2 km uphill from near the bottom of Leaping Lizard. Difficult corners.

Nikau Valley: grade 4, 2 km, mostly downhill from the middle of Leaping Lizard to the middle of Missing Link.

Skills Area: great place to kill time while waiting for a friend. It was revamped and reopened in 2007 and includes a number of obstacles and jumps to hone your skills on.

For an excellent intro to the park, try this 14-km loop: ride up Koru, along Sally Alley, through Missing Link, up Aratihi to the top. Take in the views, then either head down the Ridgeline (grade 4+) or the 4WD road (grade 2) and hook into Ridgeline Extension. Finish off with SWIGG (grade 3+) or Lazy Fern (grade 2).

Notes Drop a donation into the box at the car park. The main car park is usually full in the weekend. Consider riding to the park on the sweet single tracks described below!

Connecting Tracks to and from Makara Peak

Wahine (Makara Peak to Karori Park)

Grade 3, 20 minutes, 1 km   ★ ★

From the bottom of Varley's Track, cross the road and ride through the gravel car parking area and around a gate onto a gravelly 4WD track. Veer right at the first fork, and then 50 metres later turn hard right onto the Wahine single track. It's a primo route down to Karori Park. This area is heavily used by walkers, so be ready to stop quickly. Wahine also makes for a good tough climb.

Deliverance (Wrights Hill to Makara Peak)

Grade 5-, 10 minutes, 2 km, downhill only   ★ ★ ★

From the lower car park on Wrights Hill, 500 metres from the summit, there is a gnarly track called Deliverance, diving down through native bush into a valley that leads out to the end of Fitzgerald Ave in Karori. It starts 50 metres from the car park and is signposted (turn left off Skyline). At the bottom, follow

Bronwen Wall

Jonathan test riding the Skink's Back on T3.

your nose down to Makara Peak, 200 metres away (take the first left, then turn right at South Karori Road).

Salvation (Makara Peak to Wrights Hill)
Grade 2+, 30 minutes, 3 km ★ ★ ★

This sweet track climbs from the bottom of Deliverance to the top (i.e., from the end of Fitzgerald Ave almost to the top of Wrights Hill). It is part of the Skyline Track (see above) and is a two-way, dual-use track.

17 Sanctuary Fenceline

Wellington City

Grade 3, 1.5–2.5 hours, 10–12 km ★ ★

Although this is a big loop around the wildlife sanctuary, most people don't do it as a loop. They use parts of it to ride from one area to another, often on their way to town, Hawkins Hill or Makara Peak.

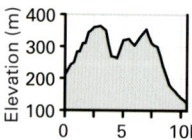

How to get there You can start this ride from the wind turbine, Denton Park, Wrights Hill or Campbell St Scout Hall (Karori), and it's good in either direction. We'll describe it from the city end, as it's the best way to ride from the city to Makara Peak. Denton Park is at the end of Highbury Road, in Highbury, 30 minutes ride from downtown Wellington.

Route description Pass through the big gate beside the park and follow the 4WD track up hill to the fence and continue south along the fenceline. The sanctuary fence will be your guide for the next half hour as you ride up the Roller Coaster to the wind turbine, down to the southern end of the sanctuary and then up again to Wrights Hill. A word of warning: the downhill to the southern end of the sanctuary has some heinously off-camber corners that have claimed many a speeding rider.

On your way up to Wrights Hill, about 500 metres from the top, the main 4WD track actually peels off to the left and sidles around the summit. Turn left and follow it if you want to ride down Deliverance (see above).

Otherwise, simply continue following the fence for a few hundred metres until you reach a signpost 'To Campbell Street'. The single track down to Campbell Street in Karori zigzags down through forest and is well worth checking out. It leads to a scout hall. However, to get to the top of Wrights Hill, you should turn left 10 metres before the Campbell Street sign and follow a single track up to a small bridge, turn left and continue climbing up to the lookout at the top. The view is a stunner on a fine day.

From the top of Wrights Hill, you can take the sealed road down into Karori (boring), try Deliverance (exciting) or head back the way you came and take the single track down to Campbell Street (fun).

Once at the scout hall on Campbell Street, you can follow the fence for another kilometre and then turn left (don't go straight ahead) onto a single track signposted 'Birdwood Steps'. It takes you either to the long set of steps above Birdwood Street, or there is a right-hand fork (just before a bridge) leading down to St Johns Pool and on up to Waiapu Road near the Sanctuary entrance. This last section of track is grade 4—very narrow and steep with extremely tight corners (not recommended when wet).

Straight across Waiapu Road, the perimeter track continues up a concrete path, past some houses and back into the bush. Although some of this last section is too steep to ride up, it is the most direct route back to Denton Park.

Track conditions 70% 4WD track, 30% single track

Notes Be prepared to meet other bikers or walkers around any corner—this is a popular area.

18 Long Gully

INTERMEDIATE

6 km southwest of Wellington City

Grade 3, 1 hour, 20 km ★ ★

Long Gully is privately owned and provides access on a farm road from the Karori Sanctuary fenceline to the south coast.

Landowners Long Gully used to be completely out of bounds. Nowadays the landowners don't mind mountain bikers riding across their land as long as you ask for permission and leave all gates as you find them. Phone Steve Watson on 027 442 7334 or (04) 476 5296.

Route description From Brooklyn, head up to Hawkins Hill (see below). About 50 metres before reaching the first building near the top, turn right onto a farm track and follow the 'goat track' down to Long Gully. Several full-on DH tracks have been built here since 2001. Unless you're into big jumps, avoid them (they aren't built for standard mountain bikes). Head left at the bottom and ride to the farmhouse at the top of the valley. Stop to say hello if the farmer is around.

From the farmhouse, head south over a gate and follow the main 4WD track down to the coast. From the bottom, ride east around the coast past Hell's Gate and Red Rocks to Owhiro Bay.

Notes The downhill tracks are built by the Wellington [Downhill] Mountain Bike Club for club members. They are not open to the general public.

19 Hawkins Hill

Te Kopahou Reserve, South Wellington

Grades 3–4, 1–4 hours, 10–30 km ★ ★ ★

This is one of the largest mountain bike destinations within riding distance of Wellington City. The tracks are well signposted with map boards and marker posts.

Hawkins Hill to Red Rocks

Grade 3+, 2–4 hours, 15 km ★ ★ ★

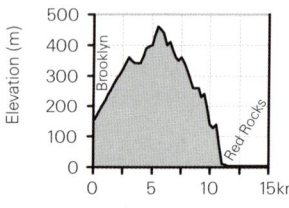

From the Brooklyn shops, follow the signs to the wind turbine. At the car park, squeeze around the gate and continue along the sealed road nearly all the way to the top of Hawkins Hill—the one to the south with the large golf ball on top.

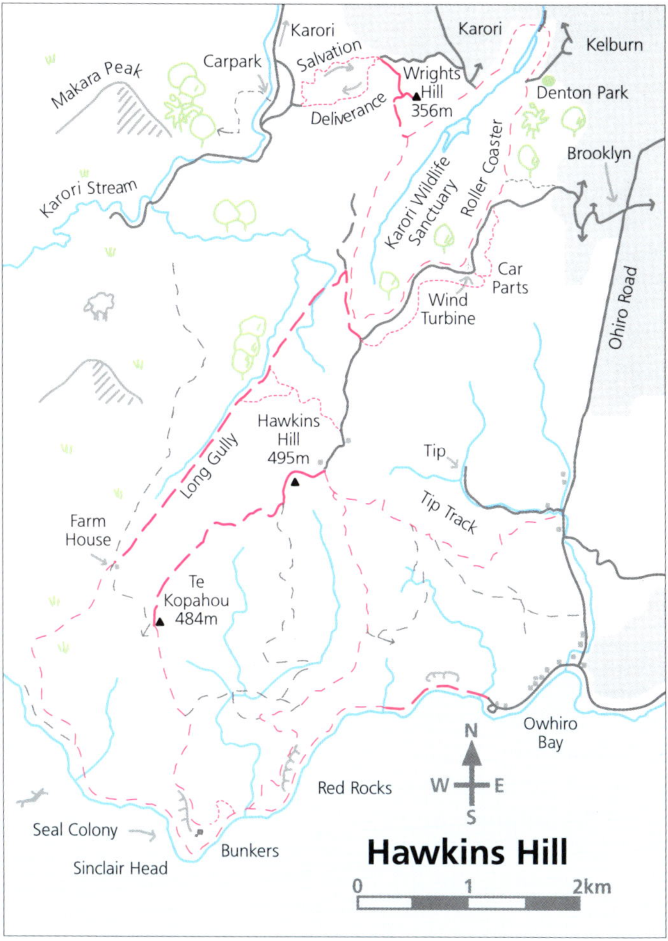

Makara Peak

Carpark

Karori
Salvation

Karori

Kelburn

Deliverance

Wrights
Hill
▲356m

Denton Park

Karori Stream

Brooklyn

Karori Wildlife Sanctuary

Roller Coaster

Ohiro Road

Car
Parts

Wind
Turbine

Hawkins
Hill
▲495m

Tip

Long Gully

Tip Track

Farm
House

Te
Kopahou
▲484m

Owhiro
Bay

Red Rocks

N
W   E
S

Seal Colony

Bunkers

Hawkins Hill

Sinclair Head

0   1   2km

As you approach the top, you'll pass a building on your left, followed 250 metres on by a castle-type building on your right. Go a further 100 metres and turn left down a 4WD track called the Tip Track (see below). Ride down this rough route for 500 metres before turning right up hill (off the Tip Track).

This track leads to the coast and is signposted all the way. Watch out for the loose bouldery section near the bottom.

Once you reach the coast, turn left and head past Red Rocks and the old quarry site to Owhiro Bay.

Tip Track

Grade 3+, 30–60 minutes, 4.5 km, 400 vertical metres ★ ★

This is the shortest possible route to the top of Hawkins Hill. In other words, it's damn steep; which is great if you're after a lung-searing hill-climb workout.

Start at the large steel gate beside the turn-off to the Happy Valley Tip (aka Southern Landfill). There is a council map board at the bottom, and from there you can see a pukey-coloured castle-type building on the ridgeline—that's the top! This much loved climb is 100% rideable (on a good day).

There are four common ways down from the top:

1. Head down to Red Rocks (see above).
2. Ride to the south coast via the bunkers (see below).
3. Head north on the sealed road to the wind turbine, then hop onto the single track directly opposite the car park. This lovely piece of single track is called Car Parts (see below). At the end, cross the road and follow the Roller Coaster (beside the Sanctuary Fenceline) down to Denton Park, Highbury.
4. Check out Long Gully to your west (see above).

Hawkins Hill Bunkers

Grade 5-, 2–4 hours, 11 km from the top ★ ★

Ready for an adventure? Ride up to the golfball-like radar on the top of Hawkins Hill and continue south on the sealed road for 1 km before veering left onto a 4WD track (signposted). After a few hundred metres, this track becomes very rutted, and some riders may have to walk a bit. When the 4WD track turns sharply to the left, go straight ahead, following an even rougher track heading south. After a short climb, the track drops steeply down a really, really rough grass slope to the concrete bunkers that can be seen in the distance to the south. As you approach them, you'll see the head of a small valley on your left.

After checking out the bunkers, follow a barely discernible track down into that valley. It soon becomes unrideable as it drops to the coast beside a very steep stream. After grovelling down to the coast, turn left and follow the gravel road round past Red Rocks to Owhiro Bay.

Car Parts

Grade 4, 10 minutes, 1 km ★ ★ ★

This track is barely long enough to write about, but it's a lot of fun, and it's being extended. This excellent track starts from the wind turbine (across the road from the car park) and sidles down the hill beside the road. It's worth hunting out. Now, a group of locals are extending the fun by developing the track from the wind turbine *up* Hawkins Hill beside the sealed road. It's likely to be finished in 2009 and will be about 1 km long.

20 Mt Victoria

Wellington City

Grades 2–3, 1–2 hours, up to 8 km ★ ★

The condensed maze of tracks on Mt Victoria is good fun once you know your way around. First timers usually feel bamboozled within 10 minutes.

Route description Mt Victoria, actually only 196 m high, encompasses a fair chunk of Wellington's town belt and is heavily used by walkers and runners. There is a myriad of parallel tracks traversing the sunsoaked northwest side of the hill, just east of downtown Wellington. Pick any one of a dozen routes up to the Mt Victoria lookout for panoramic views. Then enjoy the rush of a pine-scented descent—the best aromatherapy.

Paul Kennett

You can easily spend from 30 minutes to 2 hours exploring. If that area starts to become a bit too familiar, follow tracks south along the Southern Walkway to Mt Albert behind the zoo.

Track conditions 30% 4WD track, 70% single track

Other users Walkers of all ages, runners, dogs

Notes Remember, a cheery 'hellooo' tends to disarm even the most fervent anti-biker.

21 Pencarrow Head

Eastbourne, 10 km south of Petone

Grade 1, 2–3 hours, 20 km return ★

On a fine weekend day, this completely flat ride is popular with families and beginner riders.

How to get there Ride/drive around Wellington Harbour to Eastbourne. A nice alternative is to take the East by West Ferry to Days Bay (2 km north of Eastbourne). Phone (04) 494 3339 for ferry times.

Route description Follow the main road south through Eastbourne to the gate at the end of the sealed road. From there, follow the gravel road beside the coast for 5 km to Pencarrow Head and then another 5 km to Baring Head. The last 200 metres to the rocks at Baring Head are too sandy to ride.

Most people return the same way.

For some added adventure, explore the Lake Kohangapiripiri and Cameron Ridge tracks. They can add up to 5 km to your trip. Pick up a copy of the East Harbour Regional Park pamphlet from your local Greater Wellington regional council office or log on to www.gw.govt.nz/section400.cfm for more information.

Notes This normally tame ride can turn wild on a windy day. The armadillo-like rocks at Baring Head are popular for rock climbing.

Nelson

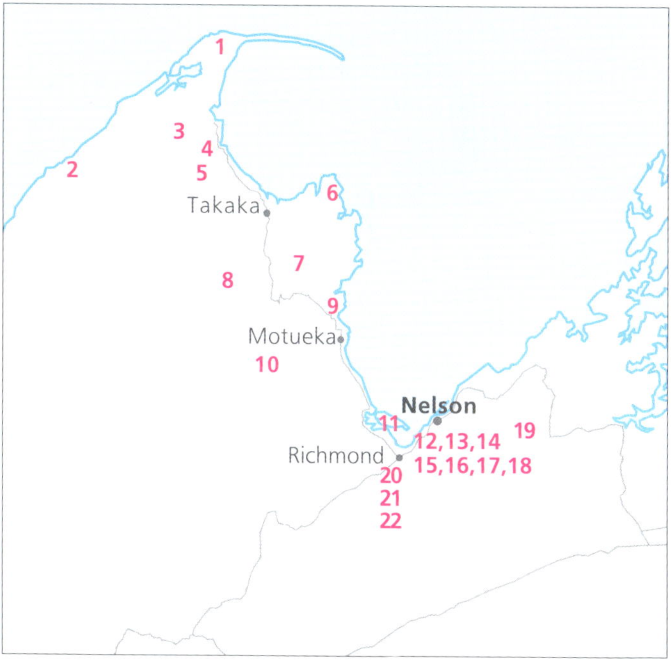

Takaka

Motueka

Nelson

Richmond

1 Puponga Farm Park	12 Centre of NZ to Walters Bluff
2 Kahurangi Lighthouse	13 Hira Forest MTB Park
3 Aorere Goldfields	14 Fireball Road
4 Parapara MTB Tracks	15 Dun Mountain
5 Ye Old Mill Road	16 Fringed Hill
6 Gibbs Hill	17 Peaking Ridge
7 Rameka Track	18 Maitai South Branch
8 Kill Devil	19 Maungatapu Track
9 Marble Mountain	20 Barnicoat Range
10 Flora Saddle	21 Kingsland Forest
11 Rabbit Island	22 Aniseed Valley

NELSON HIGHLIGHTS

Nelson has it all, the lucky buggers! From downtown cafes, you can ride out to primo purpose-built single tracks or awesome back-country trails with fantastic scenery. The sheer number and excellence of tracks makes Nelson one of the top three MTB cities in the country.

1 Puponga Farm Park

Farewell Spit, 50 km north of Takaka

Grades 3–4, 1 hour, up to 10 km ★

This isn't a long ride, but if you're doing the touristy thing and need to check out Cape Farewell, it's worth it.

Route description From Collingwood, drive up to Farewell Spit and park at the Paddle Crab Café (great food and stunning views). You can buy a DOC pamphlet on the area, which has a map showing the tracks that are open for riding. We

Martin Langley says 'Hello' to Farewell Spit.

recommend heading out along Wharanaki Road, up to the woolshed in Puponga Farm Park and then east to Pillar Point Lighthouse. From there, head up past the high point, Old Man (155 m) and soon after, veer left and drop down to a farm track on Triangle Flat that leads back to the café.

Track conditions a mix of farm roads and sheep tracks

Notes You can also explore further west on the Green Hills Route. After crossing Green Hills Stream, the track splits in two—go right (the left branch is poxy!).

2 Kahurangi Lighthouse

50 km northwest of Takaka

Grade 2, 1–2 days, up to 120 km ★ ★

This is a remote and beautiful part of New Zealand. The cycling is on gravel roads, beaches and a small amount of single track.

How to get there We recommend basing yourself at Collingwood or Pakawau and taking the time to explore the area by bicycle from there.

Route description Ride north out of Collingwood, past Pakawau, then west over to the remote and beautiful West Coast beaches. The roads are quiet, and generally you can have the beaches and glorious sunsets all to yourself. An excellent overnight trip is to head south from the Anatori River mouth to the lighthouse at Kahurangi Point. To get there, you must cross Big River 1 hour either side of low tide.

Knuckle Hill.

There is an old farmhouse to stay in hidden in the trees 1 km east of the lighthouse. It's now managed by DOC. There are beds, but no cooking equipment.

Notes There are also lots of old logging roads to be explored at the end of Dry Road, or you could try a side trip to Knuckle Hill (506 m) south of Whanganui Inlet (this involves walking the top couple of kilometres).

Refer to Topomap M25 Collingwood and/or drop in to The Quiet Revolution Cycle Shop in Takaka to get information and a pamphlet of rides in the Bay.

3 Aorere Goldfields

INTERMEDIATE

11 km southwest of Collingwood

Grade 3+, 2–5 hours, 20-km loop ★ ★ ★

On a dry day, this is one of the best rides in Golden Bay. Some of the single track is excellent, and it's an interesting area both historically and scenically.

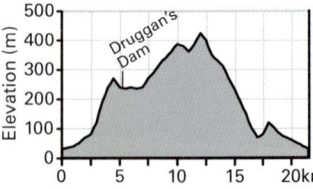

How to get there From Collingwood, head west on the road to Rockville for about 10 km. Go straight onto Caves Road and park at Devils Boots (large upside down boot-shaped limestone formations).

Route description You can either do the full 20-km loop or ride up to Druggan's Dam and back. There is a cave, old gold workings and a dam to visit on this ride.

From the boots, ride up the rough road for 15 minutes before turning left up a steep 4WD track at the 'Aorere Goldfields' signpost.

What follows is a tough climb that will require the odd bit of walking. Turn right at the 'Goldfields Walk' sign and then veer left at the 'Caves 5 min' sign.

A glimpse of the magic that is Aorere Goldfields.   Dave Mitchell

For an interesting 20-minute diversion, we walked down to the Ballroom cave and climbed through to the Stafford cave (torch essential) before walking back to our bikes.

From the caves, a water-race track leads on to Druggan's Dam. It's technical in places, so don't race it on your first time through. The dam is a common rest spot, as is the great look-out spot 5 minutes past it.

For a great 2–3 hour ride, turn around at the dam (or look-out spot) and enjoy the single track you rode up.

Alternatively, complete the grand loop by riding round to Red Hill, and down towards Plain Road on a wide fast 4WD track. At the bottom, hop over a gate, coast down to Plain Road, then turn left to return to Devils Boots.

Track conditions 60% 4WD track, 38% single track, 2% unrideable

Notes The ride is best done in dry weather. Take a torch for the caves and Topomap M25 Collingwood if you want to do the full loop.

4 Parapara MTB Tracks

20 km north of Takaka

Grades 3–4, 1 hour, up to 10 km ★ ★

This was the first collection of MTB tracks built in Golden Bay. The area may be logged in future, so it's best to check at The Quiet Revolution Cycle Shop in Takaka before heading out.

How to get there Parapara Forest is 20 km north of Takaka. The tracks start from the south end of the Parapara Inlet bridge.

Route description From the bridge, ride back towards Takaka for 100 metres. Take the old road on your right around the inlet to head into the forest on an easy track. After a few minutes, turn right at an arrow to follow a single track that zigzags up onto the main ridge, climbing for 10 minutes. Turn left when you hit the old forestry road to cruise along the ridge and then drop down to a little lake. You can ride halfway around the lake for some views and then backtrack to the pines.

From the lake, follow a squiggly single track to the swimming hole in the Parapara River. On a hot summer's day, this is the place to be. Head out from the river and turn left to finish off with the best bit of single track in the forest.

Notes The Quiet Revolution Cycle Shop sells a MTB pamphlet with a map of rides in this area.

5 Ye Old Mill Road

EASY

19 km northwest of Takaka

Grade 2+, 1 hour, 6 km return ★

A pleasant uphill workout to a good lookout over Golden Bay.

How to get there Start from a nondescript driveway 19 km northwest of Takaka on Highway 60. Four hundred metres after passing Tukurua Road, you'll reach two letterboxes on the left near the top of a small hill. This is where the ride starts.

Route description Take the driveway 10 metres before the letterboxes and follow the gravel 4WD track up into the hills for half an hour. Regroup at the park bench (290 m) for a brilliant vista of Golden Bay.

You can continue climbing for another few minutes to a 'Private Property' sign before turning around and enjoying the downhill. After about 10 minutes downhill, at the end of a long flattish section, take a sharp left-hander for a more challenging descent. Just go straight ahead after crossing a ford, then turn right at the major gravel road. This leads back to Highway 60, 1 km from the start of the ride.

6 Gibbs Hill

INTERMEDIATE

25 km northeast of Takaka

Grade 3, 3–4 hour loop, 23 km ★

Don't miss this turn-off!

How to get there From Takaka, drive out towards Totaranui, turn left onto McShane Road and drive to the road end.

Route description From the Wainui Bay car park, follow the track north to the first saddle, then turn right and settle in for a 20-minute climb — it involves a few steep sections that we didn't quite manage to ride. At the small saddle 100 metres from the top, leave your bike and follow a narrow track to the summit a few minutes away–great views and funky rocks.

The downhill from here is both fast and dangerous. You've really got to control your speed. After 1 km, there is a sharp left and the track becomes quite rough in places. It takes 30 minutes to get from the top to Totaranui — Golden Bay's most over-populated campground in the summer. From there, it's a scenic 13-km road ride back to the Wainui Bay car park.

Notes This ride has only just been opened up to cyclists. Please support the cause and respect other users.

7 Rameka Track

36 km from Motueka or 47 km from Takaka

Grade 3+, 3–4 hours, 31 km ★ ★ ★

The Rameka Track is an old classic with exciting new tracks being built at both ends—Canaan Downs and Project Rameka.

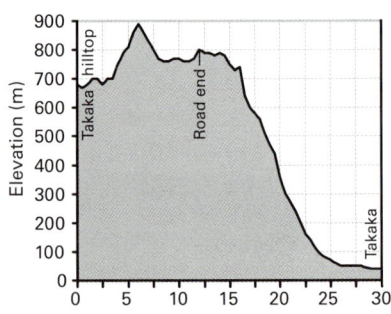

How to get there Most people get dropped off at the start of Canaan Road, which is near the top of the Takaka Hill, then ride through to Takaka. Contact Southern Link K Bus, phone 0800 881 188, for transport from Takaka or Motueka. Some people shuttle it, but the shuttle is so long (1 hour one way) that locals often make this a there-and-back ride.

Route description Near the top of Takaka Hill, turn north onto the twisty Canaan Road. Cycle to the road end 11 km away (there is a toilet and camping area there). At the far end of the camping area, hop over a gate and head past an 'Abel Tasman National Park' sign on a grassy 4WD track.

One kilometre from the camping area, turn left at a 'Rameka Track' signpost. In the next few kilometres, you'll wind down through native bush on an excellent single track.

When you break out of the bush, the track steepens, and there is a short grade-5 section that requires walking. From there, follow orange markers all the way down to Rameka Creek Road and Takaka. Some people choose to turn around at the bush edge and ride back to Canaan Downs.

At the bottom of the Rameka Creek Road, you'll reach a three-way intersection with several letterboxes. Continue following orange markers to Highway 60, about 10 minutes away. Cross the highway and take Dodson Road (to avoid highway traffic). Takaka township is only 2 km away.

Track conditions 25% sealed road, 40% gravel road, 15% 4WD track, 20% single track

Notes There is a 30-minute walk (no bikes allowed) from Canaan Road car park to Harwoods Hole, a 176 m deep tomo that is popular with cavers. Local riders are also developing mountain bike tracks at Canaan Downs (see below). Take Topomap N26 Takaka.

Canaan Downs

In 2007, Golden Bay mountain bikers began building tracks at Canaan Downs. From the end of Cannan Road, ride up past the start of the Rameka Track to Wainui Saddle (3 km). From the saddle, head to your right to a fence 50 metres away. Veer left and follow markers on a long sidle track that drops in and out of creeks as it heads south to Gold Creek.

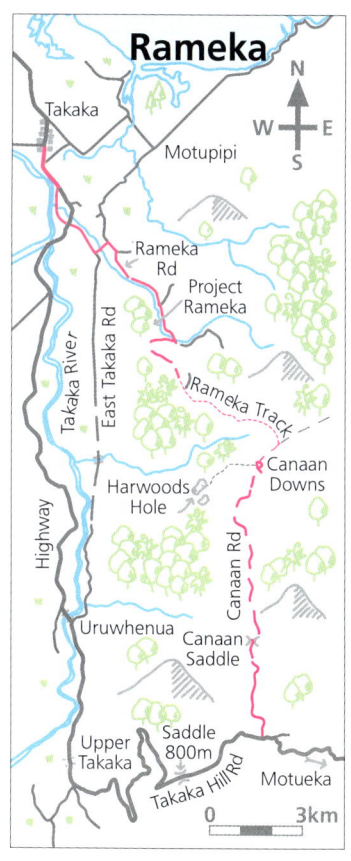

From Gold Creek, you have two options. The easy option: Follow the orange markers down to some stock yards and along farm roads to Canaan Road. That makes the whole ride a grade 3+, 6-km loop. The hard option: Follow less obvious markers across Gold Creek and up to a lookout at the highest point on Canaan Downs. After taking in the view, a tricky downhill zigzags through to the Downs and across to Canaan Road. This raw grade 4+, 12-km loop, is an excellent tour of Canaan Downs.

Project Rameka

Bronwen Wall

Track-design mission, Canaan Downs.

At the time of writing, Jonathan and his partner Bronnie had just bought a large chunk of land halfway down Rameka Road to create a carbon sink. They soon discovered that the original Rameka Track (built in the 1850s) actually runs right through the property! So it's being cleared, marked with purple arrows and opened up to walkers and cyclists.

Eventually they hope to add 4 km of single track to the Rameka experience. It will be a two-way track, so if you're based in Golden Bay, you will be able to ride it from the bottom, rather than do a huge shuttle. From the 'Project Rameka' sign, follow purple arrows down through the carbon sink and back out onto Rameka Creek Road. Then follow orange arrows to Takaka.

If you would like to assist with Project Rameka (track building or tree planting) drop into The Quiet Revolution Cycle Shop in Takaka or check out www.kennett.co.nz/rameka

8 Kill Devil

EXPERT

10 km from Takaka

Grade 5-, 4–8 hours, 24 km return ★ ★ ★

This tough ride has fantastic scenery, and countless technical challenges, with 57 switchbacks packed into a 700-m climb.

How to get there From Upper Takaka, head north for 6 km, turn left at Uruwhenua Road and head south for 3 km to the signposted start of the track.

Route description Follow a farm road for a few hundred metres to the base of the hills, then triangle markers will lead you across a stream and up a steep spur on a challenging single track. After 2 hours of riding and walking, you'll reach the top of the climb at almost 1000 m height. The next part of the ride involves quite a bit of walking—most people turn back at this point.

Riordans Hut is still another 1–2 hours away. Ride along the ridge until you reach a '15 min' signpost. This is the turn-off to the historic hut, 1 km away.

From the hut, take in the views before tackling the short climb back to the ridge and then the awesome return down to Uruwhenua Road.

Notes Check out Topomap N26 Takaka and M26 Cobb. In winter, this track can be plastered with snow.

Here's a challenge; all but two of the switchbacks have been ridden up hill!

Murray Drake

Chow down at Riordans Hut.

9 Marble Mountain

12 km north of Motueka

Grade 4-, 2–3 hours, 35 km   ★★

You only get one chance a year to ride the Marble Mountain, so don't miss the opportunity to explore this unique landscape.

How to get there   The race starts at Kaiteriteri Beach.

Route description   Each April, local landowners give permission for this event to be run over their properties. After skirting around the coast for a while, the route climbs up farm tracks and crosses some funky marble limestone landscape before diving back down to Kaiteriteri.

Although officially it's a race, that doesn't mean you have to do it at race pace. Just enter and cruise. Enjoy the views from the top of the 700-metre climb, then let it go all the way back to the coast. There are a couple of grunty climbs and one ripper of a single track downhill section at the end.

Notes   For more info, see www.marblemountainclassic.org.nz

10 Flora Saddle

34 km southwest of Motueka

Grade 3+, 2 hours, 15 km return   ★★

This is a short ride, but it runs through stunning beech forest.

How to get there   From Motueka, head southwest on Highway 61 for 18 km to Ngatimoti.

Cross the Motueka River and follow the Mt Arthur track signs up Graham Valley Road to the car park. This gravel road gains 850 m altitude and is so steep in parts that concrete slabs have been laid down for traction.

Route description   From the road end, it's an easy 1 km on a 4WD track to Flora Saddle (975 m). Now veer right to head to Flora Valley. In a matter of minutes, the track reaches Flora Hut. Veer left at the 'Flora Track to Takaka Valley' sign to follow a beautiful, leaf-littered 4WD track towards Takaka Valley. Another cruisy 5 km will bring you to 'Gridiron Gulch —

Population 2', an impressive rock bivvy. This is where the legal road ends, so, after taking in the awesome scenery, head back to the car park.

11 Rabbit Island

30 km west of Nelson

Grade 1+, 30 minutes, 2 km ★

This is a veritable rabbit warren of mountain bike tracks.

Route description Rabbit Island is a flat, forested recreation reserve about 40 minutes drive from Nelson. The Tasman District Council have built a small network of easy mountain bike tracks here. It's a neat wee area for kids and beginner mountain bikers but a bit of a baffling maze until you've ridden there a few times.

There is a map board but no signs on the tracks, so riding can become a bit aimless. Absolute beginners can start with a marked 9-km loop on flat wide forestry roads.

Note There are some nice picnic spots close to the beach.

12 Centre of NZ to Walters Bluff

Downtown Nelson

Grade 3, 1 hour, 6-km loop ★

Tourist flock here, but we don't rate it as a great ride.

How to get there From Nelson City, ride out to Maitai Road and take the first 4WD track on the left, signposted 'Centre of NZ Walkway'.

Route description Follow the main track to the top of the hill, a steep 20 minutes away. If there are lots of walkers near the top, it's best to hop off your bike and walk.

After taking in the fine views, backtrack 500 metres to the Walters Bluff sign. Follow a farm track north across the hillside to a gravelly track that dives down to Walters Bluff. Before the top of the downhill, you can turn right and climb up onto the main ridge that leads back to the Centre of New Zealand.

13 **Hira Forest MTB Park**

2 km east of Nelson

Grades 3–5, 2–5 hours, 15–37 km ★ ★ ★

Hira Forest is within easy riding distance of town and has purpose-built as well as old-school tracks. Most are awesome fun.

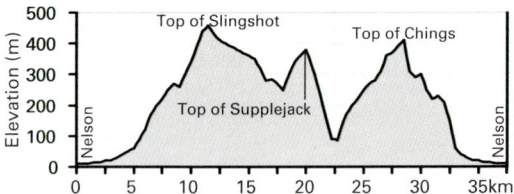

How to get there Ride down Maitai Valley Road for 2 km and turn left into Sharlands Road.

Route description This is now the main riding area in Nelson. The tracks are marked on a map board up Sharlands Road.

Ground Effect Slingshot and Scottwood Wiggles
Grade 3+, 2 hours

First timers should start with these excellent purpose-built single tracks. Climb for almost an hour up Sharlands Road and Bobs Fern Road (the second Bobs Fern Road, not the first one) to reach the 'Mtb Track' sign near the trig at the top. Trust us—there are few tracks in New Zealand that return as much for your hard-earned elevation as Ground Effect Slingshot. It weaves back and forth down the valley, providing a long, flowing ride. After 15 minutes, it connects with Scottwood Wiggles, which is a bit steep and more difficult in places and leads out to Sharlands Road at the '5 km' sign.

Now you have three options:

1 Cruise down the road and back to town.

2 Ride up Sharlands Road to a huge flat clearing. Cross the clearing and ride Chings Highway (grade 4, 1 hour). This is an intermediate ride, but there are several difficult sections that simply don't flow. It leads back to Sharlands Road.

3 Tackle the Supplejack track (grade 5, 1 hour). Coast down Sharlands for 5 minutes and then turn off up 'Bobs Fern Road'. Within 2 minutes, turn left onto the first 4WD track you see. When you reach the main ridge, turn right and climb a bit more. You're aiming for a lookout next to a skid site (spot height 388 on the topomap). The track is signposted 'Rimu and Matai Trail' at the far side of the skid site. After 5 minutes, you will meet a 4WD track and should nip up to the signposted 'Supplejack'. This technical downhill will test your cornering ability to the max. Please don't skid or cut the corners. Avoid when wet. Supplejack leads back to Sharlands Road.

Notes The Nelson MTB club maintains and builds tracks here.

14 Fireball Road

2 km southeast of Nelson

Grades 2–4, 1–2 hours, 5–20 km ★ ★

Many mountain bike tracks have been built through this pine forest over the last decade and have proved extremely popular for racing and recreation.

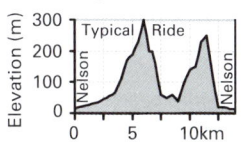

Landowners Hancock Forests Ltd, phone (03) 541 7037.

Route description At the time of writing, this area was temporarily closed to biking. A massive storm in 2008 left a jumble of trees across all tracks and roads, and the forestry company had plans for logging. They say that the forest will eventually be reopened to bikers during the weekends only and people should drop into a main bike shop in town for an update on information.

The shop will be able to sell you a map showing most of the trails around Fireball Road, and hopefully point out which ones have been opened again by the time you get there.

Notes If you live in Nelson, we recommend you check out www.nelsonmountainbikeclub.org.nz and join this progressive club.

15 Dun Mountain

EASY   ADVANCED

1 km south of Nelson

Grades 2–4, 2–4 hours, 22 km return ★ ★ ★

This much-loved ride follows a historic tramline deep into beech forest. Several other great rides peel off the Dun Mountain trail. If you're new to Nelson, start here.

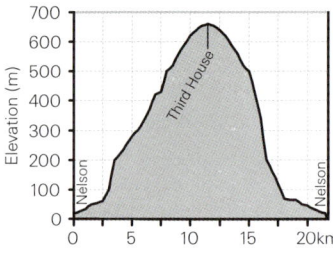

Route description Only 1 km from downtown Nelson, you'll find the start of the 'Dun Mountain Walkway' sign-posted opposite 130 Brook Street. The first section of the walkway is also known as (Old) Codgers Track. Follow the easy climb for 20 minutes till you pop out onto the gravel Tantragee Road. Ride up the road for 300 metres till you see another Dun Mountain Walkway sign heading off to your right.

After about an hour's riding on an easy gradient, you'll come to a well-signposted four-way intersection. Follow the 'Dun

Third House, Dun Mountain.

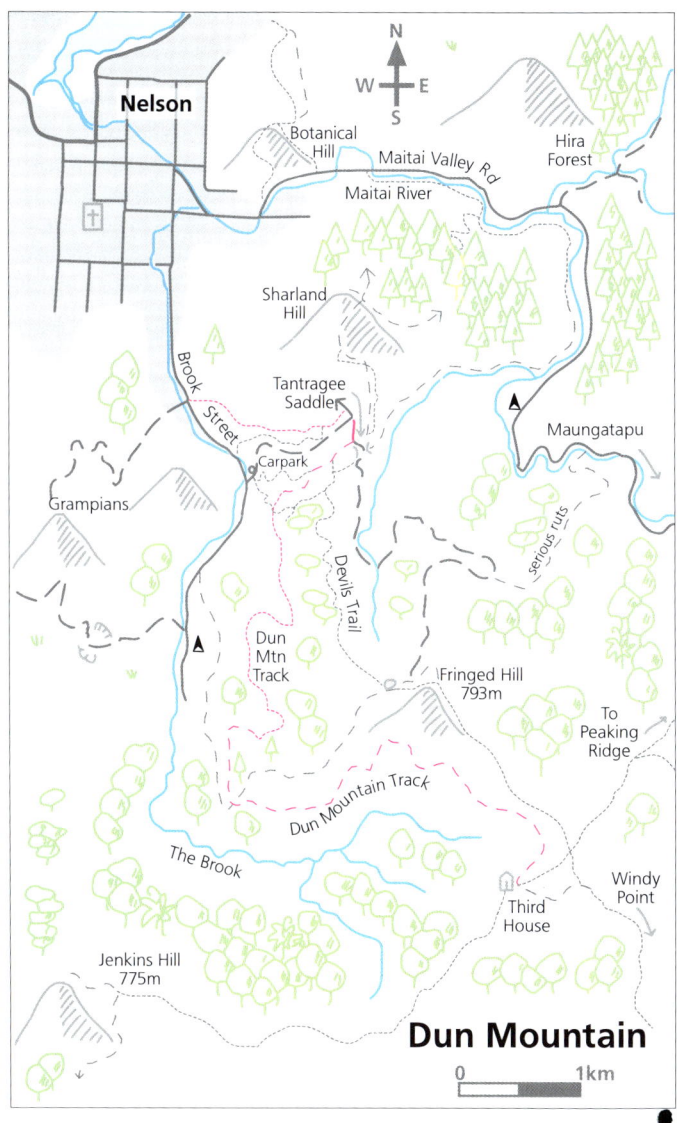

Nelson

Botanical Hill

Maitai Valley Rd

Maitai River

Hira Forest

Sharland Hill

Tantragee Saddle

Carpark

Grampians

Maungatapu

serious ruts

Devils Trail

Dun Mtn Track

Fringed Hill 793m

To Peaking Ridge

Dun Mountain Track

The Brook

Windy Point

Third House

Jenkins Hill 775m

Dun Mountain

0   1km

Mountain' track straight ahead—it just gets sweeter and sweeter, all the way to Third House. Sitting at the top of a grassy clearing, this shelter overlooks Nelson Bay.

From Third House, you now have four great options:

1 Return the way you came.

2 Pedal off to Peaking Ridge (see below).

3 Howl along to Windy Point (see Maitai South Branch below).

4 Leg it even further and do the whole Maitai South Branch ride.

Track conditions 60% 4WD track, 40% single track

Notes The Dun Mountain Walkway is popular with walkers–avoid it at busy holiday times and remember to give way.

16 Fringed Hill

1 km southeast of Nelson

Grades 4 and 5, 2–4 hours, 12–18 km ★ ★

A generally easy but long climb will give your lungs a good clear out and earn you a huge descent.

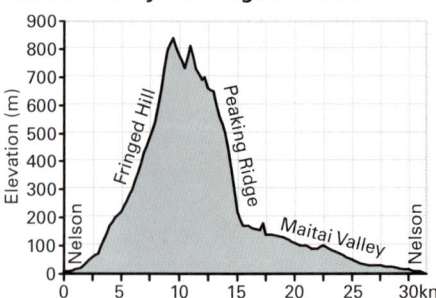

How to get there Ride out to the bottom of the Dun Mtn Walkway on Brook Street, a 10-minute ride from town.

Route description Follow the gravel road up to Tantragee Saddle, and on up to Fringed Hill. Be warned: it's over 700 m to the top. Ah, but the view! On a fine day, it's worth every bead of sweat.

About 500 metres from the top, you'll reach a T-intersection. Turn left to climb the last and nastiest stretch to the top or right to cruise to the car park 50 metres away. If the weather is dry as a bone, you have a choice of two routes down (Note: there is a steep 4WD track signposted 'Brook Valley' between the trig and the car park)

Brook Valley

A dry-weather 4WD track (grade 4) leaves from the left of the car park and descends to the four-way intersection half-way along the Dun Mountain Walkway. From there, you can carry on straight ahead to get to Brook Street. Watch out for the nasty drainage channels. This is not the best option.

Third House

From the very top of Fringed Hill, there is a rough, grade-5 single track that weaves its way through native forest towards Third House. After 2 km, you'll reach a four-way intersection with a 'Rocks Hut' sign. To ride to Third House, go straight ahead and sidle down to the Dun Mountain Track and then turn right. From Third House, you can follow the Dun Mountain Walkway back to Brook Valley (see above).

Alternatively, at the intersection, you can head left and tackle Peaking Ridge (see below).

Notes This track is fragile when wet; avoid skidding.

17 Peaking Ridge

EXPERT

1 km southeast of Nelson

Grade 5, 4–8 hours, 30-km loop from Nelson ★ ★ ★

This is a ruggedly technical route down from Fringed Hill, guaranteed to keep expert riders on the edge of their seats.

How to get there From downtown Nelson ride up to Fringed Hill (see above).

Route description From the Fringed Hill radio masts, take the Black Diamond Ridge single track. After pedalling for 30 minutes, turn left at the 'Maitai Caves' sign, and 15 minutes later, you'll come across another Maitai Caves signposted turn-off that includes a small 'to Peaking Ridge' sign. Follow that sign, and after another 30–40 minutes, you'll reach an obvious 'Peaking Ridge' sign that points off to the right.

The first 500 metres is loose and steep and follows a series of fading pink spray-painted dots on trees. After 30 minutes

Squeezing down Peaking Ridge.

of no mucking around, you'll pop out on a smooth 4WD track that runs down alongside the Maitai River South Branch.

Turn left and take the 4WD track until you reach a ford, where you will see a single track to the left. Take that track, to avoid crossing the river, all the way to a T-intersection at the main Maitai River. Turn right, then left and cross over a footbridge to the Maitai gravel road. This is the same exit as the Maitai South Branch ride.

Take a breather as you pedal the 45 minutes back to the centre of Nelson.

Notes Refer to the Fringed Hill elevation chart.

18 Maitai South Branch

Nelson

Grades 4–5+, 7–9 hours, 36-km loop ★ ★ ★ ★

Without a doubt, this is one of Nelson's greatest epic trail rides. High levels of fitness and technical skills, as well as a good bike, will all help to make this ride enjoyable.

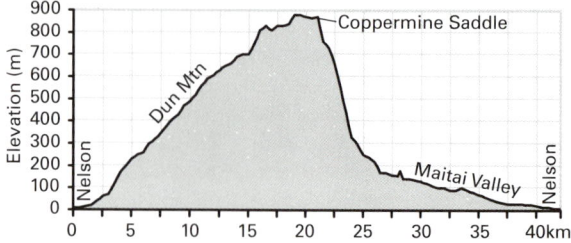

How to get there Ride the Dun Mountain Walkway all the way up to Third House (see above).

Route description From Third House, carry on up the Dun Mountain Walkway, past Junction Saddle. Beyond here, the track goes through a rough patch. Half an hour later, you'll break out above the bushline, then another 15 minutes of sweet single track will bring you to Windy Point.

This is a good time to reassess the weather—you've got another 2 hours of exposure above the bushline to complete this marathon.

If the weather looks good, then carry on to Coppermine Saddle. From the sign at the saddle (with your back to the sign) go straight ahead, down into the scrub where you will find a cleared track (this is a shortcut alternative to going up to Dun Saddle). You will have to walk for 1 km till you connect with the South Branch Track.

From here it's pretty much all down hill. The first half of the descent into Boulder Valley is grade 5. If you like the Karapoti Rock Garden, you'll love this! The second half gets faster and smoother as you descend.

The Maitai South Branch—Paul's favourite Nelson ride.

The council is gradually upgrading the track from the Maitai end. Eventually you reach, and cross, the Maitai River South Branch. From here, there's even more sweet smooth riding, then 4WD to a second ford, where a single track takes off to the left. To avoid getting wet take the single track to a T-intersection at the main Maitai River. Turn right and then left, then swing over a footbridge to hit the Maitai gravel road.

From here, it's 45 minutes pedalling back to the center of Nelson.

Notes Check out www.coppermine.co.nz if you are interested in racing this mighty ride. Take Topomap O27 Nelson.

19 Maungatapu Track

Pelorus Bridge to Nelson

Grade 3+, 4–6 hours, 35 km   ★ ★

This popular 'short cut' to Nelson crosses the Bryant Range on a 4WD pylon track steeped in gruesome history—murders most foul!

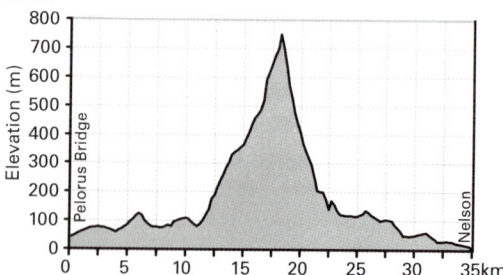

Route description Turn west off Highway 6 at Pelorus Bridge and ride up Maungatapu Road. There are two major forks in the road—both are well signposted. The gravel road turns into a 4WD track 12 km from the highway and climbs steadily out of the Pelorus Valley. Carry on straight ahead at a four-way intersection. The last few kilometres up to Maungatapu Saddle (740 m) are very steep and, depending on the condition of the track, may be unrideable in places.

At the saddle, check your brakes before heading straight down past the 'Water Catchment Area' sign on an even steeper 4WD track. Watch out for the ruts and drainage channels!

The track improves as it heads down into the Maitai Valley, and almost all the major intersections are signposted. The one exception occurs a long way down, when you think you are at the bottom of the hill. The track splits in two and you must turn right to follow an obvious 4WD track up a steep but short hill.

After passing the Maitai reservoir and climbing another minor hill, you coast down into the Maitai Valley again. Follow the valley road for about 10 km, then turn right at the first intersection in Nelson to go to the town centre.

Track conditions 20% sealed road, 45% gravel road, 35% 4WD track

Notes Pelorus Bridge is 53 km from Picton via Queen Charlotte Drive and 57 km from Nelson via Highway 6. Pelorus Bridge has a shop/cafe and camping ground. Refer to Terrainmap 9 Nelson.

20 Barnicoat Range

3 km east of Stoke

Grade 2, 1 hour, 6 km ★

This easy ride is a good workout that rewards with great views.

How to get there Ride up Marsden Road, off Main Road, Stoke, to the quarry gates.

Route description Take the little bridge on your right, then, after 100 metres, take another bridge on your right. Now climb on a good 4WD track for around 40 minutes. Hang a right when you hit the ridge to get to a high point (604 m), where there is a big pole and some wind socks. This is where paragliders take off from. The views of the Nelson region are awesome. Head back down the way you came.

21 **Kingsland Forest**

Richmond

Grade 3–4, 1–2 hours, 4–8 km   ★ ★

Richmond locals have built a bunch of fun single tracks in Kingsland Forest, in the hills above town.

How to get there   Ride up Queen Street towards the hills. Carry on around Churchill Ave till you see Marlborough Crescent on your right. At the far end is the entrance to Easby Park.

Route description   From Easby Park, climb steeply up Tower Road for 15 minutes. When you reach the power lines, turn right at the 'Lost Time' sign. From the bottom of this single track, veer left and climb up another steep road.

At an intersection at the top, veer right to head down Pylon Road for 200 metres before turning right onto Walter's Wiggles, the second single track. This leads down to The Escalator. At the bottom of it, you should turn right and climb to a lookout area at a 'Kingsland Forest' sign.

From the lookout, head right onto a grassy track (not the 4WD track) and follow it for 150 metres to the last and best

Rarified air from the top of Kingsland Forest.

single track, 'Lodestone Gully'. This sweet trail leads to the bottom of Lost Time. Drop down the gravel road for a few hundred metres before turning left to follow a track back to Tower Road and Easby Park.

Track conditions A mixture of gravel roads and single tracks
Note Parts of the forest were being logged Monday to Friday in early 2008, so some areas may still be closed.

22 Aniseed Valley

16 km south of Richmond

Grades 2–5, 2–4 hours, 6–10 km return ★ ★ ★

There are three good back-country trips heading up the Aniseed Valley from a large picnic area.

How to get there Head south from Richmond on Highway 6 for 4 km then turn left at the 'Hackett Picnic Area' sign. After another 12 km on Aniseed Valley Road, you will reach the signposted 'Roding River Recreation Reserve'. This is the starting point for the following three rides.

Whispering Falls
Grade 2, 1 hour, 8 km

Cross the bridge and pass the 'Hackett Hut 2 hours' sign. After 30 metres of single track, veer left onto a gravel road and follow it up valley for 10 minutes to a swing bridge (ignore a climb off to the left). Once across the swing bridge, follow a grade-2 single track to a signposted fork. Keep left to head up to a bridge, from where you can see the Whispering Falls.

Hackett Hut
Grade 3, 2 hours, 12 km

On the way to Whispering Falls, there is a signposted fork where you can veer right and ride a grade-3 track to Hackett Hut, 30 minutes away. There is one shortish steep climb and descent to tackle before reaching the hut at an idyllic picnic spot. The hut lies just across a stream. Head back the same way.

Browning Hut
Grade 5, 3–4 hours, 18 km

From Hackett Hut (or from the signposted fork 10 minutes before Hackett Hut), a difficult grade-5 track leads to Browning Hut. It's one of those pay-before-you-ride type tracks. In other words, there's lots of bike carrying on the way up, but riders who have a few trials skills will love the ride back down. Hot tips: Take the track below the slip, not above. This ride is only worth riding after a long dry spell.

Notes The huts are marked on Topomap O28 Wairau. These tracks are popular with elderly walkers and families.

Dave Mitchell at Druggins Dam, Aorere Goldfields.

Marlborough

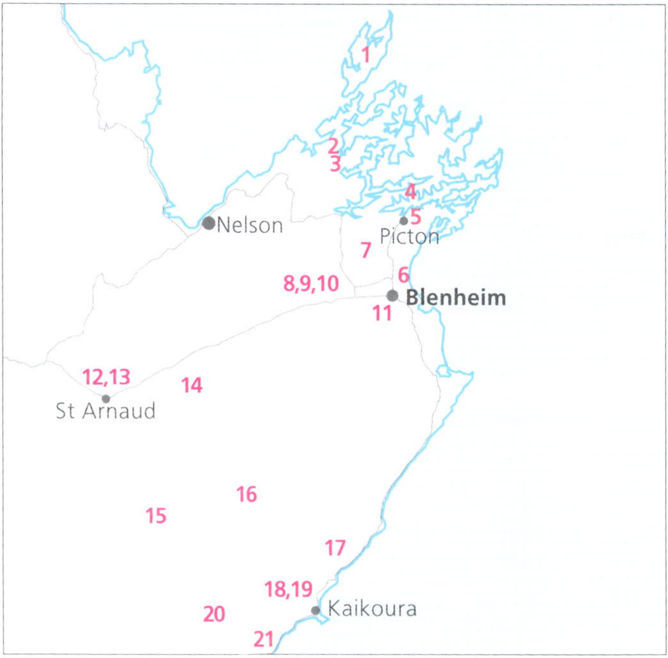
1
2
3
4
5
Nelson
Picton
7
6
8,9,10
Blenheim
11
12,13
14
St Arnaud
16
15
17
18,19
20
Kaikoura
21

1 D'Urville Island
2 Archers Track
3 Nydia Bay
4 Queen Charlotte Track
5 Picton Tracks
6 Whites Bay Loop Track
7 Linkwater Long Cut
8 Wakamarina
9 Onamalutu Intro
10 Mt Patriarch
11 Wither Hills
12 Teetotal Trails
13 Beebys Knob
14 Branch and Leatham Valleys
15 Rainbow
16 Molesworth
17 Okiwi Bay-Half Moon Bay
18 Mt Fyffe
19 Kaikoura MTB Park
20 Clarence Expedition
21 Kaikoura Coast Track

MARLBOROUGH HIGHLIGHTS

Marlborough is a back-country trail rider's dream. Queen Charlotte Track is the longest single-track in the country, Wakamarina and Nydia Bay are stunning technical bush rides, and the Rainbow and Molesworth are trips through BIG mountain country. A few training rides before you visit will help. Most single track in this region is on clay, which is treacherous when wet.

1 D'Urville Island

Northwestern tip of Marlborough Sounds

Grade 2, 2 cruisy days, 53 km plus ★ ★ ★

This remote island is a great place for a few days holiday. The riding is technically easy but requires some fitness.

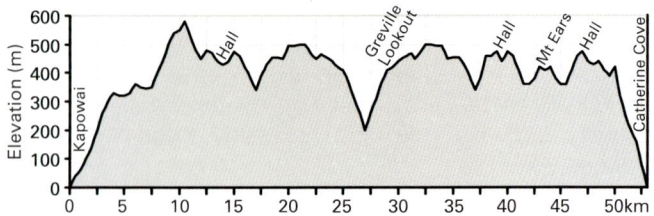

Landowners Most of the 4WD tracks on the island end up on private land. Check with your transport across to the island if you plan to explore beyond the trip described below.

How to get there From Rai Valley, halfway between Picton and Nelson, ride/drive north to French Pass, at the end of a windy 60-km road (it takes 2 hours to drive). A 10-minute boat trip from French Pass gets you to Kapowai Wharf on D'Urville

Island. Contact French Pass Sea Safaris, phone (03) 576 5204, or French Pass Sea Link, (03) 576 5337, to book a trip across.

Route   description
D'Urville Island has a network of smooth gravel roads passing through a large, scenic reserve. The almost complete lack of traffic makes this an ideal sanctuary for cyclists.

Riding the main ridge on D'Urville Island.

From Kapowai Bay, follow the 'Main Road' up a large climb onto the spine of D'Urville. After about 45 minutes of straining the chain, you should turn right. It's another 2 hours to the D'Urville Island Community Hall—an ideal spot to break for lunch.

In the afternoon/evening, head west to Greville Harbour. If you appreciate good views but don't like hard climbs, stop just past the bush edge. The sunsets from here can be stunning. Return to the hall for the night (the sunrises from the hall are equally impressive).

The next morning, ride up to Mt Ears for more great views. On a clear day, you can see the lower North Island. Head back to the hall again for lunch.

In the afternoon, ride south from the hall for 1 km before turning left onto a 4WD track signposted 'WILDERNESS RESORT'. This track follows power poles down to the Wilderness Resort at Catherine Cove. A few hundred metres from the bottom, there is a fork in the track—turn right. Then, after another 100 metres, turn left.

At Catherine Cove, you can catch the boat straight back to French Pass or stay the night and enjoy swimming, short walks and fine food at the restaurant. The trip described here is only 53 km long, so you'll have time to explore.

Accommodation There is accommodation at French Pass (from $120 for 2 people), at D'Urville Island Community Hall in the middle of the island (minimum charge of $40/group) and at the Wilderness Resort at Catherine Cove (from $80 for 2 people). Camping is available at French Pass (DOC campsite, $5/person) and Catherine Cove (Wilderness Resort, $35/person, including a two-course meal). Accommodation can be booked through French Pass Sea Safaris, phone (03) 576 5204.

Track conditions 85% smooth gravel road, 15% 4WD track

Notes There is a total fire ban on D'Urville. Catherine Cove even bans camp stoves. If you like table tennis, there's a table and bats at the hall. French Pass has swimming, short walks, dolphins, etc. Take Topomap O26-P26 D'Urville or Parkmap Marlborough Sounds.

2 Archers Track

96 km northwest of Blenheim

Grades 2–4, 2–3 hours, 16 km return ★★

This is a good complementary ride for the driver in a group doing Nydia Bay (see below). If you park your car at Opouri Saddle, it takes about the same time to do this ride and drive around to Nydia Bay as it does to do the hard-core Nydia Bay track.

How to get there From Rai Valley township (halfway between Blenheim and Nelson), drive north for 1 km and turn right onto Opouri Road. Turn right again shortly afterwards to follow the road all the way to Opouri Saddle, another 25 km away.

Route desciption From Opouri Saddle, either ride the technical downhill single track (on your right) or coast down Tennyson Inlet Road. The single track rejoins the road near the bottom. A minute later, turn north onto Archers Road and follow it for 6 km to Penzance Bay.

Now follow a single track around to Deep Bay. Eventually the single track turns into a 4WD forestry road that traverses naked logged hillsides on the way to Elaine Bay.

Return to Penzance Bay the same way and back up to Opouri Saddle (500 m).

3 Nydia Bay

ADVANCED

96 km northwest of Blenheim

Grade 4, 4–7 hours, 34 km   ★ ★ ★

If this ride wasn't so hard to get to, it would be one of the most popular technical rides in the country. If you've got great riding skills and an eye for fine scenery, you'll love it.

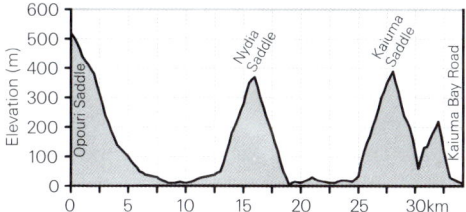

How to get there Drive 26 km northeast from Rai Valley to the top of Opouri Saddle (500 m). We recommend you take a driver who would be happy doing the much easier Archers Track then driving to the finish of this ride to pick you up.

Route description From Opouri Saddle, experienced single track riders can head down the gnarly bridle track to the right, while intermediate riders should descend via Tennyson Inlet Road. At the bottom, turn right and cruise 3 km to Tennyson Inlet settlement. Carry on around the bay to the start of the Nydia Bay Track.

This rock and root riddled track will lead you over Nydia Saddle (370 m) and down to Nydia Bay. At the far end of the bay, head inland through farm paddocks, then up and over a second saddle, Kaiuma (387 m). Overall, the ride is technical and rewarding. If you can average 7 km per hour, you'll be doing well. Part of the track follows the route of a 1910 timber railway line.

The track finishes on Kaiuma Bay Road, a gravel road 23 km from Highway 6 and another 3 km from Canvastown. There is a plan to build a bridge over the Pelorus River near Havelock—thus cutting out at least 10 km of tedious riding/driving.

Track conditions 25% 4WD track, 75% single track

Notes In dry weather, it's 98% rideable north to south, much less from south to north. In wet weather, it's mostly unrideable either way. There's a backpackers' hostel and DOC lodge at Nydia Bay but no shops. Take Topomap P27 Picton or Parkmap Marlborough Sounds.

4 Queen Charlotte Track

Picton, Marlborough Sounds

Grade 3+, 2–3 days, 63–86 km ★ ★ ★ ★

This is the longest single track in the country. Add to that lovely coastal scenery, good cafes and accommodation stops along the way and a brilliant beech forest section at the end, and you have a recipe for one of the best weekend rides in New Zealand.

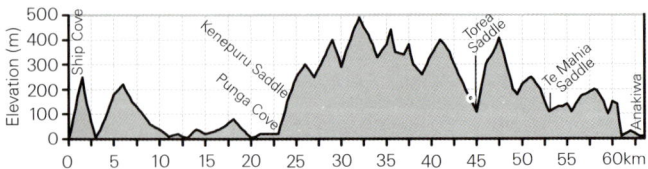

How to get there Catch the Beachcomber, phone (03) 573 6175 and www.mailboat.co.nz, or Arrow Water Taxi, phone (03) 573 8229, from Picton to Ship Cove, for around $50 per person and bike. Or you can get dropped off at any one of several bays along the way to shorten your trip.

Route description The northern section from Ship Cove to Punga Cove (much of it on private land) is closed to mountain bikes during the peak walking season—December to the end of February (a helluva lot better than permanent closure).

Apart from the steep climb out of Ship Cove, the track to Punga Cove is generally quite rideable and fills the first day nicely. From Punga Cove, things get hillier, and many riders

Jonathan Kennett

Taking time out for the Queen Charlotte.

choose to avoid the middle section by riding along the road from Kenepuru Saddle to Te Mahia. If you stick to the track, be aware that it's very exposed in places (i.e., has awesome views) and water is scarce. Those who take the road generally make it back to Picton on the second day; those who go over the top often stop at Te Mahia for the night and finish the ride the next day.

The last section from Te Mahia to Anakiwa (the Anakiwa Track) is biking at its best—exhilarating single track through beautiful native forest.

Picton is 23 km from Anakiwa via Queen Charlotte Drive; a meandering and scenic sealed road.

Track conditions 2% gravel road, 96% single track, 2% unrideable

Other users This track is very popular with walkers — be ready for them to appear around any corner.

Accommodation Punga Cove Resort, phone (03) 579 8561; Portage Hotel Resort, phone (03) 573 4309; Portage Bay Shop, phone (03) 573 4445; Te Mahia Resort, phone (03) 573 4089. There are also many good camping areas. There is a shop and camping ground at Momorangi Bay, 9 km from Anakiwa, en route to Picton.

Notes The percentage of this track that is unrideable increases dramatically when wet. If it rains, we recommend taking the boat to Resolution Bay rather than Ship Cove. A DOC survey found that while most people are happy to share the track with bikes, they don't appreciate them in large groups. Refer to Parkmap Marlborough Sounds.

5 Picton Tracks

INTERMEDIATE   ADVANCED

Grades 3–4, 1 hour, 10 km   ★

This area is a mixed bag—from unrideable rubbish to very sweet single track—but it's worth a look if you're killing time in Picton.

How to get there Head around the marina to Victoria Domain.

Simon Kennett

The tracks start at a map board near the boat sheds.

Route description From the map board, a semi-rideable track sidles around a steep hillside and drops to a large grass playing field just around the corner. The track crosses the grass and meets up with a road that goes up to the ridge on your left.

There are two good tracks from the lookout on the ridge. One goes back down to the Waikawa Valley and is quite steep. The other is an excellent sidle track that draws you around the side of the ridge to meet up with the ridge road again. Roughly 50 metres on from where you re-meet the road, there is a 4WD track heading north further along the ridge. This leads the way to the other mountain bike tracks on this small hillside. These tracks were a bit gorsy but worth exploring.

When you get back down to the valley, head right to return to Picton or left for Waikawa.

Notes You can pick up a free map of Victoria Domain at the information centre near the Picton ferry terminal.

6 Whites Bay Loop Track

20 km northeast of Blenheim
Grade 4, 2–3 hours, 12-km loop   ★ ★

Half this ride involves physically and technically challenging single track through native bush.

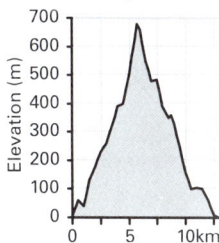

How to get there From Blenheim, take Highway 1 north to Tuamarina, turn east and go past Rarangi to Whites Bay.

Route description Park your car at the historic cable station in Whites Bay then ride back to the road and north up the hill for 2.5 km. On the left side of the road, 50 metres past the crest of the hill, is a pylon track signposted 'Whites Bay Loop Track'. That's where you want to head.

After 1 km, you pass a pylon and then the track narrows to single track. It takes about an hour to ride and push your bike to a signposted fork on top of the ridge. From there, turn left towards Whites Bay and follow a tight squiggly downhill through native bush. At the end, follow a pylon track down to a fork, turn sharp left and you'll soon reach the road between Whites Bay and Rarangi. Turn left to return to your car, 2 km away.

Track conditions 40% sealed road, 10% 4WD track, 50% single track

Notes You'll need to carry plenty of water as there are no streams along the way and riding can become hot work in the dry Marlborough region.

7 Linkwater Long Cut

20 km northwest of Blenheim

Grade 4+, 4–6 hours, 33 km ★ ★

This is the long way from Tuamarina (10 km north of Blenheim) to Linkwater over the Waikakaho Walkway. It is enjoyed by jungle riders willing to walk for a technically demanding downhill.

Route description From Tuamarina (10 km north of Blenheim on Highway 1), head west on Bush Road and Kaituna-Tuamarina Road for 6 km. Turn north up the Waikakaho Valley gravel road and ride for another 12 km. Pass the farm buildings and continue for 3 km. The track starts on the left of the river soon after the road peters out (100 metres past a hay barn) and climbs steadily up a spur.

  The track up to the saddle (800 m) is a granny-gear grind and will take 1–2 hours. Then, the following 2 km section to Cullens bush edge is rutted, rooty and largely unrideable.

  From here, follow the zigzag track down to the valley floor. If you plan to ride from north to south, this steep section will require at least an hour of bike carrying. From the valley floor, it's a further 5 km on sealed road to the Linkwater store.

Track conditions 35% sealed road, 35% gravel road, 30% semi-rideable single track

Notes Take Topomap P27 Picton.

8 Wakamarina

25 km northwest of Blenheim

Grade 3 or 5-, 2 or 5 hours, 20 or 35 km ★ ★ ★

We suggest two options for this once-busy goldminers' track: a fun trip to the tops and back or the full hardcore crossing of the Richmond Range from Onamalutu to Canvastown.

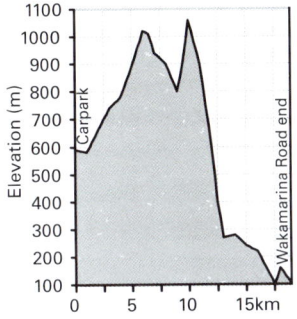

How to get there From Renwick (just east of Blenheim) follow Highway 6 for 4 km. Then turn left onto Northbank Road and after 5 km veer right onto Onamalutu Rd. You will pass Onamalutu Reserve and after another 7 km hang a sharp left turn at the 'Wakamarina Track' sign. The road end is then 100 metres away.

Route description The two great options for the Wakamarina are:

There and back Ride up to Fosters Clearing for the views and an endorphine hit. DOC has upgraded this section of track, so it is now grade 3 when dry. There is a 10-minute, grade 4+ diversion to Fosters Hut, where the views are breathtaking. Head back the same way. That will take 2–3 hours. Some fit locals lengthen this ride by starting from Onamalutu Reserve.

The full crossing Ride up to Fosters Clearing for your first rest stop (there is a water supply at the clearing). Next, descend and sidle about 2 km before walking to the top of the crossing (at 1066 m). This is rugged country, and you will have earned every metre of elevation. Now fine-tune your brakes and clear your mind in preparation for switchback-city Arizona. You're about to descend over 800 m in 2.5 km of twisting, turning single track.

Near the bottom, turn right at the turn off to 'Stone Huts'. Shortly after, you'll reach Devils Creek Hut turn off. Pop down for a squizz at the hut, then sidle down the Wakamarina river valley. Four kilometres on, after the Doom Creek Hut site, veer left down to the footbridge, cross Doom Creek and veer left again. The Wakamarina road end is 2 km further on. From there, it's 15 easy km to Canvastown.

Track conditions 5% sealed road, 45% gravel road, 45% single track, 5% unrideable

Other users Trampers

Dave Mitchell

Following in the miners' tracks, Wakamarina.

Notes This track has a clay surface—avoid when wet. Get through in a day if possible, but be prepared to be benighted.

There's a motor camp in the Wakamarina Valley, 10 km from Canvastown. Canvastown itself has a pub, and that's it. Take Topomap O28 Wairau or Parkmap Mount Richmond (but note that Doom Creek Hut has been removed).

9 Onamalutu Intro

28 km northwest of Blenheim

Grade 2, 2.5–4.5 hours, 40 km ★

This is a relatively easy ride for anyone who may be suckered into dropping their friends off at the start of the gnarly Wakamarina track (see above) or for riders after a shorter workout.

How to get there From Renwick, head north for 4 km. After crossing the Wairau River, turn left onto Northbank Road. Ride 5 km, then turn northwest into the hills on Onamalutu Road. Onamalutu Reserve is about 18 km of pleasant road riding northwest of Renwick.

Route description From the reserve, head southwest on Onamalutu Road. Veer left at the 'Mt Richmond Forest Park' sign, then 1 km on, cross Flowers Creek ford. Don't turn left to 'Scollays Ltd'. At the next intersection, veer left following Kiwi Road (alternatively, turn right onto Nutmeg Road for a very hilly 13 km back to the reserve).

Carry on up Kiwi Road, past the Wakamarina car park turn off, and straight ahead at the top (560 m). A few minutes on from the top, veer onto Bartletts Road. Keep following this road down to Bartletts Creek. After crossing the ford, simply veer or turn left all the way to Northbank Road. Follow that road down the valley back to Onamalutu Road.

Track conditions 50% sealed road, 50% gravel & dirt road

Notes Refer to Topomap O28 Wairau.

10 **Mt Patriarch**

47 km west of Blenheim

Grade 3, 4–6 hours return, 66 km return ★ ★

Another essential trip for mountain biking peak baggers. The views from the 1656 m summit are amazing!

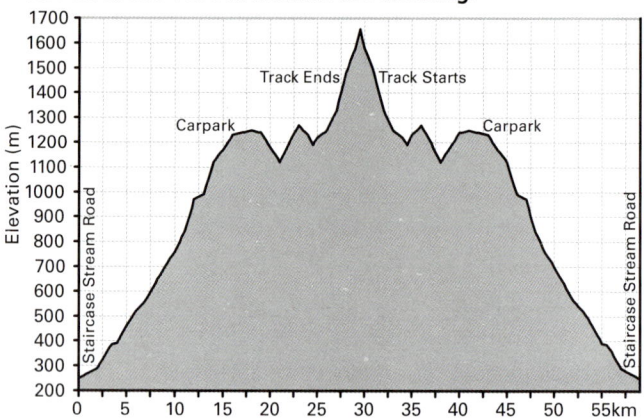

How to get there About 4 km north of Renwick on Highway 6, turn left (just north of the Wairau River bridge) and follow Northbank Road for 33 km, to Top Valley Road.

Route description Ride up Top Valley Road for 6 km, then turn left onto Staircase Stream Road and climb through forest, then alpine scrub for 12 km to the Lake Chalice car park.

From the car park, continue for another 12 km to the road end on the flanks of Mt Patriarch. At an altitude of 1460 m, there are stunning views of the Wairau Valley and inland Marlborough.

You can walk the last 3 km to the summit of Mt Patriarch (1656 m) by negotiating a demanding rocky ridge and then sidling across a shingle slope. The route is marked with poles, and there is a trig at the top. This is a very exposed area.

Track conditions 85% gravel road and 4WD track, 15% unrideable tramping route

Notes Staircase Stream Road is impassable to vehicles after heavy rain. Refer to Parkmap Mount Richmond.

Dave Mitchell

The long and winding road to Mt Patriarch.

11 Wither Hills

Blenheim

Grades 2–4, anything up to 3 hours, 5–20 km ★ ★

This mountain bike park in Blenheim will keep you fit and prepare you for the longer track to Mt Vernon.

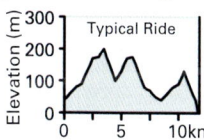

How to get there Ride south out of Blenheim on Maxwell Road (it becomes Taylor Pass Road). The Wither Hills Mountain Bike Park is well signposted 2 km south of the hospital. It's 1 km south of the main walking area car park.

Note: The local council has developed a track from central Blenheim along the Taylor river bank out to the mountain bike tracks car park; it's more fun than the road.

Route description At the mountain bike car park, there is a map board that shows all the main tracks. The layout is very clear, so it's easy to plan your trip. Start off with the 'Main Track'. It's a 20-minute, grade-2 loop that climbs to the top of

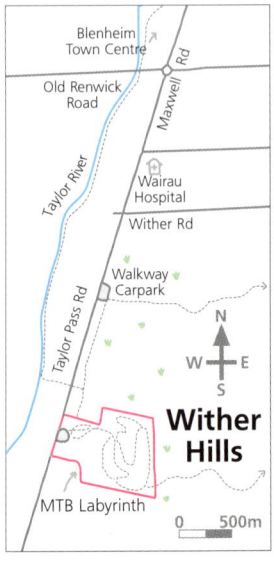

the park and back. You'll then know what the whole area looks like.

Next, move on to the grade-3+ 'Technical single track'. It's narrow and off camber in places. After that try the tracks not marked on the map. There are many bus stops beside the main track and a technical downhill in the main valley.

Mt Vernon Loop
Grade 3-, 1–3 hr

This ride climbs almost to the top of Wither Hills just south of Blenheim. From near the centre of town, follow Redwood Street south right to the last house. There you'll see a sign introducing the ride. Follow the markers up to the top of Mt Vernon (422 m) for some great views. Then either carry on around to the Taylor View Track and to the Wither Hills Mountain Bike Park or head downhill via the Cob Cottage Track followed by a cruise along Mapp Track back to Redwood Street. The tracks described here are nearly all farm tracks.

The council has added a sidle track around the bottom of Wither Hills to the mountain bike car park.

Notes If you are new to this area, get a copy of the Marlborough District Council's 'Wither Hills' map from the information centre at the railway station. It was updated in 2006. Mt Vernon is extremely exposed to the elements—go prepared.

12 Teetotal Trails

St Arnaud, Nelson Lakes
Grades 2 and 4, 1–3 hours, up to 35 km ★ ★

Mountain biking isn't the main attraction at St Arnaud, but if you are there with a bike, these tracks are worth riding.

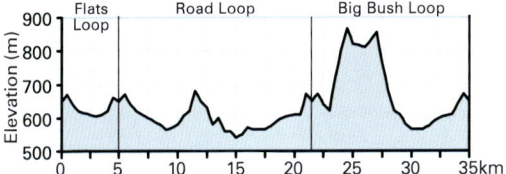

How to get there   Ride from St Arnaud towards Murchison for 1 km, then turn right at the 'Teetotal Mountain Bike Trails' sign. There is a car parking area 30 metres off the highway, but the sandflies there are terrible (better to ride from town and just keep moving).

Route description   There are three main loops to try:

Teetotal Flats Loop Trail
Grade 2, 1 hour, 5 km

From the car park, follow the DOC signs around this easy loop. It twists across farmland, through a few stands of manuka and past a lake.

Teetotal Road Loop Trail
Grade 2, 1–2 hours, 16 km

This is a good trip for those who want to stretch their legs on an easy trail. Start with the first half of the Flats Loop Trail and then head west when you hit the farm road (it's signposted). At the far end of this loop, you can nip up the signposted 'Teetotal Summit' road for a decent workout and some good views. Give yourself up to half an hour for this return trip to the summit.

Big Bush Loop Trail
Grade 4, 2 hours, 13 km

This loop also branches off the Flats Loop Trail and is well signposted. The initial climb is getting rutted out by 4WDs, so unless you are really fit and the track is as dry as a bone, you will have to walk most of it. After half an hour climbing, you should reach a high point (856 m) on a gentle, forested ridge. Check your brakes and let the fun begin. But beware: the track becomes a very steep and fast single track!

Simon Kennett

Between a rut and a twiggy place on Big Bush Loop.

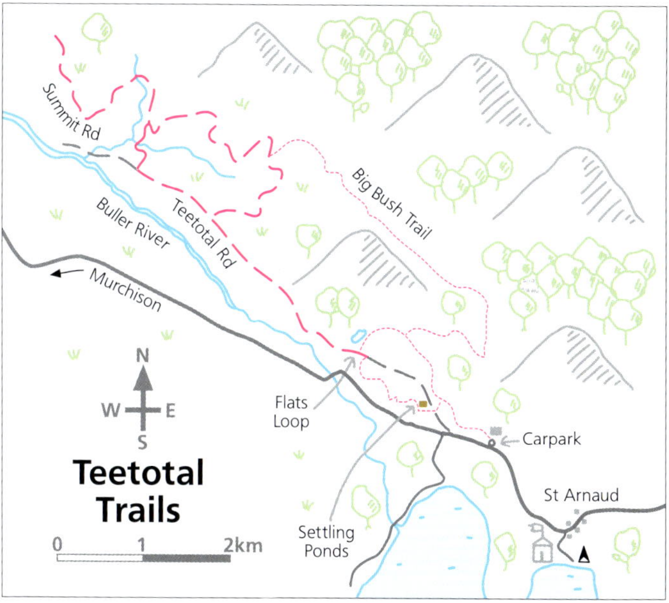

Teetotal Trails

0   1   2km

When you hit Teetotal Road, turn left for the quick route back to St Arnaud or right to lengthen your ride by 5 km. There are signposts to guide you back to the highway.

Track conditions Mixture of farm tracks, forestry roads and single track

13 Beebys Knob

ADVANCED

9 km northeast of St Arnaud

Grade 4, 2–5 hours, 15+ km return   ★ ★

Looking for a BIG hill to test your lungs and then your brakes? Then Beebys Knob is for you. The summit vista is spectacular!

How to get there Head out of St Arnaud on Highway 63 towards Blenheim. After 8 km, turn left, then follow Tophouse Road for 800 metres. DOC signs show the bottom of the track on your right.

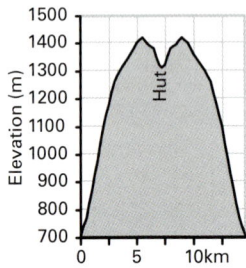

Route description Hop over the gate by the signs and change down. This is a very tough climb up to the tops at 1400m (alongside the Beebys Knob TV transmitter). Beebys Hut is another 1.5 km beyond the Knob, descending along the ridge. We turned around at the hut, but you can carry on along the ridge for another 5 km before turning back.

Keep an eye out for 4WDs and other riders on the descent.

Track conditions 100% 4WD track

Notes This ride is covered in one of DOC's two pamphlets about local MTB tracks, available from the St Arnaud Info Centre. Avoid this ride in winter (when it is likely to be under snow) and go prepared for freezing alpine conditions any time of the year. The 4WD vehicle access season is 1 Dec to 30 April.

14 Branch and Leatham Valleys

70 km west of Blenheim

Grade 2, half to one and a half days, 30–95 km ★ ★

These two valleys offer riders the chance to get into the base of some remote mountains without taking on anything particularly technical or mountainous.

How to get there Turn south off Highway 63 onto Leatham Road, 70 km west of Blenheim and look for a place to park.

Route description Ride along the gravel Leatham Road for 7 km to the confluence of the Branch and Leatham rivers (where a new footbridge over the Branch River was being built in 2008). This spot is another option for parking.

There are 4WD tracks heading up both of these mountainous, bush-clad valleys. Allow half a day to explore the Branch Valley as far as Greigs Hut and back (a total of 30 km). From the hut, Tourist Track is ideal for those in search of their new maximum heart rate.

David Drake dropping off Beebys Knob.

Give yourself a day to explore the Leatham Valley–it's over 50 km to the Lower Gordon Hut and back. The scenery is more of a mixed bag up this valley, with farmland early on, but it is spectacular up the top end. The track becomes unrideable shortly after the hut.

Notes Take Topomap N29 St Arnaud. If you want to spend the weekend exploring these valleys, you can stay overnight at one of the huts or camp at the confluence of the Branch and Leatham (7 km from Highway 63).

15 Rainbow

INTERMEDIATE

Hanmer to St Arnaud

Grade 3, 1–2 days, 120 km ★ ★ ★

The Rainbow follows a pylon road through mountainous country, along the original stock route from Marlborough to Canterbury. It is now one of New Zealand's best mountain bike touring rides.

Landowners Permission to cross Rainbow Station must be obtained from Star Holdings Ltd, phone (03) 545 7600. The Road

An Easter ride up Leatham Valley.

is open annually from the end of December to the end of March, with a gold coin donation for mountain bike access.

Route description Hammer out of Hanmer on Jacks Pass Road. Cycle over Jacks Pass (869 m) and down to the Clarence River valley, then turn left. From here it is 35 very corrugated

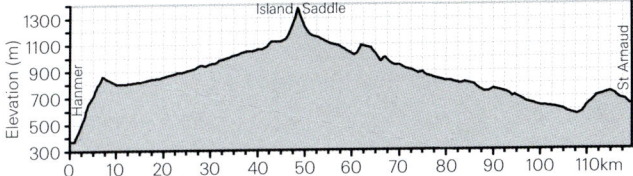

kilometres to the turn off to Lake Tennyson (a 3-km detour). Lake Tennyson is as exposed to bad weather as it is beautiful. You may want to camp near the Clarence River bridge or even head over Island Saddle (8 km further on) to Coldwater Creek where there are more pleasant camping areas. The last few kilometres up to Island Saddle (1372 m) are steep and unrelenting, but even if you walk, the rewards of a great downhill and excellent views make it worthwhile.

From Island Saddle, it is another 50 km passing through tussock, then beech forest, to Highway 63. About 5 km on from Island Saddle and 400 metres before reaching the Wairau River, a 4WD track on your left leads to a hut 400 metres away, which can't be seen from the road. It has four bunks, a toilet and space for camping next to it.

Continuing down the valley, there are several fords that may be impassable after heavy rain. About half an hour after crossing Rough Creek, veer left at the 'Rainbow Forest Park' sign and climb the last few kilometres to the highway.

Once you reach Highway 63, it's an easy 10 km west to St Arnaud where you will find the tranquil Lake Rotoiti, a general store, a motor camp, a backpackers' hostel and lots of sandflies.

Track conditions 10% sealed road, 70% gravel road, 20% 4WD track

Notes Doing the ride in the direction we've described is great for linking up with the Molesworth ride (see below), but if you do this ride the opposite way, from St Arnaud to Hanmer, there is often a tail wind, making it an excellent day's riding. This is the route of one of New Zealand's most popular mountain bike events, The Rainbow Rage, held the third Saturday in every March, phone Stoke Cycles, (03) 547 6361.

Island Saddle Hut.

Go well equipped and be prepared for snow at any time of year. No fires are allowed in the precious remnants of native bush north of Coldwater Creek. Leave all gates as found. Take Terrainmap 11 Kaikoura.

16 Molesworth

Blenheim to Hanmer

Grade 3, 2–4 days, approx 205 km ★ ★

INTERMEDIATE

This ride passes through the country's largest farm, Molesworth Station and runs alongside the massive Kaikoura mountains.

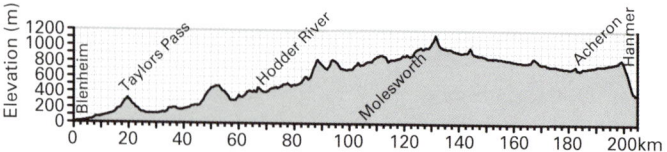

Landowners Molesworth Station is usually open to the public in January and February. Outside this time, permission is required from Jim Ward, Molesworth Station, Private Bag, Blenheim, phone (03) 575 7043.

The station is closed for mustering in November and March, in winter because of deep snow and sometimes in summer because of high fire risk. Recently it's also been closed over Easter for a goose shoot.

Route description From Blenheim, ride south on Maxwell Road and head over Taylors Pass on a gravel road. This takes you to the main sealed road heading southwest up the Awatere Valley. (You can avoid this first hill by riding around on Highway 1 to the Awatere Valley.) After about an hour's cycling, the road climbs high above the Awatere River before dropping down to Jordan. There are several newly sealed stretches, but the road is still very hilly—try to travel light and pace yourself.

At the Hodder River bridge (72 km from Blenheim), there is a public toilet and some good trees to rest under on a hot day. Cyclists and mountain climbers often camp here for the night. There is also a reasonable camping spot among trees further on near Upcot. Not far past Upcot, you must tackle the formidable Upcot Saddle—a steep, crank-bending, knee-grinding, granny-gear climb.

From Hodder River, it takes 3–5 hours of riding to reach the old Molesworth Homestead, which has a pleasant DOC camping area (but no safe water supply). From here you enter the massive Molesworth Station.

Within Molesworth Station, camping is only permitted here and at the historic Acheron Accommodation House, a good 5 hours away. After climbing to the top of Wards Pass, it's downhill all the way to the Acheron River. From Isolated Saddle, undulate along to the Acheron Accommodation House, at the confluence of the Acheron and Clarence rivers, where there is more good camping and a drinkable water supply.

It's about an hour's cycling from Acheron Accommodation House to the Hanmer Springs turn off. Those who are heading back to Blenheim via the Rainbow Valley (see above) can carry on straight ahead at this fork. Otherwise, cycle from Jollies Pass down to Hanmer about an hour away. Hot pools, ice creams and a camping ground await at the bottom of a long fast downhill.

Track conditions 15% sealed road, 85% gravel road

Notes This is BIG country. Gigantic hills and valleys are guaranteed to make even the most confident rider feel very, very small. Take a gas cooker as open fires are not allowed on Molesworth Station. Also take an extra water bottle; summer temperatures often rise into the 30s, and the river water is not always palatable. Leave all gates as you find them.

Go well equipped and be prepared for snow any time of year. Further information can be obtained from DOC in Renwick, phone (03) 572 9100. Take Terrainmap 11 Kaikoura.

Due reverence should be paid to Kennet Peak between Upcot and Molesworth (even if it is spelt wrong).

17 Okiwi Bay-Half Moon Bay

31 km northeast of Kaikoura

Grade 3, 4–5 hours, 20-km loop ★

This is a good ride for locals looking for a lot of borderline granny gear climbing to push their fitness.

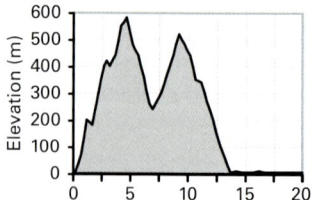

How to get there Okiwi Bay is 98 km south of Blenheim, or 31 km northeast of Kaikoura, and the track is signposted "Okiwi Bay Walkway Tracks" on Highway 1.

Route description The route is well signposted all the way up to a grassy saddle and fence line. A further 20 metres on, go straight through another fence opening (the gates have been removed) and head towards Kaikoura.

From here, just follow the main 4WD track through multiple fence lines down, up and then down again to Half Moon Bay and Highway 1. Turn left and ride the 7 km back on Highway 1 to Okiwi Bay.

Notes This track is used mainly by hunters on 4X4 quad bikes so it is a bit rutted.

Paul Kennett

Patrick slogs his way out of Okiwi Bay.

18 Mt Fyffe

ADVANCED

Kaikoura

Grade 4, 3–5 hours, 16 km return   ★ ★ ★

Mt Fyffe is the pinnacle of hill climbing in New Zealand, but your suffering is amply rewarded.

How to get there Head out of Kaikoura on Ludstone Road, turn right onto Mt Fyffe Road, left at Postmans Road, then follow the DOC signs to a car park/picnic area 12 km from town. There was a sign or two missing when we last did this, so a map came in handy.

Route description Nip round the side of the locked gate and change straight down to granny gear. The 4WD track ahead climbs from 180 m to 1602 m in 8 cruel kilometres. There is a DOC hut shortly after the halfway mark (1100 m), past which the track deteriorates and a significant bike push is necessary (but only on the ascent).

Dave Mitchell

Just a hint of the view to come from Mt Fyffe.

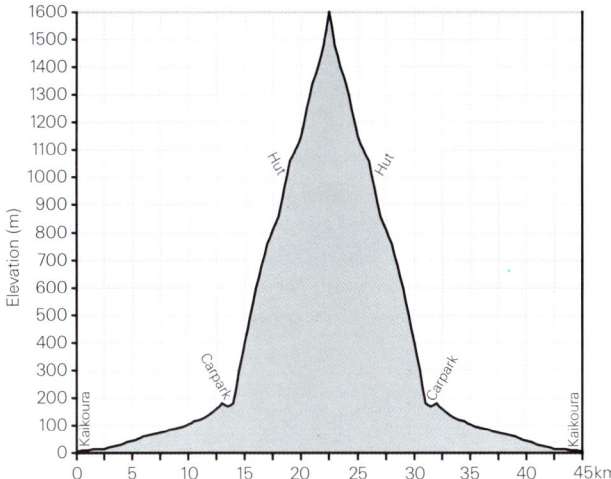

The view from the top is fantastic, but it can get very chilly up there, even on a fine day. Take extra clothes as well as food and water.

The ride takes 2–4 hours up from the car park and about half an hour back down.

Notes Walkers and 4WD vehicles regularly use this track.

19 Kaikoura MTB Park

2 km north of Kaikoura

Grade 1 and 4, 10–30 mins, 0.5 km 👎

We rode this tiny pine plantation area in May 2008. It comprised a few North Shore ramps, some nasty jumps and about 500 metres of abandoned single track. It has suffered from a bad storm which dropped a lot of debris all over the place. Sadly, the area just isn't worth going to.

However, 'Si' from R&R Sport in Kaikoura can point you in the direction of two local walking tracks that are not (yet) signed 'no mountain bikes' but that the local information centre isn't keen for us to promote in this guide.

20 **Clarence Expedition**

25 km west of Kaikoura

Grade 3+, 1–2 days, 50–100 km ★★

Wedged between the seaward and inland Kaikoura ranges, with a breathtaking mountainous landscape, good campsites and DOC huts, the Clarence Reserve provides great scope for exploration.

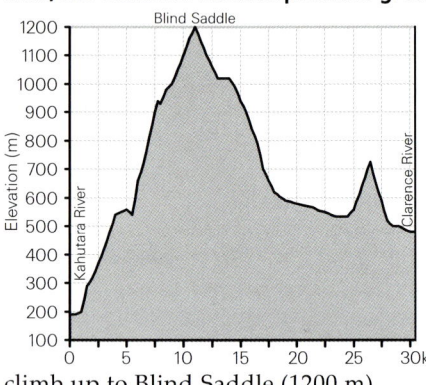

Route description

The track starts from the northern side of the Kahutara River bridge (the topomap marks this incorrectly), on Highway 70, 25 km west of Kaikoura township. Almost straight away, you'll have to tackle the formidable climb up to Blind Saddle (1200 m).

On the way down, you'll pass Tentpoles Hut, which is rough and basic, some weird rock formations showing a fault line, and near the bottom, Bluff Dump Hut (four bunks, basic but tidy). Another kilometre down valley, on your left, you'll see an unusual, small hill. Behind it is hidden a lovely little hut nestled among some willows beside a small creek.

After carrying on down the valley for a few kilometres, you'll reach a signposted intersection. Continue straight ahead to the Clarence River (via a 200-m hill).

From Quail Flat, beside the Clarence, you must follow the markers to avoid the farm buildings and private property. It is 20 km down the Clarence River valley to Goose Flat Hut (6 bunks) and another 6 km dead-end ride on to Fidget Hut (4 bunks). There's also a lovely campsite among some willows beside the Clarence, about 1 km north of Tytler Point. The easiest way out is back the way you came!

Track conditions 80% gravelled farm track, 20% 4WD track

Exploring the back of beyond in the Clarence Reserve.

Notes For more information, pick up a copy of the DOC pamphlet on the Clarence Reserve or contact DOC in Renwick, phone (03) 572 9100. You can also go www.doc.govt.nz then search 'Clarence'. Access beyond the Conservation Area is currently verboten! Unfortunately two of the landowners are having a battle over public access. Topomap O31 is essential.

21 Kaikoura Coast Track

50 km south of Kaikoura

Grade 3+, 2 days, 43 km ★

This privately-owned track offers plenty of great views and points of historic interest.

Landowners The track is open from October to April and costs $75 per rider, including overnight accommodation at Ngaroma Station. Your gear is transported for you. For bookings, contact Sally Handyside, phone (03) 319 2715, fax (03) 319 2724. Also check out their website at www.kaikouratrack.co.nz

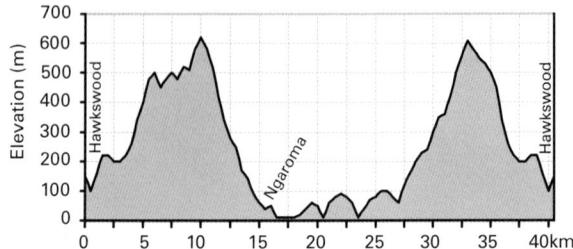

How to get there The ride starts and finishes at the Staging Post at Hawkswood, just off Highway 1. This is a fascinating place to stay and has cheap campsites and funky backpackers' accommodation (www.stagingpost.co.nz). It's worth heading up the night before your ride just to check it out.

Route description From the Staging Post, you head north on Highway 1 for a few kilometres before turning up a steep forestry track. From here on, you'll be following a marked route along farm tracks, climbing for an hour or two. The views of the coast and the Kaikoura mountains are awesome.

After some rolling terrain along the tops, it's a fast downhill to Ngaroma Station, not far from the coast; but be warned, there is likely to be stock on the track, and if you're going too fast, you could miss some of the turn offs.

After overnighting at Ngaroma Station your day starts with a cruisy gravel road ride down to Medina Station, a good spot for a break. Then, it's time to tackle the big hill up to Mt Wilson Hut, which has water and a view of Mt Tapuae-O-Uenuku. It's quite a difficult scramble to get right to the top of Mt Wilson (642 m) but well worth it on a calm clear day.

From Mt Wilson, it's mostly downhill back to the Staging Post, less than an hour away.

Track conditions 5% sealed road, 25% gravel road, 65% 4WD track, 5% single track

Notes Bookings are essential. A guide booklet is provided that outlines the route in detail. The Crayfish Trail mountain bike race is held in October on the Kaikoura Coast Track.

West Coast

Karamea 1

2
3
Westport 4
5
7
6
Reefton 8
10 9
12
11
13
Greymouth
15 14
Hokitika 17
18 16
19
Arthur's Pass
20

Haast 21

1	K Road	12	Moonlight Track
2	Charming Creek	13	Croesus Track
3	Britannia Track	14	Napoleon Hill
4	Denniston Plateau	15	Noname/Kumara Mud Plug
5	Denniston Short Cut	16	Taipo Valley
6	Tiropahi Tram Track	17	Tunnels Tracks/Blue Spur
7	Pioneer Heritage Trail	18	Kaniere Water Race
8	Kirwans Track	19	Totara Valley
9	Blacks Point	20	Okarito Forest
10	Reefton Lookout	21	Paringa-Haast Cattle Track
11	Big River		

WEST COAST HIGHLIGHTS

Reefton is the hub for mountain biking on the West Coast. Within an hour's drive of town are several fantastic forest rides along old mining trails. And this just whets the appetite for the multitude that the West Coast has to offer. If the weather is fine, you'll think you've died and gone to MTB heaven.

1 K Road

110 km north of Westport

Grade 4-, 1–2 hours, 6 km

Ironically, this is the only mountain bike track that's been officially opened by a New Zealand Prime Minister. The Right Honorable could hardly have picked a worse one!

Route description Loads of dosh have been poured into providing a toilet, a car park, a map board and promotion. Only one thing is missing—a good mountain bike track. Instead, after hours of driving, you get to ride a steep, grovelly dead-end forestry road. In an area renowned for outstanding scenery, this ride offers virtually none. It's a logged-over, weed-infested landscape that might look good in a few decades, but the steep forestry road will still make it a 'K' for krap.

Track conditions 100% boring forestry road

Notes The one consolation is that, for just a few more kilometres of driving, you can walk to the Oparara Arch. Pity it's not rideable, but the scenery is impressive.

2 Charming Creek

30 km northeast of Westport

Grade 3, 3–5 hours, 36 km ★ ★ ★

This is a very cool ride through native bush on an old railway line. There are tunnels, bridges, waterfalls, huge trees, the whole lot. You'll love it—we did!

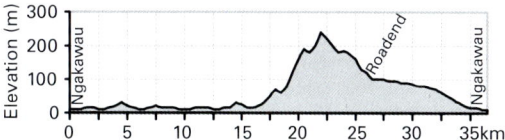

Seasonal restrictions This track is popular with walkers. It is closed to bicycles from 25 Dec to 25 Jan and during Easter.

Route description From Ngakawau, head north on Highway 67 for 13 km before turning right towards Seddonville. After another 3 km, turn right again at the Charming Creek signpost. This road soon turns into gravel and climbs steadily among scrubby bush. Follow the main road, passing several turn-offs, to the road-end car park 10 km from Seddonville.

Carry straight on over a bridge and past old coal mining machinery to a tunnel. Follow the old railway line track into the bush, and you'll soon reach a large mill shelter where there is a logbook to sign; it's a good place for a break. Navigation from here is a piece of cake. The track follows Charming Creek down through native forest, past historic sites (with shelters), through more tunnels and over swing bridges.

There are also lots of bumpy railway sleepers to rumble across, and bird life abounds in the area. The track ends at a car park at the edge of Ngakawau.

Track conditions 45% sealed rd, 30% gravel rd, 25% single track

Notes Remember, this is also a walkway—always give way to those on foot. There is still some of the original wooden centre rail (used for braking) along some of the old rail route– best try and avoid riding on it as it is fragile in places. Take Topomap L28 Mokihinui.

If the weather is terrible, locals ride from Ngakawau up the old rail line to the Seddonville road end and back as this section is sheltered most of the way.

3 Britannia Track

20 km north of Westport

Grade 3, 2 hours, 12 km return ★★

This well-graded old mining track climbs through native forest.

How to get there From Waimangaroa, 16 km north of Westport on Highway 87, drive another 2 km north and turn right at the DOC sign. A gravel road heads inland to a car park 2 km away.

Route description From the car park, a signposted track heads across paddocks and onto a lovely old benched track. This track then climbs through native forest to a waterwheel stamping battery about 1 hour away.

Jonathan jostles with the beech forest on Britannia Track.

The track is slippery when wet. There are half a dozen short walking sections, but it is worth taking your bike up to the end of the bench—the technical ride back down is a hoot.

Track conditions 100% single track

Notes Take a headlamp if you want to explore a small gold-diggings tunnel along the way.

4 Denniston Plateau

Denniston, 25 km north of Westport

Grades 2–4, 1–12 hours, over 50 km of track ★ ★ ★

The bizarre landscape around Denniston has recently attracted a lot of attention from the Buller Cycling Club. In partnership with DOC, they have signposted several interesting mountain bike routes, ideal for exploring the plateau.

How to get there Drive 16 km northeast of Westport on Highway 67 before turning right at Waimangaroa and heading up the hill to Denniston. After 7 km, turn right at a T-intersection and drive a further 1 km to the 'Friends of the Hill' museum (first driveway on your right after turning right at the top Y-intersection), where there is a MTB trails information board. Fit locals can ride up the hill in 30 minutes!

Route description The Denniston plateau is renowned for its unpredictable 'moods'. These range from wild and desolate during a storm to serene and ethereal during a fine sunset. The long history of mining also adds to the attraction and adventure of riding at Denniston.

The best way to explore the area is with a copy of the Denniston Plateau MTB tracks pamphlet. It costs $1 and is available from DOC offices and selected shops in Westport and Waimangaroa. As well as background information, it contains a high-quality aerial photo showing the main tracks. There are also comprehensive track details available on the Buller Cycling Club website (www.cyclebuller.co.nz) along with information on the latest track developments.

Typical bedrock riding on the Denniston Plateau.

Tracks marked out at the time this book went to print were:

Quarry Circuit: grades 2–3, 3 km. Short introductory ride across rocky terrain that is typical of the Denniston tracks, with good views of the plateau.

Ropers Hotel Circuit: grades 2–3, 5 km. Follows the historic track between the recreation grounds and Ropers Hotel. There is a signposted 70-metre walking-only section at the bottom end of the circuit that marks out a historically significant stretch. This is only a short section of the track, so please respect the conservation values and walk it.

Miners Track Circuit: grades 3–4, 7 km. Follows the old miners track to the Coalbrookdale Mine; a local favourite, this has the most technical single track of the current tracks on the plateau, with great historical sites to have a gander at along the way.

Drill Track Circuit: grade 3, 8 km. Follows old drill-rig exploration tracks and includes a bit of everything; a great track to link with the Miners Track Circuit.

Pig Route Circuit: grade 4, 5 km. One for the downhillers and bikes with good suspension; includes rock gardens and a 1 m high ledge drop.

Sullivan Circuit: grade 3, 9 km. The official 4WD track on the plateau; lots of ruts, rock gardens, creek crossings and mining artifacts, but no bogs or wet feet thanks to the drainage work of the local riders. Go from marker 6-6 to 5-3 at the bottom end of the circuit to get some good single track in while heading out to the main road.

Whareatea Circuit: grade 3, 11 km. The cross-country rider's favourite; a long sustained uphill with an even longer continuous rollercoaster downhill on slabby bedrock; great views of the plateau.

Mt Rochfort: grade 2+, 18 km. A tough 500-m vertical climb up the 4WD road to the communications tower at the top of Mt Rochfort. Return the same way — only much faster.

Coalbrookdale Ride: grade 1, 8 km. A family and beginners' ride to the historic Coalbrookdale and old Cascade mines; all on gravel road and easy old mining tracks; walking access only up to the Coalbrookdale fan house.

Rapid Stream Ride: grade 2+, 7 km. A more technical beginners' ride following the access road to the old Sullivan Mine and out the bottom along the old Sullivan Mine haulage road to the main road.

Track conditions 30% gravel road, 60% 4WD track, 10% single track

Notes The tracks' surfaces are suitable for riding in all weather conditions, even after a typical West Coast deluge.

The Denniston Plateau is a sensitive ecological area and is the home to endangered native species such as the great spotted kiwi and the giant carnivorous snail *Powelliphanta rossiana patrickensis*, so please keep to the formed tracks. Also, for your own safety, don't enter any mine tunnels or go near any smoke emitting from underground fires.

This is an alpine environment, so fill your riding pack with suitable clothing and don't attempt to cross flooded creeks.

5 **Denniston Short Cut**

24 km northeast of Westport

Grade 4-, 4–6 hours, 33 km ★ ★

This remote ride follows a pylon road through sub-tropical rainforest from Denniston Plateau to the Iron Bridge on the Buller River. It was pioneered by hardcore cycle tourers in the 80s.

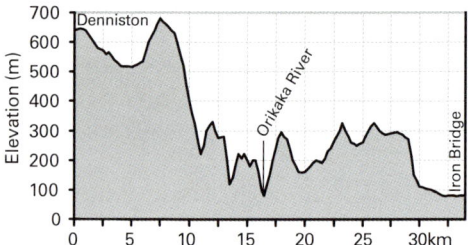

Landowners The ride passes through private land. Riders must contact DOC (Westport) or check the Buller Cycle Club website (www.cyclebuller.co.nz) for current access conditions.

How to get there Ride 20 km northeast of Westport on Highway 67 before turning inland at Waimangaroa to tackle the character-building 8-km hill climb to Denniston.

Route description A maze of rough gravel roads and 4WD tracks traverses Orikaka State Forest to Iron Bridge on the Buller River.

From Denniston, ride inland on the main sealed road towards Burnetts Face. Do not turn right towards Sullivans Mine. The seal soon ends, and you descend to Burnett Stream. At the bottom, keep left on the main road and take the bridge across Burnett Stream. The gravel road will lead you past a burning coal mine, across a surreal 'Dr Who' type landscape and into the forest.

The mine (marked on the topomap) has been burning underground since it was accidentally lit in 1953. About 5 minutes past the mine, you'll cross Cedar Stream. Take the next right turn, about 200 metres away. It's a 4WD track that takes you

Flying along the Denniston Short Cut.

up a short steep hill. When you're almost at the top, turn left at the four-way intersection. At the next fork, by the pylons, turn right then right again after 50 metres. Now just stay on the main gravel road and enjoy a fast downhill to the hut at Stevenson Stream.

Just after the top of the next steep hill, turn right down a gnarly gravel road to Mt William Stream. Cross it, climb steeply for another 15 minutes, then cruise along a short flat section to a T-intersection. Head left over a gate and down to Orikaka River (also known as Mackley River).

The Orikaka River is deadly when in flood. On the other side, tackle the last 15-minute hill climb. At the top, navigation becomes tricky—there are pylon tracks and roads heading off all over the place. Two sets of pylons head south to the Buller River, while another set (the one you should follow) heads east towards New Creek.

At the first intersection after the hill climb, veer right (south) away from a tin hut. Cruise along on the main gravel road for 500 metres until you drop to a major T-intersection. Turn sharp left (back towards your pylons) and, within 50 metres, you'll start descending fast. Stay on the main road and, in 5–10 minutes,

you'll reach an intersection by a 'Blue Duck' sign. Veer left and meander up to a saddle where you'll veer left again. Then cruise to Iron Bridge on Highway 6.

Track conditions 80% gravel road, 20% 4WD track

Other users Mining trucks at either end, occasional 4WD vehicles and motorbikes

Notes The huge shuttle is a real drag, so it's better to be super fit and do the whole loop or tackle it as part of a West Coast cycle tour. Many roads and two sets of pylons have been built since edition 1 of Topomap L29 Inangahua was printed, but its topographical information is still essential.

6 Tiropahi Tram Track

26 km south of Westport

INTERMEDIATE

Grade 3+, 2–4 hours, 25-km loop   ★ ★

As long as you don't mind an hour of road riding, the single track sweetness makes this ride well worthwhile.

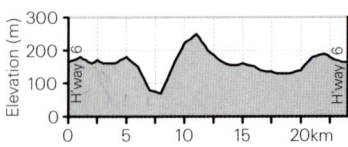

How to get there Tiropahi Tram Track car park is signposted 8 km south of Charleston on Highway 6.

Route description The car park is right next to the Tiropahi River. Check that it is crossable before starting your ride—you'll finish by crossing this river.

Ride north on Highway 6 for 5 km before turning right onto 'Four Mile Road'. Follow old forestry roads inland for 12 km. Navigation is easy—just turn right at all four intersections. There are a couple of ups and downs, and the road gradually becomes a 4WD track before dropping down to the edge of a pakihi swamp and an orange triangle marker (at grid ref 834 126).

From this orange marker, there are two ways to go:

1. The original route was to continue along the forestry road for 1 km, then turn left at a plastic bag (it now has a purple track marker) and drop down to the Tiropahi Track. This is

En route to Tiropahi Tram Track.

the best way for cyclists, and locals were working to have it cleared of gorse by the time this edition went to print.

2. The new way to go is to follow the orange triangles across the boggy swamp. This involves a fair bit of walking but no gorse bashing. It also leads to the Tiropahi Track and is the more scenic option.

The Tiropahi Tram Track heads west past a 'Track' sign. There are a few deep washouts to negotiate, but the terrain becomes easier as you go on. After 4 km, you'll need to cross Tiropahi River (dangerous in flood). The car park is on the other side.

Track conditions 20% sealed road, 50% forestry road, 25% single track, 5% unrideable

Notes The Tiropahi Tram Track is wet and boggy most of the year. Take Topomap K30 Punakaiki. Hot local tip: head to Jack's Gastof 5 km north of Charleston for excellent pizza and beer and a German-come-West Coast style 70s disco machine!

7 Pioneer Heritage Trail

Nelson Lakes to Springs Junction

Grade 2+, 2–3 days, 135 km ★ ★ ★

This is a classic, old-school, fat-tyre touring route for those wanting to pack their panniers and get away from it all.

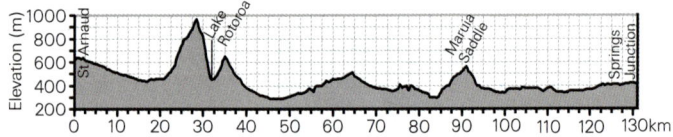

Route description From St Arnaud, head northwest up Highway 63 until you reach Howard Valley Road on your left. Ride up the valley and over the Porika Track (signposted 'Porika Road') to Lake Rotoroa. This involves climbing on a gravel road to 1000 m through native forest before descending a steep brake-block burning pylon track to the lake. There are great views on the way down, and this whole stretch of riding is beautiful. There's a camping ground at Rotoroa.

Next, head across the Gowan River and over the Braeburn Track (a gravel road). There is a good rest area at the top of the Braeburn saddle, then a cruisy downhill.

Turn left when you hit Tutaki Road North and cruise into Murchison via Mangles Valley. There are plenty of shops in Murchison, and a good camping ground by the river.

From Murchison, head south on Fairfax St, which turns into the gravel Matakitaki Rd. Eventually that turns into Maruia Saddle Rd. Follow this road through beech forest over the saddle (580 m) and down to Highway 65 just north of Maruia.

From the highway, you can ride south to Springs Junction or north to Murchison, both about 40 km away. If riding south on a busy day, then take the gravel road alternative not far past Maruia, which cuts out about 15 km of highway riding.

Track conditions 45% sealed road, 45% gravel, 10% 4WD track

Notes Take Terrainmaps 11 Kaikoura and 10 West Coast. If you have a week to spare and can handle a big dose of road

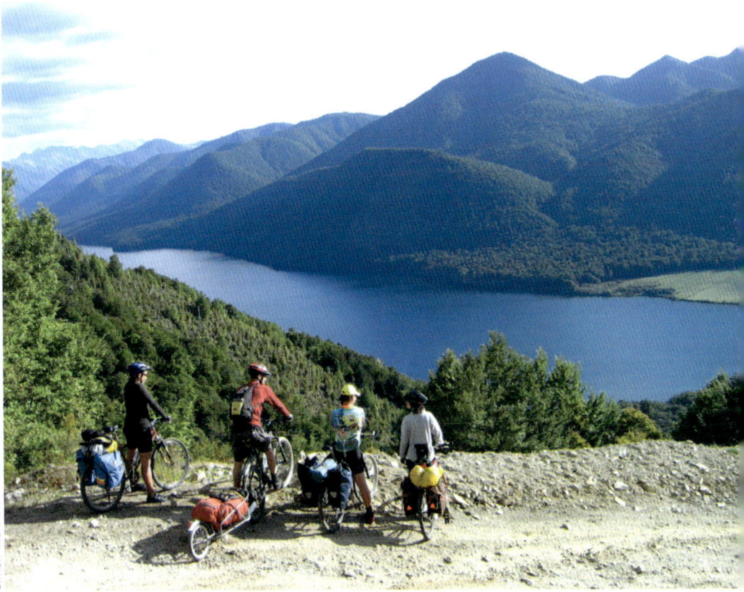

Simon Kennett

Fat-tyre tourers contemplate Lake Rotoroa from the Porika Track.

riding, we recommend heading south to Springs Junction and then east over Lewis Pass to Hanmer. Finally, make it a loop by returning to St Arnaud via the Rainbow Valley.

8 Kirwans Track

EXPERT

19 km northeast of Reefton

Grade 5, 4–6 hrs, 20 km return ★★★★

This rates as one of the most enjoyable hardcore rides in the country. The track is so fascinating that the prolonged slog in the upwards direction is actually fun; views from the top are stunning, and the technical downhill lasts for about an hour.

How to get there Head north out of Reefton for almost 12 km, turn right onto Boatmans Road and ride 6.5 km to the road end.

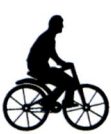

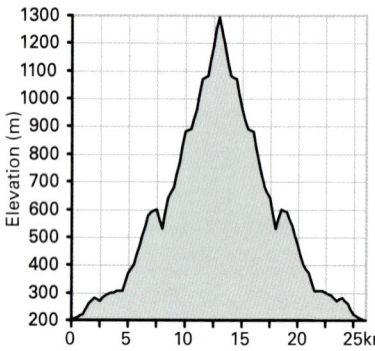

Route description Kirwans Track is signposted from the road end. Cross the rickety bridge and follow markers across the paddock to pick up the track as it enters forest. The track follows the valley for 4 km before climbing a massive hill to Kirwans Reward Mine at 1220 m.

About 1.5 km from the road end, you have to turn right, scuttle through a tunnel and scamper across a swing bridge. Next comes a mostly unrideable section, but after half an hour, the track improves again. Climb steadily for 2–3 hours to an intersection near the top. Follow the signposts to 'Kirwans Hut 30 min'. The last few hundred metres to the hut are unrideable, but the views are great.

Then tighten those brakes up for a mega-technical downhill back the same way.

Notes Watch out for walkers, as this is a popular tramping track. Sandflies at the road end have no mercy!

9 Blacks Point

Waitahu Valley, Reefton

Grade 3+, 3–6 hours, 27 km ★ ★ ★

INTERMEDIATE

Beech forest, mining remains and vintage single track make this a good outing despite the hike-n-bike sections.

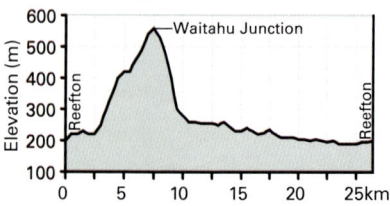

Route description From Reefton, ride east on Highway 7 for 2 km before turning left at the 'Murray Creek' sign. Follow the obvious old mining trail up to 'Energetic Junction', turn left to 'Murray Creek Track' and 10 minutes later cross the bridge to the true right of the stream.

Carry on to 'Cementown Junction' and past Chandlers mine to the top of the hill at Waitahu Junction. The climb is well graded and in good condition. For an easy (and predictable) ride, turn around here and head back the way you came.

The alternative descent to Waitahu Valley is described by DOC as a 'Tramping Track'. At the beginning of 2008, it was quite overgrown. Ask at DOC if it has been cleared before dropping down to the valley (or take a saw). Also, if river levels are up, you will not be able to cross the Waitahu River.

If you plan to continue, turn right at the 'Waitahu Junction' signpost and after 5 minutes keep your eyes peeled for a sudden left-hand turn off the main benched track. Carry your bikes down a 100-metre zigzag to where the riding starts again. If there are tree falls and slips, the downhill could take an hour.

Near the bottom, the track sidles up valley above the river for a few hundred metres before dropping down to the riverbed. Watch out for the dangerous drop-offs.

Cross the Waitahu River and head straight into the forest on the other side. After about 50 metres of bush bashing, you will hit the Waitahu 4WD track.

At the 4WD track, you can turn right for a diversion to Montgomerie Hut, 7 km up valley. But you'll have to head back the same way as, beyond the hut, the track is generally unrideable. Be warned; the track to the hut is littered with bogs.

Most people turn left and follow a good track out to Gannons Road. From the end of the 4WD track, it's a cruisy 8-km ride back into Reefton.

Track conditions   33% sealed road, 30% 4WD track, 30% single track, 7% unrideable

Notes   Take Topomap L30 Reefton and avoid the area during high rainfall.

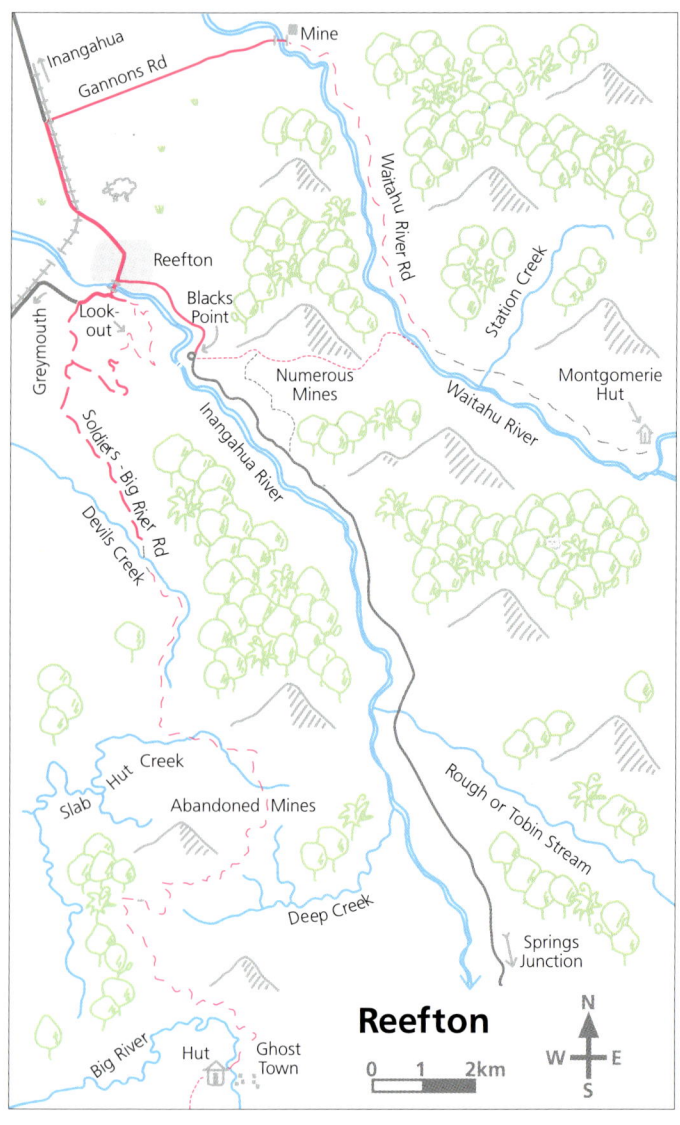

10 Reefton Lookout

Grade 2, 40 mins–1 hour, 8 km ★

A short spin on the edge of Reefton, even if the view fails to take your breath away, the climb should.

Route description Ride southwest out of Reefton on Highway 7 for 1 km. Turn left onto 'Soldiers Road' and, after another 1 km, turn left again at 'Lookout Road'. After 700 metres, veer left and cruise up to the lookout where there are some huge aerials and a brass direction dial pointing out various locations.

From the lookout, continue up the hill on the main gravel road for around 1 km. Now, pay attention or you'll end up riding down dead-end tracks like we did. Veer left just after passing a small pond on your right (which appears to be silting up fast). Two hundred metres later, turn left and coast down a good forestry road to Deadman Creek. Simple! You'll emerge from the forest, next to the last house in Rosstown. Turn left again for a flat 2-minute spin back to Reefton.

Track conditions forestry roads and 4WD tracks

11 Big River

Reefton

Grade 3, 4–8 hours, 50 km return ★ ★ ★

Historic mining road + native bush scenery + gnarly single track likely to destroy numerous bike parts = a classic old-school ride.

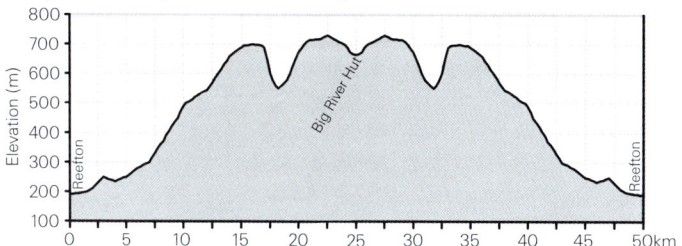

Route description Ride south from Reefton on Highway 7 and cross the Inangahua River bridge. After 1 km, turn left onto

Dave Mitchell

Moss alley, Waiuta Track.

Soldiers Road. This soon becomes a gravel road and climbs up Devils Creek valley for 9 km to the 'Alborn Coal Mine' car park. One hundred metres further on, Big River Road (signposted) veers off to the left.

The ride continues for another 2–4 hours, through native bush, on a rocky but rideable 4WD track, to Big River.

Various sites in this area were extensively mined for gold in the 1800s. Some old machinery remains and huge piles of mullock (waste rock) stand as testimony to the environmental effects of mining.

The luxurious Big River Hut is perched about 50 metres above the river, overlooking the Big River township site and surrounding countryside. It's worth staying overnight to explore various side tracks and the abandoned gold workings. Remember, this is a 4WD track—give way to those with a smaller brain-to-weight ratio.

Notes Big River Hut costs $10 per night. Refer to topomaps L30 Reefton and L31 Springs Junction.

Waiuta Track Option

The walking track from Big River to Waiuta, a mining ghost town, is now open to cyclists! It's 12 km of grade-4 riding. Expect a bit of walking, but mostly you'll strike long sections of dreamlike single track. From Waiuta, there are 10 km of gravel and 27 km of sealed road to ride back on to Reefton. Give yourself 2–4 hours to get to Waiuta and another couple of hours pedalling from there back to Reefton.

12 Moonlight Track

EXPERT

10 km northeast of Blackball

Grade 5-, 4–6 hours, 32 km return ★ ★

This half-day, grade 5- ride is similar to the Croesus Track (see below)—a full body workout uphill and down, but even more technical in places.

How to get there From Blackball, 25 km northeast of Greymouth, head south on the Taylorville Blackball Road, then northeast

on Atarau Road. About 10 km later, turn left onto Moonlight Road. If you have a car, park at the picnic area with the old sluicing cannon.

Route description Head north on the rough Moonlight Rd through beech and pine forests. After the bridge over Moonlight Creek, take the track on your right and climb up the river terrace.

Half an hour after the picnic area, you'll reach a car park and the start of Moonlight Track. You can drive to here if your car has reasonable ground clearance, but it's a better ride.

The benched single track follows Moonlight Creek through numerous old mining claims and hut sites. Many are signposted and are worth inspecting. The track climbs gently, but in many places the surface is rocky and slippery. This is challenging cycling but worth it because, with Mr Gravity on your side, the return journey will be much more enjoyable.

Beyond the hut, the track is mostly unrideable. Head back the same way for a rip-snorting downhill. Crashing aside, you should easily make it back to the car park within an hour.

Track conditions 60% gravel road, 40% single track

Notes Refer to Topomap K31 Ahaura.

13 Croesus Track

ADVANCED

Blackball, 25 km northeast of Greymouth

Grade 4+, 1 day, 38 km return   ★ ★ ★ ★

A big dose of rugged pre-mountain biking single track, through forest up to the alpine zone, makes this one of New Zealand cycling's unpolished gems.

Seasonal restrictions Because this track is so popular with walkers, it is closed to bicycles from 25 Dec to 25 Jan, and during the Easter break.

Route description Head northwest out of Blackball and follow Blackball Road for 6.5 km to the road end where the Croesus Track starts. It's sign-posted.

From there, an interesting old mining trail snakes through the forest. A few bits are rough and steep, but generally it is

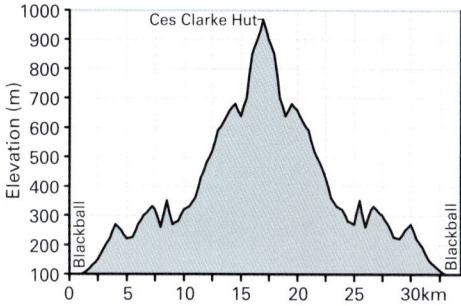

well graded and rideable—if it's dry! If it's wet, head somewhere else.

At a steady pace, it will take you 3–4 hours to reach Ces Clarke Hut, just above the bush-line. The hut is lovely, and the views are stunning. After a wee rest, it's worth wandering up to Croesus Knob 2 km away for even better views, but the track up there is mostly unrideable.

From the hut, the ride back down to Blackball is fantastic. Beautiful forest, challenging riding, good friends—what more could you ask for?

If you have time, it's worth making a diversion to Garden Gully Hut (a shack) and the abandoned mine beyond it. It is clearly signposted 3.5 km down from Ces Clarke Hut and offers great single-track riding.

Track conditions 30% gravel road, 70% primo single track

Notes The place to stay in Blackball is the famous Formerly The Blackball Hilton. This track is no fun in the wet. To stay en route, take Topomap K31 Ahaura.

14 Napoleon Hill

47 km northeast of Greymouth

Grade 3+, 2–4 hours, 23 km ★★★

This bizarre track will have you totally baffled as it swoops down narrow canyons, across several streams and through improbable tunnels.

Landowners The ride now traverses private property. If considering this route, call Malcolm Smith or Robyn Curtis-Smith on (03) 732 3849 or 021 131 4632 to apply for access and

Dave Mitchell

Brisk cycling conditions on the Croesus.

arrange payment of your $5 access fee (used for road maintenance). They will be able to tell you of changes to the track network that will effect your navigation.

How to get there From Ahaura, 35 km northeast of Greymouth on Highway 7, head inland on 'Orwell Creek Road'. Turn left after 9 km to stay on Orwell Creek Road and drive another 3 km before parking at a four-way intersection just before the end of the pines.

Route description Follow the main gravel road up Orwell Creek Road and round onto Napoleon Hill. At grid ref 021 708, turn off the track marked on the map to head north and follow a 4WD track down into Nobles Creek. This becomes a canyon that finally closes over completely. After passing through the second tunnel, head right and follow a farm track up a large stream for about 1 km and then right again to ride up Mosquito Creek.

Follow the Mosquito Creek track back up to grid ref 021 708 and then follow another 4WD track down to Orwell Creek Road where it crosses Smythes Creek. Cruise back down to your car.

Notes Topomap K31 Ahaura doesn't show the entire route but will indicate roughly where you are. Just remember you're doing a big figure of eight and you'll be fine.

15 Noname/Kumara Mud Plug

Nemona State Forest, 15 km south of Greymouth

Grade 3+, 2–4 hours, 33 km from Marsden ★ ★

Another one of our original rides that has withstood the test of time, this classic features a mix of scenery alongside old logging tracks and gravel roads. Throw some extra grease at your bottom bracket—this is a wet one.

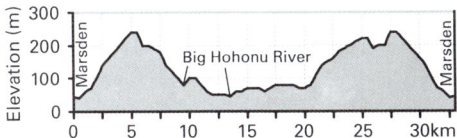

How to get there From Greymouth, the quickest way to Marsden is to head south on Highway 6 for 5 km, then turn left at the 'Shantytown' sign and ride to Marsden another 8 km away. A scenic alternative is to ride through Boddytown and on down Marsden Road. This ride can also be done from Kumara.

Route description From Marsden, head to the right and cross the bridge a few hundred metres away. On the other side, turn right at the 'Noname Rd' sign and, during the next kilometre, ignore all tracks that branch off the original road (including the big driveway at the 'Noname 0152' sign).

After about 5 km, you'll drop down a small hill and reach a T-intersection (with a left turn that may be overgrown by now). Turn right and before long you'll reach a four-way intersection.

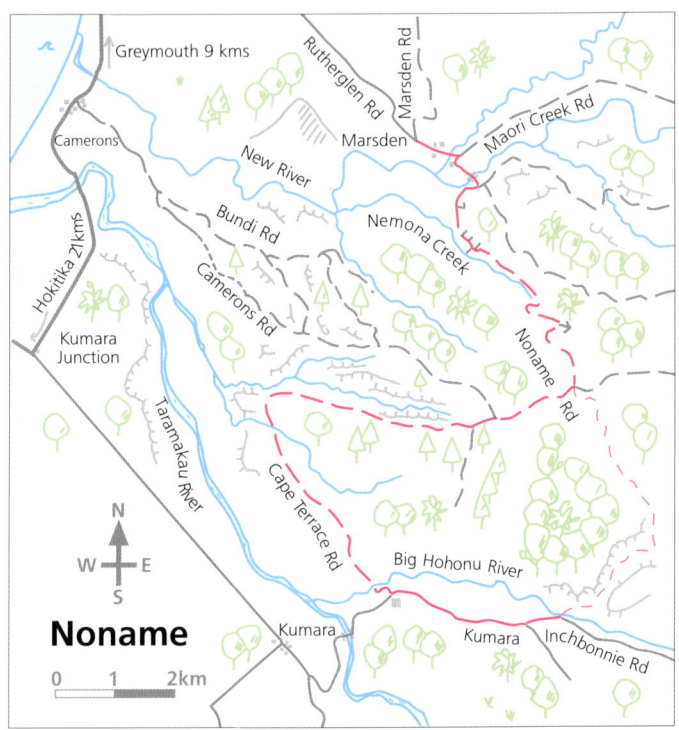

Ride straight ahead onto the 4WD track. After a few kilometres, this track becomes quite rough and nips back and forth across Blackwater Creek a few times. As long as you are not in too much of a hurry, the track is easy enough to follow and soon reaches the Big Hohonu River.

Cross the Big Hohonu and pick up a track 50 metres down river that meets the Kumara Inchbonnie Road, a stone's throw away. Turn right and follow this road for 3 km before turning right again at Cape Terrace Road, opposite some large old buildings. Head down to the river, go downstream for 100 metres and then cross the Big Hohonu River again.

Continue on Cape Terrace Road for another 10 km. About 1.5 km after passing the Bundi Road turn-off, you'll reach the four-way intersection at the start of the loop. Turn left and follow Noname Rd back to Marsden.

Track conditions 10% sealed road, 45% gravel road, 45% 4WD and single track

Notes If it's been raining, choose another ride (the Big Hohonu River will be uncrossable). Take Topomap J32 Hokitika.

16 Taipo Valley

40 km east of Kumara Junction

Grade 3, 2–4 hrs, 18 km return ★

The Taipo Valley offers a scenic half-day ride on a rough old farm track.

How to get there The track starts 40 km east of Kumara Junction on Highway 73 (2 km after crossing the Taipo River bridge) and is signposted 'Taipo Valley access 4x4 only'.

Route description After climbing for 20 mins up to a small clearing that has a logbook, you'll drop down to the valley floor and follow the main 4WD track up valley to Seven Mile Hut.

Simon Kennett

Taipo Valley—giant weta country.

From there, you can either explore further up the valley, although the riding soon becomes quite difficult, or head back out to the highway.

Notes Warning: do not attempt this trip when the river is in flood as there are several fords that will definitely be uncrossable.

17 Tunnels Tracks/Blue Spur

Hokitika

Grades 3–4, 1–2 hours, 10–20 km   ★ ★

This area, on the outskirts of Hokitika, has just been replanted in pines, and the Hokitika MTB Club are developing a track network here for the long term. It's typically hilly country, but a water-race track and two small tunnels give it a unique feel.

Route description To get there with a smile on your dial, ride out of town via the airport road and veer right just before the terminal building. A short distance down this road, turn

A new track on Blue Spur.

right onto the obvious single track. Follow that down past the race course to Hau Hau Rd. Head inland on the seal for a couple of kilometres. The road then turns to gravel and descends sharply.

At the bottom of this descent, you can turn left and start exploring. Blue Spur hill rises up to the east, and the newest tracks are south of this. This area is fairly complicated, but the local club has plans to put some sign posts in. Meanwhile, pop into Hokitika Cycles for a rough photocopied map or go for a ride with the Hokitika MTB Club.

18 Kaniere Water Race

ADVANCED

Kaniere, 19 km southeast of Hokitika

Grade 4+, 1–2 hours, 10 km   ★ ★

This is one of the best rides around Hokitika. Although most of it is flat and easy, there are a few tricky bits to keep expert riders challenged and the rest of us walking.

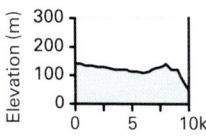

How to get there   Head southeast of Hokitika to Lake Kaniere (about 19 km). There is a little parking area at the start of the track (it's 20 metres past a 'Kokatahi' sign, just over a bridge).

Route description   Head into the bush on the narrow track that follows the water race. The first 4 km are scenic and easy. Then you'll cross a gravel road, and the track will become significantly more difficult and dangerous. Less confident riders should turn left and follow the gravel road out to Lake Kaniere Road.

Those who stick to the water-race track will soon find they have to dismount to walk half a dozen gulches. The riding in between makes up for this inconvenience though. At the end of the single track, you'll ride onto a 4WD track where you should turn right and, a few hundred metres later, left. You'll soon pop out onto Lake Kaniere Road.

Turn left to ride back to the start of the track (7 km away) or right to cruise back to Hokitika (12 km away).

Track conditions 10% 4WD track, 90% single track

Notes Refer to Topomap J33 Kaniere (it shows the track clearly.) This track is also popular with walkers, so take it easy.

19 Totara Valley

BEGINNER

27 km south of Hokitika

Grade 1+, 3–4 hours, 40 km return   ★

This is a pleasant ride up a quiet and beautiful West Coast valley.

How to get there Turn east off Highway 6 at the 'Totara Valley' sign 3 km north of Ross. If you're in a car, park 2 km further on, 50 metres before the gravel starts.

Route description The road has been fixed up, so it only becomes slightly rougher and narrower as it heads up Totara Valley towards the Mikonui River. There are just a few fords, bridges and gates to distract you from the fantastic scenery.

When you reach the Mikonui, there is an option to ride up valley for another 20 minutes on a rough stock route to a rustic homestead. Hop over the large gate and look for the route on your left just after crossing the first ford 100 metres away. It leads up valley, over a bluff and then across farmland to the old homestead. Return the same way.

Track conditions Gravel road and old farm track

20 Okarito Forest

BEGINNER

130 km south of Hokitika

Grade 1, 1–2 hours, 15–30 km   ★

Okarito is best known for its stunning lagoon, but the forest around it is a quiet wonder of its own, fizzing with flora and fauna. Old forestry roads provide easy, fun riding.

How to get there Turn west off Highway 6 at the 'Okarito' signpost 14 km south of Whataroa. The lagoon is a further 14 km away.

Route description From the lagoon, cycle back towards the highway for just over 5 km (Jonathan saw a white heron here when he did this ride). Turn left into the obvious old forestry road and, after another 1.5 km, you will reach a large clearing, which must be an ornithologist's utopia.

From this clearing, you can turn left and ride just over 1 km to another clearing. On a fine day, this is a great spot to just sit and listen before heading back the same way.

For a longer ride, park at The Forks, 2 km from the highway, and ride north on Oroko and Okutua roads for 9 km to a large clearing close to the edge of Westland National Park. There are also several side roads you could explore—Loop Road is the longest at about 4 km.

Notes The government SOE Timberlands were ripping out huge rimu from this forest right up to 2001! They dragged them from all directions into these clearings then trucked them out. That's what formed the 'corridors' that look like a giant star from above (see Google Earth). This area is also used by 4WD vehicles.

21 Paringa-Haast Cattle Track

43 km northeast of Haast (141 km north of Wanaka)

Grade 5, 1–2 days, longer than it looks!   ★

EXPERT

This ride provides gnarly bike tramping for those with sturdy footwear, a good rain jacket and an eye for lush jungle scenery.

How to get there Ride or drive 8 km south from the Lake Paringa camping area on Highway 6 to the minimal roadside parking at the start of the track. Alternatively, park near the Waita River (roughly 10 km north of Haast) and ride the scenic 33 km to the northern end of the track.

Route description To ride all the way through to the Haast River is hard work, even for fit and experienced bike thrashers. For most riders, we recommend just riding from Paringa to Blowfly Hut and back; about a 2-hour trip if the track is dry. Of course, this is the West Coast, and the track is seldom

dry. DOC warns that it is prone to flooding, so pick your day carefully.

The track deteriorates considerably from the hut, with many slips and windfalls, although it is on DOC's maintenance schedule and is due for work in spring 2008. If continuing on, make sure you have a good shoulder pad and plenty of food.

Notes   Take Topomaps F37 Haast and G37 Landsborough. Experienced rider Doug Hamilton went all the way through in 11 hours and that included 2 hours of bike carrying.

Charlie Palmer on a Kirwans' switchback.

North Canterbury

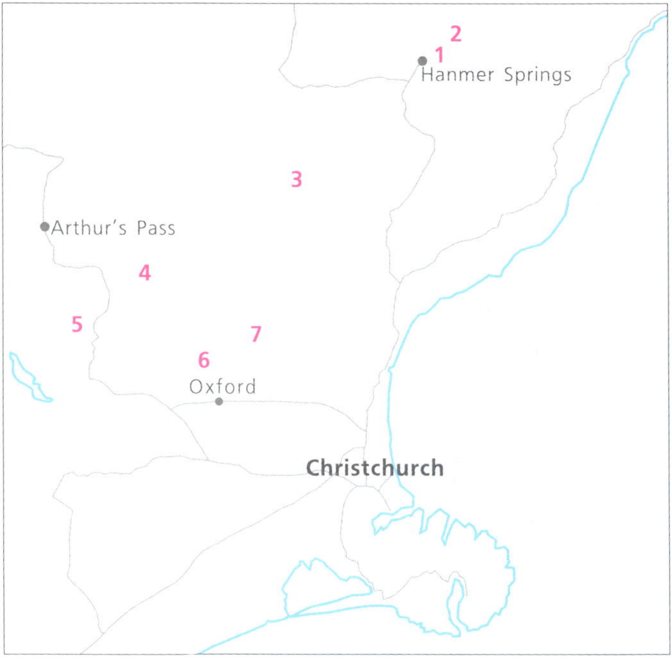

Hanmer Springs

Arthur's Pass

Oxford

Christchurch

1 Hanmer Tracks
2 Jacks and Jollies Passes
3 Lake Sumner
4 Poulter Valley
5 Craigieburn Forest
6 Wharfedale Track
7 Blowhard Track

NORTH CANTERBURY HIGHLIGHTS

Hanmer has a potpourri of tasty tracks (nicely rounded off with a marinate in the hot pools). Craigieburn Forest and Wharfedale Track offer fantastic mountain biking through beautiful beech forest for intermediate and expert level riders. And for more challenging riding, the Blowhard Track is hard to beat.

1 Hanmer Tracks

Hanmer Springs, 130 km north of Christchurch

Grade 2, 1–2 hours, 10–15 km ★ ★ ★

The hot springs and single track make this holiday town a brilliant weekend destination.

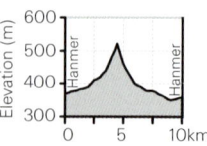

Route description Thanks to the efforts of the Hanmer MTB Club, there are a range of tracks in the Carter Holt Harvey forest from Chatterton River across to Dog Stream. A map is essential for finding the single track treasures. Pick one up from the Information Centre or across the road at Wildlife (100% of the map price goes back into the trails).

Here's a good ride for starters: Cycle 1 km out of town on Jollies Pass Road and turn left at Pawson Road. After another 300 metres, hang a right onto Dog Stream Track. This single track winds in and out of the forest, across Jolliffe Road and down beside Menzies Road before turning left onto Jolliffe Saddle Track. It isn't far to the saddle, is mostly rideable and the downhill is a hoot.

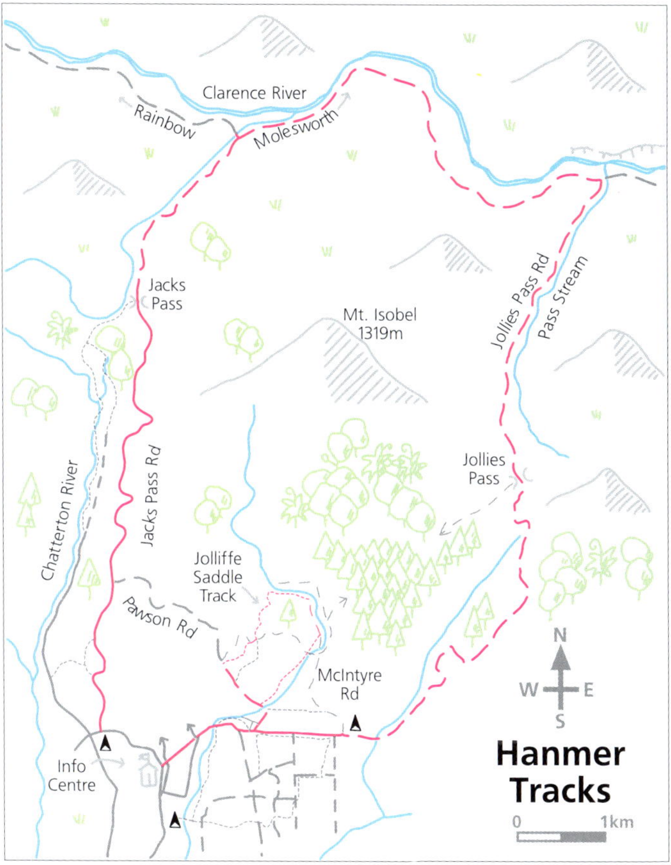

Clarence River

Rainbow

Molesworth

Jacks
Pass

Mt. Isobel
1319m

Jollies Pass Rd

Pass Stream

Jollies
Pass

Chatterton River

Jacks Pass Rd

Jolliffe
Saddle
Track

Pawson Rd

McIntyre
Rd

N
W — E
S

**Hanmer
Tracks**

0   1km

Info
Centre

At the bottom, turn right onto Jolliffe Road, head downhill for
100 metres and pick up Timberlands Trail. Turn left at Pawson
Road to get back to the start of the loop.

If you're keen for more, cross Jollies Pass Road and ride
back into town via several mountain bike tracks . The real gold,
however, is shown on the Hanmer Mountain Bike Club map.

Cruisy riding on the flats east of town.

Track conditions 5% sealed road, 30% gravel road, 65% single track

Notes This ride includes brilliant sections of single track that DOC encourages bikers to use. Their intention is to avoid conflict with other park users, so please co-operate by steering clear of walking tracks in the park.

The pine forest owners ask bikers to observe the following:
- No smoking.
- Tracks may be closed due to fire risk.

- No camping or fires.
- Respect other track users.

For a longer, old-school day ride in the Hanmer area, try Jacks and Jollies Passes (see below).

2 Jacks and Jollies Passes

Hanmer Springs, 130 km north of Christchurch

Grade 3, 2–4 hours, 25 km   ★★

This loop ride crosses two passes as it circumnavigates Mt Isobel (1319 m) from Hanmer Springs.

Route description For a clockwise loop, take Jacks Pass Road out of town for 1 km. Turn right at the ski field sign and climb over the pass.

At the Clarence River, head right again and cycle for 10 km, down to the signposted Jollies Pass Road, which takes you over the pass and back to town.

For a more exciting and technical downhill from near the top of Jollies Pass, veer right onto a pylon track. After climbing for 300 metres, enjoy a brake-searing descent through the bush.

Notes Most of this ride is covered in snow during winter, which makes it very beautiful; but if a vehicle hasn't been over the road and compacted the snow, you could be in for about 8 hours of bike pushing.

3 Lake Sumner

140 km northwest of Christchurch

Grade 1+, 3–6 hours, 36 km return   ★★

Great scenery, no big climbs and lots of good camping areas.

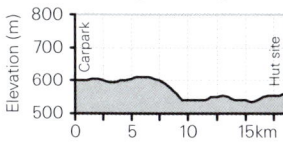

How to get there From Amberley, drive 25 km north to Waikari and head northwest past Hawarden to Horsley Down. Then follow Lake

Sumner Road for another 43 km before parking at the end of the gravel road beside Lake Taylor. Keen cyclists can start riding from Jacks Saddle (25 km before Lake Taylor).

Route description   Skirt around the southwest edge of Lake Taylor on a 4WD track before heading north to do the same again round Loch Katrine. Carry on west past the end of Lake Sumner to the remains of No.2 Hut. Admire the view over lunch and return the same way.

Alternatively, if you want to do an overnighter, carry along on a vague 4WD track 2 km up the valley to Hurunui Hut. Dump your gear here and head for the hot springs. They are 30 minutes riding plus 15 minutes walking further up the valley and are marked with an 'X' on the maps.

Track conditions   100% 4WD track

Notes   Take insect repellent. No.2 Hut burnt down and won't be replaced. Refer to Topomap L32 Lake Sumner or Parkmap Lake Sumner.

4 Poulter Valley

24 km east of Arthur's Pass

Grade 3, 5–8 hrs, 54 km return   ★ ★ ★

Here's the first track in a National Park to be opened up to mountain bikes after the DOC policy was amended to allow for such extravagances. It's all on 4WD track and riverbed.

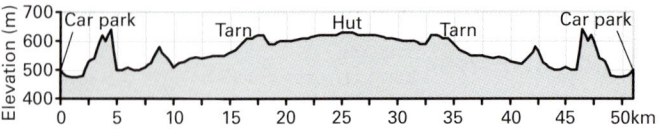

How to get there   From Highway 73, 24 km east of Arthur's Pass village, turn onto Mt White Road, then 1.5 km later, turn up Andrews Valley. You'll reach the Poulter Valley parking area, 21 km from the highway, just before the river.

Route description   The first hour of riding involves a tough climb and descent, but things get easier from the park boundary

Rob Hoult

Corrie Hoult picks his way across a side stream in the Poulter Valley.

to Casey Hut, a good spot for an overnighter.

Beyond Casey Hut, riders must follow a rough 4WD track up the braided Poulter riverbed for a couple of kilometres. This section is tricky to follow, and some walking is necessary, including two river crossings. Keep an eye out for the cairns. It's a fair bit easier on the return journey.

The Trust/Poulter Hut at the top end of the ride is tucked into the edge of the forest on the left.

Retrace your tyre tracks from the hut. Once back on the river terrace you'll come to a fork in the 4WD track—head for the small cairn in the distance and then continue connecting the markers back to the permanent 4WD track and over the big climb to the car park.

Track conditions 98% 4WD track, 2% unrideable riverbed

Notes The Poulter is a sizeable river—best avoided during heavy rain. Refer to Topomap Dampier L33 or DOC's 'Poulter Valley Mountain Biking' pamphlet.

Simon Kennett

Heading for The Edge at Craigieburn Forest.

5 Craigieburn Forest

100 km west of Christchurch

Grades 2–4, 2–4 hours, 16 km ★ ★ ★ ★

Beech forest, views to die for and mountain single track combine to make this our favourite ride in Canterbury.

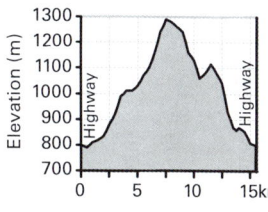

How to get there Drive northwest from Christchurch towards Arthur's Pass for about 100 km. Turn left at the 'Craigieburn Recreation Area' sign and park at the shelter/picnic area 100 metres from the highway.

Route description Ride back out to the highway, turn left and ride up the road for 1 km before turning left again onto the Craigieburn ski field road. The scenic 7-km climb up to the ski field buildings takes about an hour and is well graded.

At the bottom of the rope tow, turn left and ride down across a shingly slope. This is the start of The Edge, a hairy grade-4 track that requires some walking and includes a few sketchy drop-offs. After 4 km, you'll reach a fork in the track—veer right and climb up to Lyndon Saddle, 15 minutes away. From there, the short walk up to Lyndon Hill rewards with some massive views.

Back at the saddle, turn west to enjoy 'The Luge', a grade-3 single track that weaves through beech forest for 3 km. Some of the bridges on the way down are narrow and slippery. Turn left when you hit the gravel road at the bottom and coast down to the picnic area 2 km away.

Track conditions 5% sealed, 50% gravel road, 45% single track

Notes Take it easy on these tracks, they are popular with walkers and cyclists. The ski field roads are used regularly by 4WD vehicles. Refer to Topomap K34 Wilberforce and be prepared for cold conditions.

Dracophyllum Track
Grade 3, 2–3 hours, 14 km return ★ ★

This is an interesting there-and-back ride, best done in dry conditions.

Follow the directions given above to the Craigieburn Recreation Area. From the shelter near the highway, follow the narrow gravel road up into the forest. After 10 to 20 minutes, you'll reach an intersection with a 'Dracophyllum Flats' sign on the other side. From here, a single track leads through forest and across a river to a climb up to the flats. Although it's not marked on the map, there is a minor track, marked with poles, leading across the flats and through more forest to an ice skating rink (next to another ski field access road).

After a rest at the ice skating rink, head back the same way.

Track conditions   40% gravel road, 60% single track

Racing the storm across Dracophyllum Flat.

Martin Langley

6 Wharfedale Track

Oxford Forest, 70 km northwest of Christchurch

Grade 4, 3–8 hrs, 30 km to the hut and back; 75 km full loop ★★★

Who'd have guessed it; they knew how to build fine mountain bike tracks 130 years ago. Jolly good show!

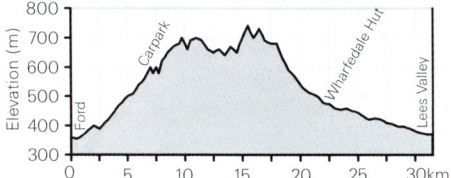

How to get there From Oxford, drive southwest (towards Arthur's Pass) for just over 3 km and turn right, onto Woodstock Road, at the 'View Hill' signpost. Drive down the road for 10 km before turning right, onto Ingrams Road, at the 'Wharfedale Track' sign and cruising down to the ford 1 km away. If it has been raining, you will have to park here. Otherwise, continue on up to the car park a further 6 km away.

Route description This track was formed as a stock route and potential road to Lees Valley in 1879. It has a cruisy gradient, and beneath a layer of beech-tree leaf litter lies a smooth, responsive riding surface. There are also plenty of fords, roots and rocks to keep you challenged.

From the car park, follow the marked Wharfedale Track through lovely beech forest to a saddle about 2 hours away. Many people just ride this far and then turn back for a mostly downhill run (total riding time about 3 hours).

For a longer ride, continue down to the far end of the track and then return the way you came (total riding time about 5 hours).

The ultimate Wharfedale ride requires continuing down valley and out to Oxford via Ashley Gorge. After following the 4WD track for about 30 minutes on from the hut, you should veer right (do not climb to your left) at an obvious Y-intersection. When you reach the gravel road, turn right again. Oxford is then 26 km away via a scenic and hilly gravel road.

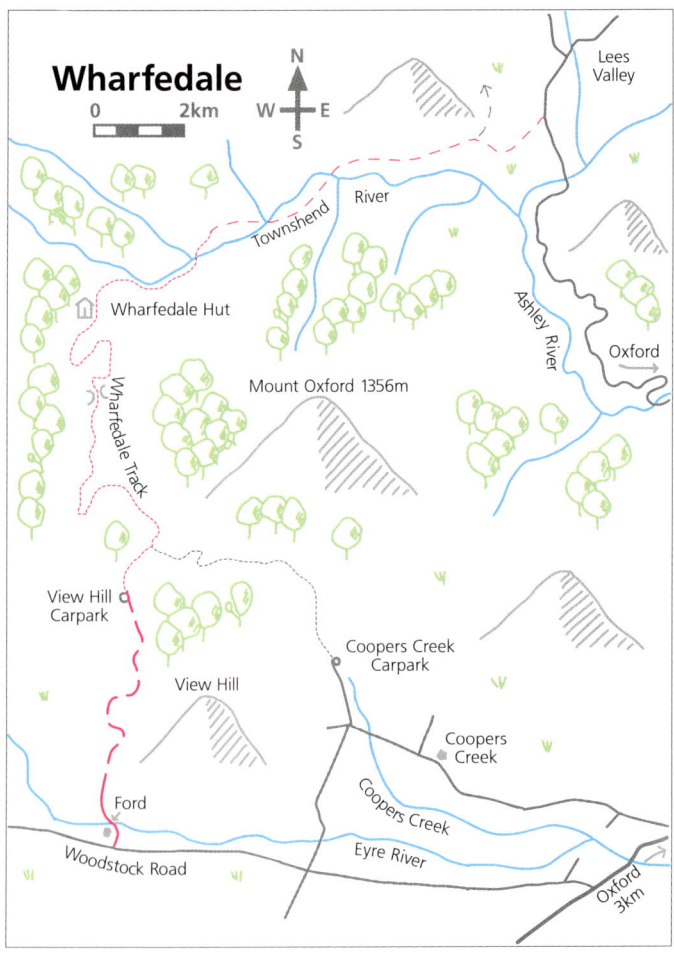

Wharfedale

0   2km

N
W — E
S

Lees Valley

Townshend River

Wharfedale Hut

Ashley River

Oxford

Mount Oxford 1356m

Wharfedale Track

View Hill Carpark

Coopers Creek Carpark

View Hill

Coopers Creek

Coopers Creek

Ford

Eyre River

Woodstock Road

Oxford 3km

Other users Walkers, some stock at either end of the track
Notes Watch out for the water channels—they get bigger and bigger as you go along, and the last two are real bike gobblers.

The track from the Coopers Creek car park, at the end of Mountain Road, (5 km northeast of View Hill) is also popular with local riders but is quite steep in places. Refer to DOC's pamphlet, 'Canterbury Foothills Forests—Oxford Forest', for more info. As with most tracks, the Wharfedale is a grade harder when wet.

7 Blowhard Track

ADVANCED

70 km northwest of Christchurch ★ ★ ★

Grade 4+, 4–5 hours, 20 km return

This is one of the best rides around for fit, technically skilled riders. The uphill is tough and requires a fair bit of bike carrying, but the view and downhill are fantastic.

How to get there From Oxford, drive north on High Street, which becomes Ashley Gorge Road (then later Birch Road), for 16 km. Then turn left onto Maori Reserve Road and drive 4 km to the road end. (It's quicker to drive via Rangiora if you live in Christchurch's northern suburbs.)

Route description The Blowhard Track is signposted at the end of the road.

Ride past the sign and up a steep 4WD track into the bush. It takes over an hour to bike and hike up to the first summit, which just peeks out above the forest. The very top of Mt Richardson is a further hour away, with some downhill respite along the ridge but mostly more hard work. On the way up, turn right when you reach a 'Bypass Track' sign. A little later, it's easy to lose the track. Keep your eyes peeled for a small cairn. Turn left when you see it to keep following the orange triangles.

The top is well signposted and at 1047 m provides a stunning vista.

The ride back down takes about an hour. All the bits you couldn't quite ride on the way up are great fun in the opposite direction—very challenging and deserving of respect.

Track conditions 10% 4WD track, 90% single track

The rear guard burns lard yard by yard up the Blowhard.

Notes This track is exposed in places, slick when wet and definitely best ridden after a week of dry weather. If you get fine weather at the top, you'll want to spend some time there; if not, you'll wish you were home patching old tubes. Don't forget to take a parka, plenty of water and your beefiest fat tyres. Refer to topomaps L34 Puketeraki and M34 Amberley. The Mt Richardson Track is out of bounds for bikers.

Christchurch

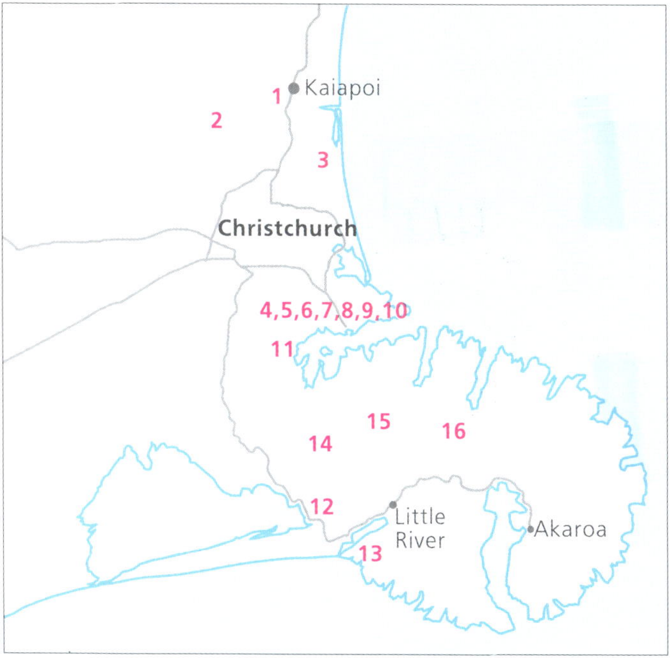

Kaiapoi

Christchurch

Little
River

Akaroa

1	Kaiapoi Island	9	Bridle Path
2	McLeans Forest	10	Godley Head Track
3	Bottle Lake Forest Park	11	Living Springs
4	Port Hills Crater Rim	12	Little River Rail Trail
5	Crocodile and Kennedys Bush	13	Lake Forsyth
6	Worsleys and Flying Nun	14	Haven MTB Park
7	Victoria Park	15	Mt Herbert
8	Rapaki Track	16	Mt Fitzgerald

CHRISTCHURCH HIGHLIGHTS

Christchurch's impressive cycling heritage continues with Council supported tracks at Bottle Lake, McLeans Forest and the Port Hills. The Little River Rail Trail is very family-friendly and Mt Fitzgerald is a back-country classic. Christchurch City Council has produced good maps of the most popular tracks, available from the info centre in The Square and www.ccc.govt.nz/Cycling/TracksRides/

1 Kaiapoi Island

BEGINNER

Kaiapoi, 12 km north of Christchurch

Grade 1+, 1–2 hours, up to 20 km ★

A few easy tracks run parallel to the Waimakariri River, along flood-banks and through pine forest. The area is fine for families and beginners.

How to get there Drive 10 km north of Christchurch City on Highway 1. Just after crossing the Waimakariri River bridge take the Tram Road exit. Turn right at Tram Road, right at Main North Road and right at Wrights Road to enter the park.

Route description There are pamphlets with maps at the information centre beside the car parking area. The tracks are signposted, so you shouldn't have trouble finding your way.

From the information boards, ride under the motorway bridge on the gravel road heading west and take the first right-hand road for 30 metres. You will see a signposted mountain bike track starting from the side of the road. This easy track weaves through forest. At the end, you can return the same way or pop up onto the stopbank road and ride back on that for a change and a view.

There is also a cycle track running from the information centre down river. It can be used for a short there-and-back riverside ride, or you can follow it all the way to Kaiapoi township.

Track conditions A mixture of gravel roads, purpose-built single track and shared cycle/walkways

Notes There are toilets and picnicking areas near the info centre.

2 McLeans Forest

24 km northwest of Christchurch

Grade 1+, 40–80 mins, 10 km ★ ★ ★

Getting bored with Bottle Lake? Then check out this new riding area on the southern banks of the Waimakariri River.

How to get there Take Highway 73 out of Christchurch. About 14 km from the Square, veer right onto Old West Coast Road. After another 4 km, turn right onto Chattertons and 5–6 km after that, turn left at the McLeans Forest entrance.

Rick Zawodny

Kaila and Trudi surfing through McLeans.

Route description Simply follow the MTB track signs into the forest and around a flat, fun 10-km loop.

The area also caters for walkers, so take care not to stray onto the walking track. If you have a copy of the McLeans Forest Map, produced by Environment Canterbury, you could use the forestry roads to shorten your ride.

Notes There are toilets and a map board at the car park, which is locked at night. This area may be closed from time to time due to flooding or logging.

3 Bottle Lake Forest Park

Christchurch

Grades 1–2, 1–2 hrs, 5–30 km return ★★★

The tracks at Bottle Lake have been so well developed that the forest is now one of the most popular riding destinations in New Zealand. It's especially good for families and night riding.

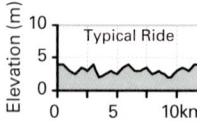

How to get there Head north out of town on Marshland Road. Turn right onto Prestons Road, left onto Alpine View Lane and left again onto Waitikiri Drive. After 700 metres, turn right into the car park.

Route description Pick up one of the maps at the info centre by the car park and plan a loop trip around any two of the three main tracks shown. It will take up to an hour to do one loop. The far track along the coast is fairly straight and sandy. The rest are twisty, firm and fun.

Because this is a production forest, short sections of track are continually being logged out and replaced with new track, so don't presume you'll always have the whole area sussed.

There is also a jumps area beside the car park and a skills area on the way.

Track conditions Mostly gravelled single track

Other users Runners, walkers, dogs, horses

Notes In case of emergencies or for up-to-date information, contact the park ranger on phone 026 252 5093, or (03) 383 3795 after hours. The park is owned by the Christchurch City Council. This is a great wet weather riding area.

4 Port Hills Crater Rim

ADVANCED

Christchurch

Grade 4, 4–8 hrs, 40 km ★★★★

The Port Hills has one of the most impressive track networks in the country. Over 40 km of trails, mostly flowing single track with stunning views, traverse the crater rim of the extinct volcano. If you only have one day to ride the Port Hills, this is the ultimate ride.

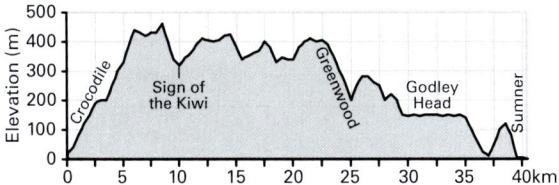

Route description Start at Halswell Quarry and ride up the Crocodile Track and Kennedys Bush Track. Then cruise along to the Flying Nun, which leads to the Sign of the Kiwi Tearooms.

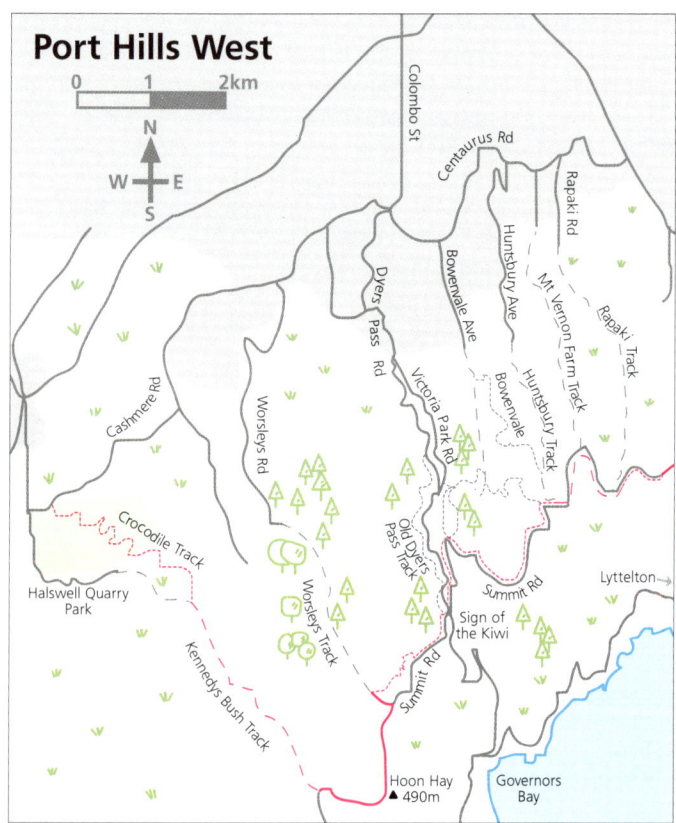

From there, you will be alternating between the Summit Road and single tracks that run parallel with the Summit Road. The main single tracks all start at obvious roadside signs and are, in order, The Bowenvale Traverse Track, Mt Vernon Track, Witch Hill Track, Castle Rock Track, John Britten Track, and the longest of them all, the Greenwood Track.

From Evans Pass, take the Godley Head Track, followed by the Anaconda Track, down to Taylors Mistake.

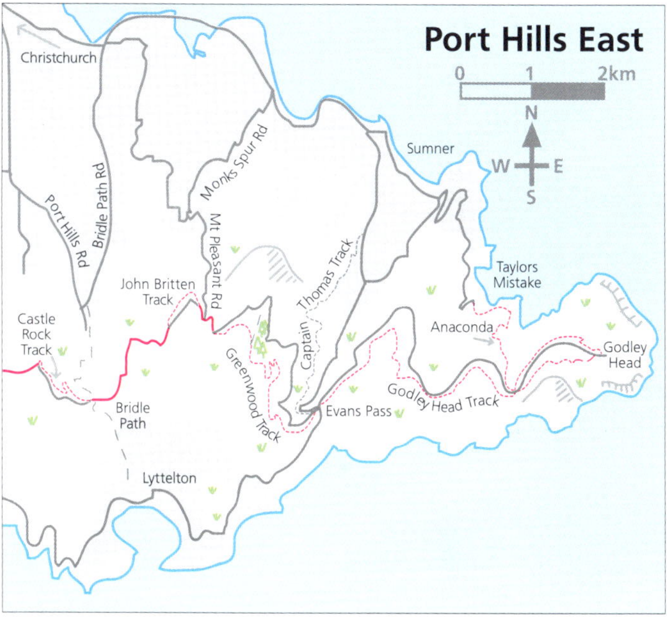

Port Hills East

0   1   2km

N
W — E
S

Christchurch

Sumner

Monks Spur Rd

Bridle Path Rd

Port Hills Rd

Mt Pleasant Rd

Thomas Track

Taylors Mistake

John Britten Track

Castle Rock Track

Anaconda

Godley Head

Greenwood Track

Latadale

Godley Head Track

Bridle Path

Evans Pass

Lyttelton

Notes This is one of the best day's mountain biking in the country. One word of warning though—all of us have had big crashes on these tracks (speed might have been a factor... possibly).

All these tracks are described in the following write-ups.

5 Crocodile and Kennedys Bush

Cashmere, Christchurch

Grade 2, 1 hour up/15 min down, 9 km ★★

A satisfying plug uphill has you honing your turning skills on a series of tight corners.

Route description Start by heading up the Crocodile Track. It begins at Halswell Quarry Park on Cashmere Road and is well signposted. After crossing a valley near the bottom, this track is a steady grind up a series of switchbacks. When you

Simon Kennett

Rick escapes the crocodile.

get to the top of the single track, hop onto the Kennedys Bush 4WD track and keep on climbing. Once at the Summit Road, turn left to head for Flying Nun.

Track conditions 4WD track and single track

Other users Walkers, runners, farm stock

Notes Both tracks are closed during lambing; August–September. The Crocodile track was built by Dan van Asch on his farmland. It's the ideal place to start a traverse of the Port Hills. Christchurch City Council have produced a map of the tracks in this area.

6 Worsleys and Flying Nun

INTERMEDIATE

Hoon Hay, Christchurch

Grade 3, 20 minutes down hill, 6 km ★ ★ ★

This makes for an excellent round trip when linked in with Kennedys Bush Track (see above).

Route description After chugging up Kennedys Bush Track (see above), cycle left along the Summit Road for 1.5 km. Just after crossing a cattle stop, turn left up a sealed road that leads to the top of Worsleys Track, 300 metres away.

Next, either hop over the white rusty iron gate and head down Worsleys Track to Hoon Hay or carry along the Crater Rim on Flying Nun. The Flying Nun single track is 50 metres east of the gate and sidles down to the Sign of the Kiwi tearooms.

Alternatively, if you're feeling like a challenge, try riding up Worsleys Track . The last 100 metres to the top, aptly named The Body Bag, are extreme—give it heaps! At the top, hop over an old gate and, after 50 metres, you'll see the Flying Nun heading off on your left.

From the Sign of the Kiwi, you can dive down to the city via a single track below Dyers Pass Road (you passed the start of it just before reaching the Kiwi) or continue along the Port Hills—you can follow single track from the Sign of the Kiwi almost continuously to Godley Head.

Other users Walkers, runners and horses also use the track, so take care if going down hill.

7 Victoria Park

Cashmere, Christchurch

Grades 2–5, 1.5–2 hours, 8 km ★★★

Victoria Park, on the side of the Port Hills, is riddled with tracks, including several downhill tracks and lots of jumps.

How to get there From Cashmere, head up Dyers Pass Road to the Sign of the Kiwi tearooms or ride up Kennedys.

Route description From the Sign of the Kiwi tearooms, head north on the Summit Road and pop onto the single track on the left almost straight away. Follow this for a few hundred metres, and you'll reach a clearing just below a carpark. This is the top of the Victoria Park Tracks.

Follow the most obvious track down towards the city for 50 metres and you'll cross a fence (via a see-saw or a cattle stop).

Breaking free on the Port Hills.

This is the top of 'Brake Free', a really cool track for learning what flow and jumps are all about. It's only a few hundred metres long, but people just ride it over and over and over.

From there, you bomb down through Victoria Park and explore the downhill tracks and jumps area, or head back up towards the Summit Road and follow Thomson's Track round to the top of the Huntsbury/Bowenvale Track—a much easier way down.

Notes Christchurch City Council has produced a pamphlet showing these tracks and is building a bit more track in this area every year. In 2008 the tracks were also shown at www.vorb.org.nz/ftopict-73251.html

8 Rapaki Track

EASY

Opawa, Christchurch to Port Hills, Summit Road

Grade 2-, 30–60 minutes, 5 km ★

This is the easiest track from Christchurch up onto the Port Hills.

Route description From the end of Rapaki Road, in Opawa, a smooth 4WD track climbs gradually 260 m to the Summit Road.

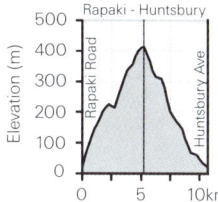

Either backtrack or make this a loop trip by cycling around to one of the other Port Hill tracks (eg. Huntsbury or Mt Vernon). **Notes** This track is well trod by walkers, runners and horses—take it easy on the way down.

9 Bridle Path

Lyttelton to Christchurch

Grade 3, 30–90 minutes, 3 km ★

This is the steepest route up to the Summit Road. It's a great test of the old legs and lungs (and brakes!).

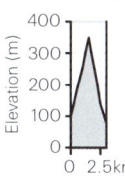

Route description From the Lyttelton side, turn left at the west end of London Street, then right up Bridle Path Road. The climb is a sealed road for the first few hundred metres. It starts from just above the road tunnel entrance, climbs over the Port Hills and drops down the Christchurch side to the other end of the road tunnel. The track takes you to the Gondola carpark.

Notes Keep a look out for walkers and joggers. Create a loop with one of the other tracks from the Summit Road (see above).

10 Godley Head Track

Taylors Mistake, Christchurch

Grade 3-, 2–3 hour loop, 12 km ★★★★

How to get there You can drive to Evans Pass, or ride there from Sumner via the Captain Thomas Track (which starts from Wakefield Street), or the Greenwood MTB Track (which starts 200 metres east of the top of Mt Pleasant Road).

Route description From Evans Pass car park, ride up the road for 30 metres and then turn hard right to ride up a steep track and over a MTB stile. This is the Scarborough Reserve Track, and it's sweet! It spits you out at Breeze Col.

Murray Drake slithers down the Anaconda.

From Breeze Col, continue climbing one of the two tracks on the other side of the Col—we recommend the left one. The steep one on the right is for wannabe pro racers—we had a go at the bottom half and then decided to remain amateurs.

Once back at the road, take a look at the view from the car park (or just beyond), then head back to Breeze Col. It is worth stretching the legs with a walk down to Godley Head if you've never been there.

Once back at Breeze Col, check out DOC's roadside map for more info. You can either head back on the track you've already ridden or turn right and descend to Taylors Mistake. Heading for Taylors Mistake gives you the chance to ride the fantastic Anaconda—fast, flowy and fun. It's the best option, so here are the directions: from Breeze Col follow the shared use track signposted 'Taylors Mistake Beach' for 2 minutes, then turn onto the signposted 'Anaconda MTB' track. Near the bottom, just before meeting a walking track, turn left onto the 'Mountain Bike Track' and sidle down to Taylors Mistake. It's easy to follow your nose from there over to Sumner.

Notes Don't forget your camera!

11 Living Springs

15 km south of Christchurch

Grades 3–4, developing track network ★

Living Springs is a private initiative involving several intermediate tracks being built over a mixture of farmland and forestry.

Jonathan Kennett

Martin and Craig living it up on Zane.

How to get there From Christchurch, drive south over Dyers Pass, turn right at Governors Bay Road and then right again at Bamfords Road. The mountain bike tracks start 900 metres up the road.

Route description It's early days at Living Springs. Check out www.mountainbike.orconhosting.net.nz before your ride.

At the time of writing, there were a few grade 3 and 4 tracks to explore, such as The Pines, Mississippi, and Zane. They are all 500 metres to 1 km in length and are very well built. In late 2008, signs will be put in place making it clear where to go.

Track conditions mostly purpose-built single track

Notes The best way to get to know this area is to attend a dig day and cap it off with a ride. Big thanks to Craig and Rebekah Tregurtha for opening up the area.

12 Little River Rail Trail

BEGINNER

Christchurch to Little River

Grade 1, 1–4 hours, 45 km when completed ★ ★ ★

This ride is mighty popular for the simple reason that it is so easy that anyone can, and will, enjoy it. The trail is wide, flat, smooth and scenic. There is no traffic to contend with but plenty of interesting history and wildlife to enjoy.

Route description Of the planned 45 km, only 26 km had been completed by the middle of 2008.

The best part is 20 km long and runs from Little River down beside Lake Forsyth and then north, past Lake Ellesmere to Motukarara. There are lots of interpretation panels explaining the history and wildlife of the area along the way. Anyone, no matter what their fitness or age, will enjoy this ride.

The second part that is open runs from Prebbleton, just southwest of Christchurch, to Lincoln. It's also easy to ride, but the scenic values are not as high.

Track conditions 100% wide, flat, smooth path

Notes The track is exposed to the sun and wind. For maps and an update on this ride, check out www.littleriverrailtrail.co.nz

Follow the leader on the rail trail.

13 Lake Forsyth

Birdlings Flat, 41 km south of Christchurch

Grade 2+, 2–3 hours, 35 km ★★

This grand loop of Lake Forsyth is technically easy and scenically rewarding but requires good fitness. It can only be done when the outlet from Lake Forsyth is blocked (about half the year).

How to get there From Christchurch head towards Banks Peninsula, and turn off to Birdlings Flat village.

Route description From Birdlings Flat, go to the coast and follow a 4WD track left across the lake outlet and up a gravel road, past farm houses and on to a long hill climb on Bossu Road. This is very quiet and affords great views.

Once on the ridge, you'll pass Kinloch Road on your left. Carry on for another 4 km, then turn left down Reynolds Valley Road. Prepare for a flying 7 km descent. At the bottom turn left and cruise to Little River 3.5 km away.

For most of the ride back to Birdlings Flat you can follow the Little River Rail Trail, which skirts along the edge of Lake Forsyth.

Track conditions A mixture of sealed and gravel roads and rail trail

Notes Sometimes you can find out the condition of the lake outlet by checking www.canterburymtbclub.org

14 Haven MTB Park

EXPERT

Banks Peninsula

Various grades and track lengths ★

This is a small, privately owned mountain bike park with several neat tracks under construction.

Route description In 2008, only one short loop was ready to ride in this new park, but there are plans for several more tracks as well as general forest restoration. To ride here, you must be a club member; check out www.havenmtb.org.nz to find out more and join up. Membership is cheap, and you get a free map.

Notes As with any developing mountain bike park, the etiquette is 'dig before you ride'. A big thanks to landowners Shailer Hart and Lisa Carter for expanding the mountain biking possibilities in Christchurch.

15 Mt Herbert

ADVANCED

43 km southeast of Christchurch

Grade 4-, 4–6 hours, 43-km loop ★

At 920 m, this is the highest point on Banks Peninsula, so if you're a peak bagger, you'll just have to force yourself up here.

How to get there From Diamond Harbour, head southeast through Purau. Take the Port Levy Road over Purau Saddle (passing the Monument Track on your right) and almost all the way down to Port Levy. At the bottom of the hill, turn right and climb up Little River Road to Port Levy Saddle.

Route description From the saddle, follow the marked track west across farmland. After about half an hour, you'll reach the signposted 'Monument Track' turn off. The track from here to Mt Herbert requires considerable bike pushing on the way up and good technical riding skills on the way back down. There is a trig and two large aerials at the top.

From the summit, backtrack to the 'Monument Track' signpost and head down past the imposing cliffs, called The Monument, to Purau Saddle.

Notes The tracks are closed during lambing (August–September). On a cloudy day, navigation is difficult. The weather changes very quickly on Mt Herbert, so take an extra warm layer. Refer to Infomap 336 Banks Peninsula.

16 Mt Fitzgerald

aka Double Fenceline

51 km southeast of Christchurch

Grade 3+, 4–8 hours, 34 km ★★★

This ride provides a rewarding journey over Banks Peninsula high country.

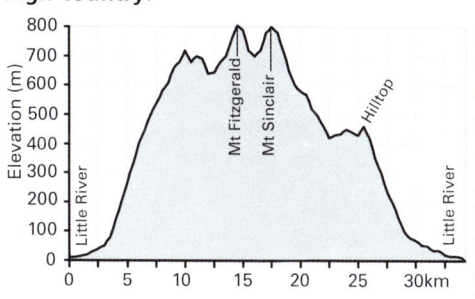

Landowners Although this track follows a paper road, it is closed during lambing, August–October.

Route description From Little River, follow the Port Levy Road and climb steeply for 1–2 hours to the saddle. Take the 4WD track east, following a paper road (often between a double fence line) along an undulating ridge to Mt Fitzgerald (826 m). As you approach Mt Fitzgerald, cross a metal stile. Turn left, cross another fence and keep going for 200 metres, then turn right down a 4WD track, which sidles around the Mt Fitzgerald summit and avoids an unrideable bit of walking track.

The Mt Fitzgerald ride can affect riders in most peculiar ways.

After a short descent, carry on up towards Mt Sinclair (841 m), from where the track drops towards Pettigrews Road. Soon after a small green hut comes into view, you'll reach a pair of gates. Hop over the left-hand gate. Don't climb the track to the TV transmitter–take the grassy 4WD track to the left for 1 km, and you'll link up with Pettigrews Road.

Once at the road, turn right, then after 500 metres, turn right again to get onto the Summit Road, which is sealed. From Hilltop, take Harmans '4WD Vehicles Only' Track and Puaha Road back to Little River.

Track conditions 35% sealed road, 20% gravel road, 35% 4WD track, 10% semi-rideable single track

Notes The downhill from Mt Sinclair passes through one of the last remaining patches of totara forest on the peninsula. This is also a well used walkway–don't rile other users.

The farmer at the Pettigrews end has insurance to cover the possibility of his bulls goring a mountain biker. If this worries you, phone (03) 304 6819 to check their whereabouts. Refer to Infomap 336 Banks Peninsula or Topomap N36 Akaroa.

South Canterbury

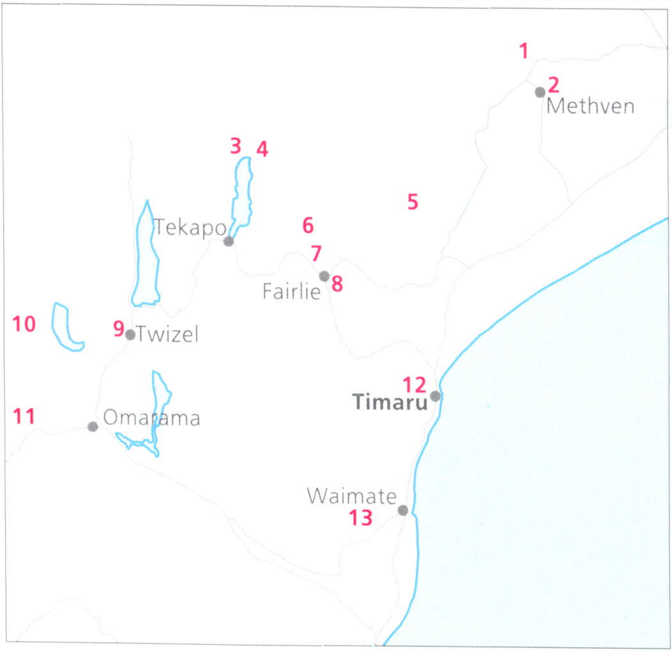

1 Mt Hutt
2 Methven

3 4

5

Tekapo

6

7

Fairlie 8

10 9 Twizel

11 Omarama

12
Timaru

Waimate
13

1	Mt Hutt	**8**	Fairlie Walkway
2	Methven Walkway	**9**	Twizel Area Tracks
3	Godley Glacier	**10**	Parsons MTB Track
4	Macaulay Valley	**11**	Ahuriri Valley
5	Mt Peel MTB Marathon	**12**	Centennial Park
6	North Opuha	**13**	White Horse Trail
7	Opuha Dam		

SOUTH CANTERBURY HIGHLIGHTS

Twizel is the centre for track development through high-country land in South Canterbury. The region offers many rides up huge valleys into the Southern Alps—mostly crossing barren tundra-like terrain with expansive views.

1 Mt Hutt

110 km west of Christchurch

Grades 4–6, 1–2 hours, up to 6 km ★

Several downhill tracks have been built below the ski field at Mount Hutt, but you don't need a DH rig to ride the easier ones.

How to get there From Mount Hutt township, drive south for 6 km then turn right onto McLennans road and follow the signs towards the ski field. Just drive up the hill for a couple of kilometres and then park at the toll gate building.

Route description There are up to 10 tracks in this area, most include jumps and structures for downhilling, but all the really gnarly stuff can be avoided. The best tracks are higher up. From the toll gate, ride up the ski field road for at least 2 km. Then you will see a DOC MTB sign on your left. This is a grade 3+ track that heads back towards the toll gate. You can also ride another 1.5 km up the road and start higher up.

On the way down, turn left to ride FUZZ, one of the easier tracks at grade 4. The area south of (below) the toll gate has recently been logged, and gorse is growing fast; don't be surprised if these tracks become overgrown.

Track conditions a mixture of gravel roads, forestry roads and single track

Notes These tracks become horrendously muddy after a bit of rain. Drop in to Big Als Snow Sports in Methven for an update on track conditions.

2 Methven Walkway

Methven

Grade 1+, 30–60 mins, 8 km ★

If you are stuck in Methven, waiting for it to snow, try this short, flat jaunt. Parts of it are quite a lot of fun.

Route description Ride northeast out of Methven on Barkers Road for 1 km. At Holmes Road, ride into the forest and enjoy the first few hundred metres of purpose-built mountain bike track. It weaves tightly through the trees and has some cool dips and jumps.

When you reach the canal, either backtrack or turn left onto the 4WD track beside the canal and carry on to the second road, turn left there and follow Pudding Hill Road back into town.

Notes Remember, most of this is a walkway—be ready to give way. For a pamphlet on the walkway (50 cents), drop in to the information centre in town.

3 Godley Glacier

Lake Tekapo

Grade 3, 1–3 days, 140 km return ★ ★

Gravel roads and bumpy 4WD tracks provide a complete circumnavigation of Lake Tekapo, offering access to spectacular mountain scenery and an optional side trip to Godley Glacier.

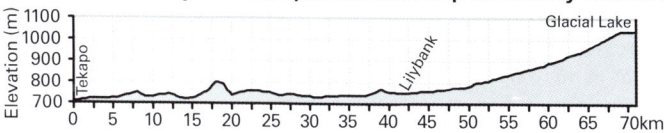

Landowners If you plan to cross the Godley, phone Les Scott on (03) 680 6919 before your ride for permission to go through

Godley Peaks Station and to confirm the condition of the river crossing.

Route description   Ride east from Tekapo Village and take the first turn on the left. This gravel road heads along Lake Tekapo and up the Macaulay River. Cross the Macaulay River to Lilybank Station and go straight to the Godley River valley (do not take the right turn, which heads further up the Macaulay — see Macaulay Valley below).

Follow a rough 4WD track past a few 'Public Access' signs and on up the huge Godley River flats. Cycle over Lucifer Flat. Dump your gear and head up to Godley Glacier Lake about 6 km north — there are usually icebergs floating in the terminal lake. Godley Hut is 600 metres from the lake. It's a basic tramping hut, with mattresses but not much else.

You can either head back the same way or, during times of low temperature and low rainfall, carefully cross the Godley River and ride down the other side of the lake. The river is fed by glacial melt and rises with temperature as well as rainfall. On your way back to Tekapo, it's worth heading over to visit Lake Alexandrina (signposted from the road). It's a lovely lake, and a lot warmer for swimming in than the glacial ones in this district.

Track conditions   50% gravel road, 50% 4WD track

Notes   Tekapo Village has shops, backpackers and a camping ground. This ride is raced once a year (see www.mtbpursuits.com). Take Topomap I36 Godley and Terrainmap 12 Mount Cook.

4 Macaulay Valley

EASY

39 km north of Tekapo township

Grade 2+, 3–6 hrs, 40 km return ★ ★

This valley, to the east of Godley River valley, sees regular 4WD vehicle use, making it a fairly well-worn route into the foothills of the Southern Alps.

Route description   Leave Tekapo as per the Godley Glacier ride (see above). There is a 'courtesy car park' by a shed 38.5 km from Tekapo, just before the first Macaulay River ford. From

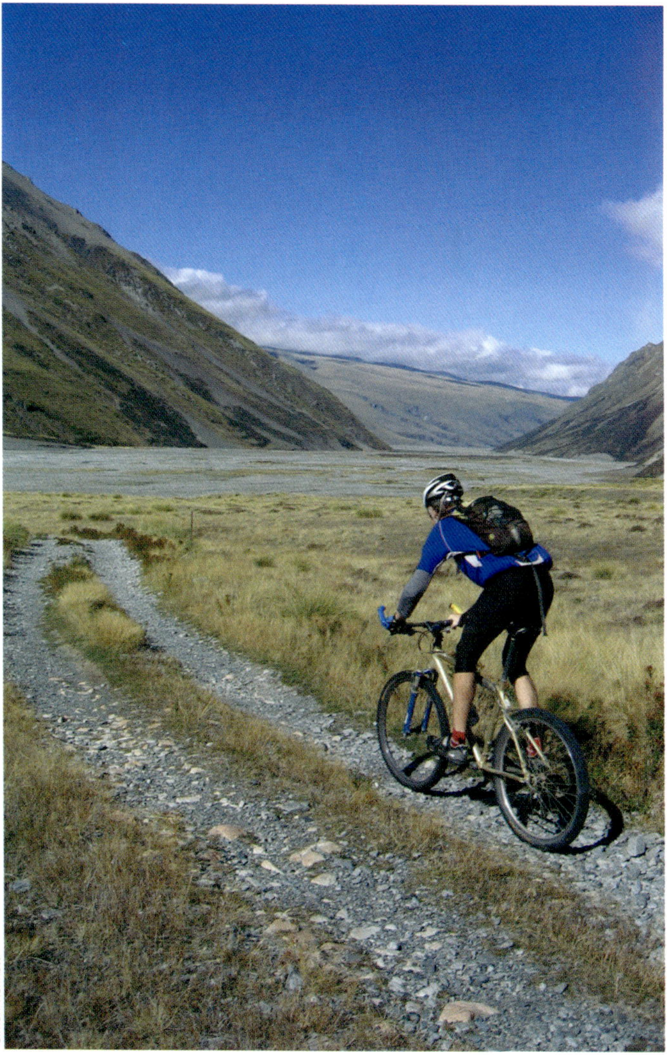

Taking to the high road, up the Macaulay.

there, cross the Macaulay River, hang a right and then follow orange markers up to the flash Macaulay Hut, 20 km away.

After about an hour's cycling, the track becomes very hard to find as it negotiates its way up the middle of the braided river valley — keep your eye on the orange markers not the transient 4WD tracks. Return the same way.

Notes Macaulay Hut is free to stay at (although donations are welcome). Don't forget your camera — there are some mighty fine mountains at the top end of this ride.

5 Mt Peel MTB Marathon

70 km north of Timaru

Grade 4+, 5–10 hours, 85 km ★ ★

This fantastic adventure ride can only be done once a year, in April, during the Mt Peel MTB Marathon.

Route description Although this event is supposed to be a race, the course is so good that it attracts many non-competitive entrants, hence its inclusion in this book.

It starts and finishes at Peel Forest (20 km north of Geraldine) and circumnavigates Mt Peel on some very rugged high-country farm tracks. This involves over 2000 m of climbing, massive views of South Canterbury high country and the Southern Alps, one mammoth downhill, and some lovely valley riding.

For less masochistic mountain bikers, the easier Blue Mountain Gorges race is held at the same time. Once again, the scenery is great, but there are only a few medium-sized hills as the 60-km route hops from one valley over to the next.

Track conditions Mostly farm tracks, plus a bit of gravel road

Notes The Mt Peel race is the hardest annual mountain bike race in New Zealand (and one of the oldest, dating back to the late 1980s).

For more details, visit www.mtpeelmtb.co.nz

6 North Opuha

29 km north of Fairlie

Grade 2+, approx 2 hrs, 18 km return ★★

This is a classic there-and-back high-country ride that will leave you hankering for more.

How to get there Head north out of Fairlie township on Highway 79 and take the first left after crossing the Opihi River bridge, onto Clayton Road. After 25 km, turn onto Fax Peak Skifield Road. Twenty-nine kilometres from Fairlie, park by the conservation area signs.

Route description It's a 7-km ride up through high-country pasture to the North Opuha Conservation Area and then another 2 km to Spurs Hut (built in 1890). Just follow the orange markers, and don't turn left at the saddle.

   The hut sleeps 4 and is a perfect spot for a break. From there, turn around to head back the same way.

Track conditions 100% 4WD track

7 Opuha Dam

13 km northeast of Fairlie

Grade 1+, 1 hour, less than 16 km

The Fairlie District MTB pamphlet promotes this as a 16-km loop ride. Be warned: in 2008, this was not a complete loop.

How to get there Head out of town on Clayton Road for 12 km, turn right at monument corner, then left at the picnic area sign.

Route description From the lakeside picnic area, there is 4 km of reasonable 4WD track on your right that leads to the dam. Beyond the dam, however, there is little more than faint sheep tracks, and a bike is a hindrance.

Notes The same pamphlet promotes several gravel roads and some single tracks at the Raincliff Forest and Pioneer Park. The single tracks are far too short or unrideable to be worth burning the fuel to get there.

8 Fairlie Walkway

Fairlie

Grade 1+, 1–2hrs, 13 km return ★★

Despite being surrounded by the worst weed infestations we've ever seen, this is a surprisingly fun track.

Route description Start on the Opihi river bank between the Top 10 Holiday Park and the main bridge out of town on Highway 79. Head downstream, following the Fairlie Walkway east and then the Opihi River Track to Opihi Gorge Road. Return the way you came.

This is an excellent introduction to single-track riding, but beginners should take care on the footbridges.

Track conditions 100% single track

9 Twizel Area Tracks

In the early 21st century, DOC started making real progress in securing new biking opportunities throughout the South Island high country. This was a result of the High Country Tenure Review process, which directed some leasehold land into the conservation estate and created access easements through the land that has become freehold.

The result is several routes in the Twizel area that you have a right to bike. With that right comes the responsibility of sticking to the marked route, leaving gates as you find them, not panicking stock and, of course, not littering. The process is ongoing, so more easements will be created in future. Pop into the Twizel information centre for the latest maps and pamphlets.

Darts Bush Stream Loop

6 km northwest of Twizel
Grade 2+, 1.5–2.5 hr, 22 km ★

This ride heads up to Darts Bush Stream and back around The Pyramid hill on a mix of farm roads, 4WD tracks and single track.

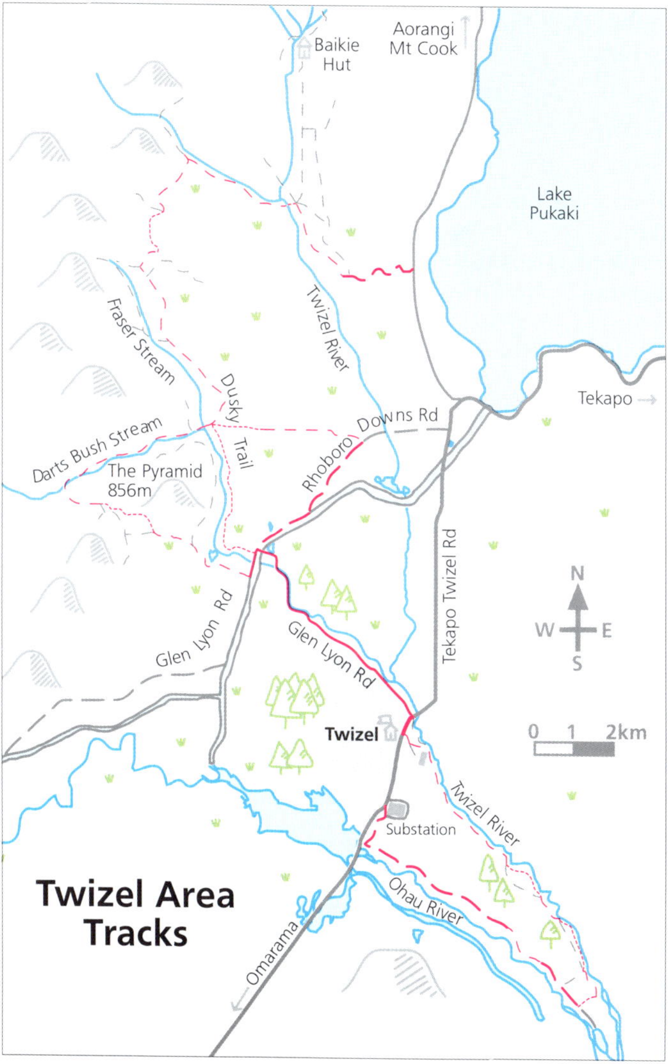

Baikie
Hut

Aorangi
Mt Cook

Lake
Pukaki

Fraser Stream

Twizel River

Dusky Trail

Darts Bush Stream

Rhoboro Downs Rd

Tekapo →

The Pyramid
856m

Glen Lyon Rd

Glen Lyon Rd

Tekapo Twizel Rd

N
W — E
S

0   1   2km

Twizel

Twizel River

Substation

Twizel Area Tracks

Ohau River

Omarama

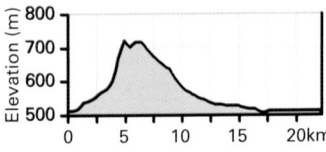

Head northwest along Glen Lyon Road on the north edge of Twizel for 6 km, cross the canal and turn left. After another 500 metres, you'll find the car park on your right.

Follow the orange markers into the hills, along a 4WD track next to Darts Bush Stream and then back to Rhoboro Downs Road. At one point, late in the ride, you'll cross a couple of streams in quick succession and then head across the flats away from the DOC sign (if you want to complete the full loop).

When you reach the gravel road, turn right to get back to the canal and then follow it back to the start of the loop. Debate rages over whether this loop is best done clockwise or anticlockwise ... take your pick.

We recommend shortcutting the last part of this ride by heading down Dusky Trail next to Fraser Stream (see below)—much more fun and convenient as it brings you back to within 200 metres of the trail-head car park where you started.

Dusky Trail

6 km northwest of Twizel

Grade 3, 2–5 hrs, 22–38 km ★★★

INTERMEDIATE

This new ride is sandwiched between Gladstone Stream and the Darts Bush Stream Loop (see above). While its scenery is similar, the Dusky Trail is a step up from that ride as it contains some sweet flowing single track. Check out the Dusky Trail pamphlet available from the Twizel DOC office.

Ride from town or start from the Dusky Trail sign on Glen Lyon Road—a couple of hundred metres before the Darts Bush car park. Follow the markers up Fraser Stream and into the foothills. This ride offers an interesting mix of new single track and old farm track passing through open tussock country.

You'll reach a picnic table at the ride's high point after 11 km. Either turn back here (the sheep track is excellent at 30 km/hr) or carry on to Gladstone Stream, which ends with a road bash back to Twizel or your parked car.

Simon Kennett

Softcore 'North Shore' on the Twizel River Trail.

Note This ride includes a few stream crossings and is best avoided during or immediately after heavy rain.

Twizel River Trail
Grade 1, 1–2.5 hrs, 16–25 km ★★

This rather brilliant little gem is one of the best beginner-grade single tracks in New Zealand. During autumn, the turning leaves are a bonus.

From the Twizel DOC centre, head out to the highway and then towards Tekapo for about 100 metres. Look for the trail-head sign on the right side of the road. Head through the gate, onto the gravel road for 300 m and then follow the orange poles to some sweet new single track.

Hobo's Camp, at the 8-km mark, is a nice picnic spot and turn-around point.

Alternatively, ride on to the far end of the track and then turn right to return via the gravel road and Highway 8.

10 Parsons MTB Track
30 km west of Twizel

Grade 2, 40–80 minutes, 10-km loop ★

Here's a short single-track blast for those desperate for a fix.

How to get there Head south from Twizel on Highway 8 for 13 km and then turn right up the road to the Ohau Ski Field village. Park just after the Glen Mary Ski Club, 20 km from the highway.

Route description Ride another 3 km up the road and then turn left up the Ohau Ski Field Road. After pedalling 1.4 km up this road, you'll cross a ford and see the start of the single track (it's marked). Follow the markers to Sawyers Creek and then the 4WD track down to the ski club.

Track conditions 30% sealed road, 15% gravel road, 20% 4WD track, 35% single track

11 Ahuriri Valley

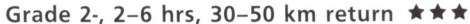

39 km west of Omarama

Grade 2-, 2–6 hrs, 30–50 km return ★★★

Here's another simple valley ride with stunning scenery. As with so many South Island valleys, this one is huge.

How to get there From Omarama drive 15 km west on Highway 8, then veer right onto Birchwood Road. It is a further 24 km to the DOC intentions booth and Ahuriri Conservation Park boundary—a good place to park.

Route description The next 10-odd kilometres provide a good warm-up on a gravelly 4WD road that leads to the Ahuriri Base Hut. Then it's 5 km on a more natural 4WD track to the Canyon Creek camping area, another 3.5 km to Shamrock Hut and another 6 km to Hagens Hut. If you're feeling keen, carry on to Top Hut, 4.5 km up the valley.

Watch out for the devilishly slippery fords. Once you've had enough, turn around and ride back the way you came in.

Track conditions gravel roads and 4WD tracks

Simon Kennett

Cruising up the Ahuriri Valley.

12 Centennial Park

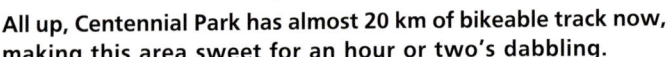

Church St, Timaru

Grade 2+, 30–60 mins, up to 20 km ★★★

All up, Centennial Park has almost 20 km of bikeable track now, making this area sweet for an hour or two's dabbling.

Route decription From the centre of Timaru, ride west all the way down Church Street and into Centennial Park. There are map boards a short distance in from the main entrances.

The park comprises several dirt tracks scattered among the exotic trees and grass fields; they include a couple of mountain bike tracks built by the local club. Also, the walking tracks have recently been opened up to mountain bikers—enjoy, but remember to give way to pedestrians.

Centenial Park to the coast

If the tracks at Centennial Park aren't long enough for you, head back past the jumps area (near the Church Street entrance) and follow the three walkways listed below out to the coast.

Otipua Creek Walkway, 1 km: From the BMX track near the entrance to Centennial Park, ride a newish track down beside the creek to Coonoor Road. Cross this road and head right for 100 metres to the next track.

Saltwater Creek Walkway to King St, 3 km: This track leads from Coonoor Road downstream to King St. It is flat and easy. Cross the road at the end to continue.

Saltwater Creek to the coast, 2.5 km: The first half of this walkway follows the creek, then crosses it, and the railway line, to the coast. It then follows the coast to the Caledonian Grounds and South Street, by the picnic grounds at Patati Point. This is 1 km from central Timaru.

13 White Horse Trail

West of Waimate

Grade 4, 1–2 hours, 10 km return from Waimate ★★

This sweet track has been built by local mountain bikers and is worth checking out, if only to break up a drive north or south. Why the name White Horse? You'll find out once you're there.

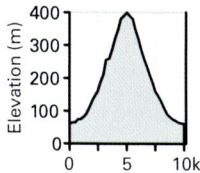

Route description From Waimate, head northwest on Mill Road, then take a left onto Point Bush Road. Follow the signs for the Waimate Walkway. The walkway starts at the car park beside Te Kiteroa homestay, 2 km out of town.

At the main gate, cross the stile and ride straight ahead, following the red and white markers to a second stile. These markers direct you to the track entrance on your left. Follow the track as it flicks back and forth up the hill. Just before the top, the trail meets up with the walkway, so be prepared for walkers from here on.

The lookout point (elevation 400 m) gives you a panoramic vista over Waimate to the Pacific Ocean. You can also spot the Waimate velodrome. Return the same way for an excellent downhill.

Track conditions 40% sealed road, 20% 4WD track, 40% single track

Notes Drop in to the Waimate information centre for an update on this and other tracks in the area. The nearby Noondale Forest has been sold, and that ride is now closed.

Dave Mitchell

Pack your mittens—we're heading for central Otago.

Otago

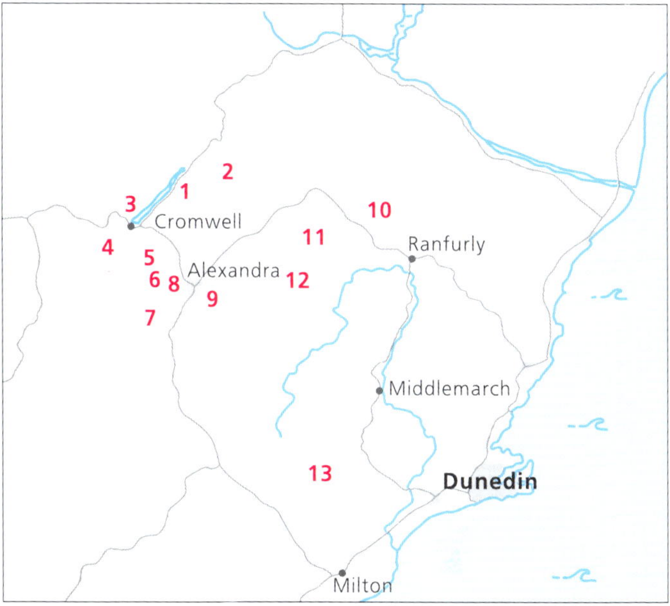

Map of Otago region showing numbered track locations near Cromwell, Alexandra, Ranfurly, Middlemarch, Dunedin, and Milton.

1	Devils Creek Track	8	Alexandra Anniversary Track
2	Rise 'n' Shine	9	Lake Roxburgh Walkway
3	Dunstan Lakeside Track	10	Naseby Forest
4	Carricktown Loop	11	Otago Central Rail Trail
5	Cairnmuir Hill	12	Dunstan Trail
6	Omeo Gully Loop	13	Government Track
7	Old Man Range Loop		

OTAGO HIGHLIGHTS

The Otago Central Rail Trail has been a huge success for the region. It provides safe riding with good food and accommodation. Naseby Forest has fun single track for intermediate and experienced riders. Alexandra has several short rides to choose from or the massive loop over the Old Man Range to push your boundaries.

1 Devils Creek Track

7 km north of Cromwell

Grade 4, 2.5–5 hours, approx 21 km return ★★

Old farm tracks in the Bendigo Conservation Area make for an excellent test of lungs and brakes.

How to get there Head 7 km north of Cromwell bridge, beside Lake Dunstan, until you see the DOC sign, 'Devils Creek Track' (there's a lakeside picnic area across the road).

Route description From the sign, a ridiculously steep track climbs up to Mt Oho and on to Mt Kinaki (1309m). Some bike pushing will be necessary on the way up, but the views and ride back down make it all worthwhile. Never mind the blurry vision as you approach the tops—that's a perfectly normal reaction to near vertical grades at this altitude.

   You can also access the Bendigo Conservation Area from near the top of Thomsons Gorge Road by riding over Mt Moka (see Rise 'n' Shine below). From there, the riding all the way to Mt Apiti is much easier.

Track conditions 100% 4WD track

Simon Kennett

David Drake deals to his demons on Devils Creek Track.

Notes For details on the extent of this new conservation area, drop in to the DOC information centre in Alexandra. Refer to Topomap Cromwell G41. Tour de France racers think 12% is a steep grade—the first kilometre of this ride averages 20%!

2 Rise 'n' Shine

aka Thomsons Saddle

15 km north of Cromwell

Grade 2, 2–4 hours, 50 km ★ ★

Here's a great ride for anyone wanting to check out the Dunstan Mountains without the challenge of tricky navigation or the hassle of contacting landowners.

How to get there From Cromwell, cross Lake Dunstan and drive north for 13 km to The Stables shop (it's marked Crippletown on the map and is 1 km north of a lakeside picnic area).

Route description From Crippletown, jump on your bike and follow the gravelly Bendigo Road east to Thomsons Gorge Road. Keep heading generally southeast, over Thomsons Saddle (980 m), through Thomsons Gorge and on to Highway 85 at Omakau and the Otago Central Rail Trail (see below). Like most of Central Otago, this trip offers expansive views but is exposed to the elements.

Track conditions 100% gravel road

Notes From Omakau, you can follow the Otago Central Rail Trail down to Alexandra, 28 km away—no hills or cars. There is an old musterers' hut about half way through the ride, just a few hundred metres from the bottom of the first big downhill, on your right. It's a good spot for a lunch stop.

3 Dunstan Lakeside Track

Cromwell

Grade 1, 30–60 mins, 7 km one way ★

An okay introduction to mountain biking for those who have never ridden off road.

Route Description From the Old Cromwell historic district, follow a mix of sealed road and dirt and gravel tracks around the lake front to Lowburn. Give yourself time to check out the sites and the fresh fruit. If you run out of time, return to Cromwell via Highway 6.

4 Carricktown Loop

Cromwell

INTERMEDIATE

Grade 3, 3–5 hours, 31 km ★★

Here's an excellent day trip from Cromwell for fit riders.

Landowners Call Don Clarke of Carrick Station, on (03) 445 0977, for permission to ride from Duffers Saddle down to Carricktown.

Route description Cycle out past Bannockburn all the way to Duffers Saddle at the top of Nevis Road. Then turn right and ride north, into the midday sun, on an undulating 4WD track. After 5 km, turn right again and enjoy the downhill past Carricktown on to Quartzville Road and Schoolhouse Road, which takes you back to Bannockburn.

Remains of stone buildings are all that are left of Carricktown, but the Young Australian waterwheel a short distance away is worth a look-see (to your right).

Notes Refer to Topomaps F41 Arrowtown and F42 Kingston.

Mark Kent and Sarah Drake descending to Carricktown.

5 Cairnmuir Hill

ADVANCED

Clyde

Grade 4-, 2.5–4 hrs, approx 30 km ★ ★

Reckon you're fit? Looking for a space so large and open it makes you feel tiny? Here's the hill for you.

Route description DOC has marked out the Cairnmuir Hill Track, from Clyde to Bannockburn, with yellow marker posts. The route (nearly all 4WD track) traverses the Cairnmuir Mountains (starting west of Clyde on Hawksburn Road). The track itself is 21 km long and climbs to 1100 m. A few kilometres of road at either end extend this trip to 30 km. There is some faint walking track involved, so have Terramap *Queenstown & Cromwell Recreation Areas* with you to be sure of your navigation. In cloudy conditions, a compass would be handy, too. Watch out for Spaniards on the walking track section!

From Clyde, cross the old Clyde Bridge and head south for a few hundred metres before turning up the 'Lookout Road'. This is steep and rutted and you'll be so deep in oxygen debt that you could be forgiven for missing the turn onto the Cairnmuir Track. Keep your eyes peeled for a DOC sign on the right 5 km from the bridge. Don't veer right until you see the DOC sign. From there, simply follow the markers.

Ten kilometres into the ride you'll be heading up towards some large torrs; head through the gate on your right just before reaching them. Another 15–20 minutes later you'll come to a hut. If you have some single track riding skills, take the sweet water race detour to the right. You'll rejoin the main route a kilometre later.

When you reach the end of the track at Cornish Point Road, turn left and cruise a few kilometres round to the Bannockburn Inlet picnic area—a nice spot to be picked up.

Track conditions 18% sealed road, 18% gravel road, 57% 4WD track, 4% single track, 3% unrideable

Notes Take plenty of water and warm clothing and be sure to leave all gates as you find them. Access is restricted during lambing (from mid-October to mid-November). If you've got

Simon Kennett

Approaching the Cairnmuir tops.

a long summer's day on your hands and are feeling particularly staunch, consider riding back to Clyde over Hawksburn Road.

6 Omeo Gully Loop

INTERMEDIATE

8 km from Alexandra

Grade 3+, 3–7 hours, 28 km ★★★

For those with good navigation and technical riding skills, this loop is a more interesting ride than the Old Man Range. Both reward a hard uphill slog with awesome views.

How to get there From Alexandra, head west over the main bridge to Blackmans (8 km away via Earnscleugh and Blackman Roads).

Route description From the Blackmans intersection, ride up Fraser Dam Road for about half an hour. Just after the crest of a hill, you'll see a DOC sign stating 'Access to Kopuwai Conservation Area' on your left. That's your invitation to start

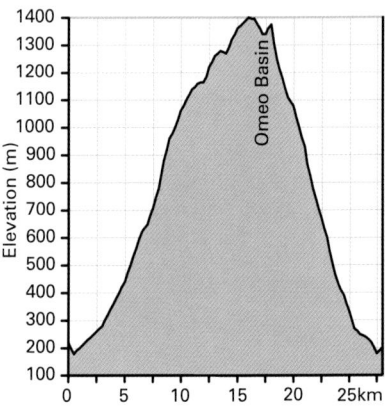

some serious climbing. Follow the yellow marker posts and leave the gates as you find them.

Keep heading up the Prospect Hill Track past some eerie rock formations and a couple of huts until you get to a locked gate at 1400 metres above sea level. Now drop into Omeo Basin and pop up to topographical map spot height 1377 on the other side. This is where the navigation starts to get tricky.

Where the 4WD track turns hard right, hop over the fence on your left. Now head northeast, directly away from the fence, aiming to keep the gully on your right and some major erosion on your left. Due to the thick Spaniard grass, you can expect to walk much of the next kilometre. After about 40 minutes, you should reach a 4WD track. Continue heading generally northeast (with a few decent zigzags thrown in for good measure) along Omeo Gully Track and then Omeo Gully Road. This stretch is a real hoot, but be careful of running stock off their legs.

At the bottom of the gully, turn right and cruise 1 km back to Blackmans.

Track conditions 65% 4WD track, 30% gravel road, 5% no track

Notes Take Terramap Queenstown & Cromwell Recreation Areas and a compass or GPS. DOC's Prospect Hill Track and Omeo Track brochures also cover this area.

Many of the tracks in this area follow access easements across private land–please stick to the marked route. Also, head elsewhere during winter (when snow covers the tops) and during lambing: mid-October to mid-November.

7 Old Man Range Loop

Alexandra

Grade 4, 4–6 hours, 52 km ★★★

The Obelisk and TV transmitter on top of the Old Man Range appear enticingly close from Alexandra on a clear day despite being over 1,500 vertical metres away. Go well prepared for a freezing alpine environment when you get there. The downhill back to town is l-o-o-o-o-ng and fast.

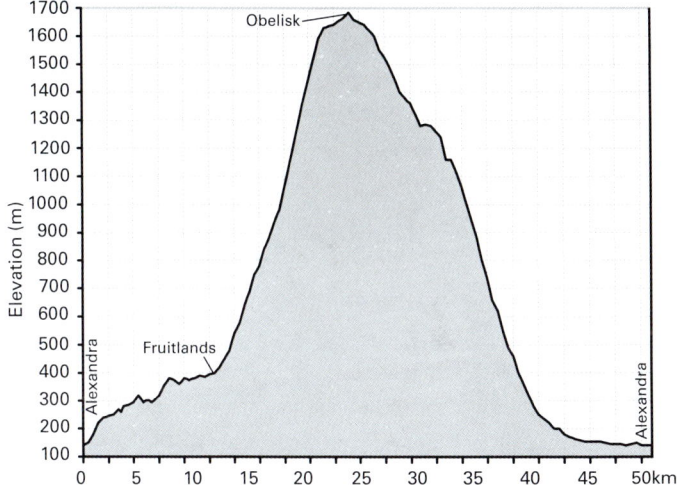

Route description Ride south out of Alexandra on Highway 8. After 13 km, turn right onto Symes Road (near Fruitlands). There is a good spot for a rest just 1 km up the road at the Historic Mitchells Cottage because, after that, it's climb time. After about a 2-hour granny-gear workout, you'll approach an intersection on the crest of the main ridge. Veer right and cruise towards the Obelisk (1695 m) 2 km to the north. There are several huge rocks to shelter beside along the way.

Continue north from the Obelisk and prepare for a massive downhill. After a few kilometres, turn left at a fence line. Two

kilometres further on, veer right (you will see a hut about 200 metres away, over your left shoulder). After another 9 km of downhilling, turn right at a T-intersection onto Fraser Dam Road.

Soon after this road flattens out, you should turn right at Blackmans Road (sealed), then right again at Earnscleugh Road, which leads you back to Alexandra.

Track conditions 35% sealed road, 30% gravel road, 35% 4WD track

Notes Take extra food and water, warm clothes and a jacket. In 1863, several miners died trying to climb over the range to avoid starving at their claims near Campbell Creek. Unless it rains, there is no water on the range, and the trip can't be done in winter due to snow. It's also closed from 15 October to 15 November for lambing. We recommend taking Topomap G42 Alexandra.

8 Alexandra Anniversary Track

Alexandra

Grade 2, 1–2 hrs, 12 km ★ ★ ★

This ride from Alexandra to Clyde is an excellent introduction to single track. Pick a fine autumn day, and you'll be rewarded with some stunning scenery.

Route description From Alexandra, cross the big iron bridge heading south, turn left and immediately duck under the bridge onto a single track beside the river. That's a short cut to the car park at the start of the Anniversary Track, which is 1 km from the shops in town.

From the car park, you can't get lost. Follow the main track to a car park and road bridge beside Clyde. The track follows the Clutha River and is a lot of fun, in a cruisy sort of way.

Cross the river at Clyde, sniff out a cafe to grab a bite to eat, then return via the Otago Central Rail Trail (on the northeast side of the highway) ... Actually, heading back the same way is more fun.

Simon Kennett

Easy riding along the Alexandra Anniversary Track.

9 Lake Roxburgh Walkway
aka Mt Rock

INTERMEDIATE

Alexandra

Grade 3, 1.5–3 hrs, approx 15 km return ★ ★

This rocky single track is ideal for riders looking to test their skills. Nice scenery, too.

Route description From Alexandra, cross the Manuherikia River on Shaky Bridge before turning right and cycling to the end of Graveyard Gully Road. From the graveyard, where there is a 'Lake Roxburgh Walkway' sign, follow a fun single track beside the Clutha River up to the historic stone huts at Butchers Point. In years gone by, one of these huts was the local hotel!

Riding becomes very difficult beyond Butchers Point, so it's best to turn around and head back the same way. Some riders choose to turn back earlier.

Notes Avoid this narrow track when it's likely to be chocka with walkers, and always give way.

10 Naseby Forest

12 km north of Ranfurly

Grades 2–5, 1–8 hours, up to 50 km ★★★

If you're looking for great single track and reliable sunshine close to Dunedin, look no further—Naseby is the place to be.

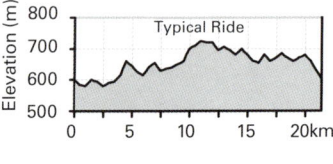

Landowners Naseby is a production forest, and logging is ongoing. Ask for an update at the forest headquarters in Naseby. The forest is occasionally closed because of fire risk. Walkers and forestry trucks always have right of way.

How to get there From Palmerston, take Highway 85 (the Pigroot) for 65 km towards Ranfurly. The historic little town of Naseby is 12 km north of there.

Serious plumbing at Naseby Forest.

Route description Most of this exotic forest lies northwest of Naseby village and is festooned with forestry roads and 4WD tracks with numerous single tracks branching off them. The 'Skatebowl', 'Ejector Seat' and 'Roller Coaster' are some of the features that local riders rave about.

According to our dodgy Internet poll, this is the most popular riding destination in Otago. Many of the tracks are cruisy and scenic; others simply 'flow' amazingly

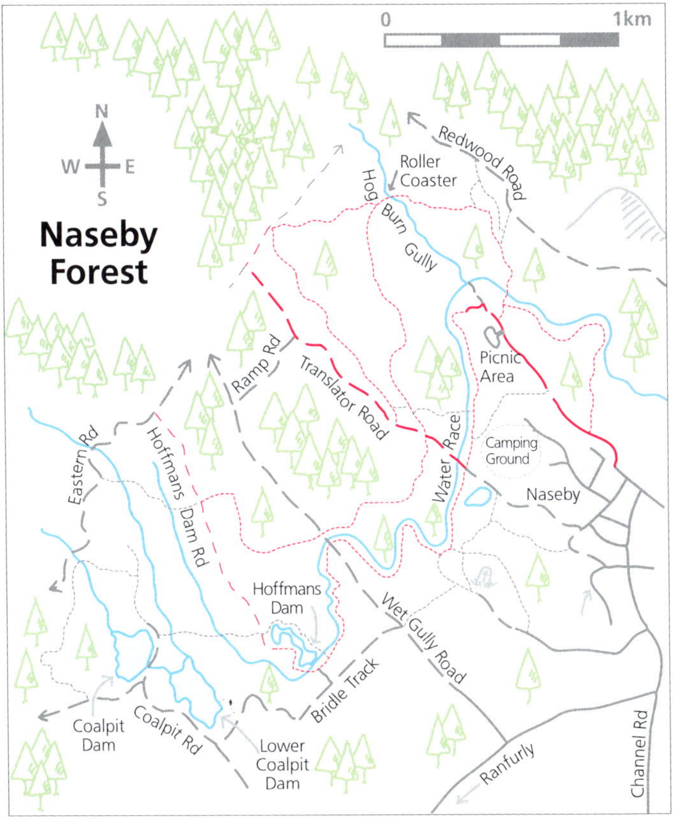

0
1km
N
W
E
S
Naseby Forest
Redwood Road
Roller Coaster
Hog Burn Gully
Ramp Rd
Translator Road
Picnic Area
Camping Ground
Water Race
Naseby
Eastern Rd
Hoffmans Dam Rd
Hoffmans Dam
Wet Gully Road
Bridle Track
Coalpit Dam
Coalpit Rd
Lower Coalpit Dam
Ranfurly
Channel Rd

well. You'll feel like riding some bits over and over again until you're knackered.

Start by heading to the top of Hog Burn gully, then explore.

Accommodation Most mountain bikers stay at the Naseby motor camp because it's right on the edge of the forest and it has well-priced cabins. There are also two hotels.

11 Otago Central Rail Trail

Alexandra to Middlemarch

Grade 2-, 2–3 days, 148 km ★ ★ ★

The disused railway from Alexandra to Middlemarch is now managed by DOC and has been modified for mountain bike use. Out-there scenery, zero traffic and unique Otago hospitality can be combined with the Dunstan Trail (see below) to make one of the best touring loops in the country.

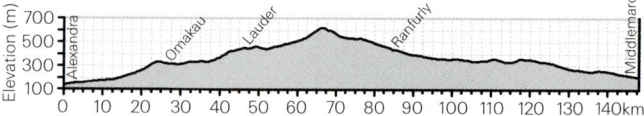

How to get there From Dunedin you can catch a shuttle or train up to Clarks Junction or Middlemarch. For details about the train, from Dunedin to Pukerangi (or Middlemarch on Sundays) during summer, phone Taieri Gorge Railway on (03) 477 4449.

Route description From Alexandra, the ride starts with a gentle climb up the huge Manuherikia Valley. On your right is the Raggedy Range, which the trail soon climbs over.

The section from Lauder Station to Ranfurly involves riding over the highest point of the trail (620 m), through gorges and tunnels and over old viaducts.

The section from Ranfurly to Daisybank includes a 96-metre-long steel truss bridge across the Taieri River. From Daisybank, at the 109 km mark, there are three more bridges en route to Hyde. There are good camping sites at various places where the trail passes close to Taieri River.

The trail has a slight downhill slope most of the way from Hyde to Middlemarch—the end of the line, so to speak. The most appealing option from here is to cycle back to Alexandra via the Dunstan Trail (140 km–see below). Alternatively, catch the train to Dunedin. Most days, it leaves from Pukerangi (25 km from Middlemarch). Dunedin is 75 km away via Highway 87.

Track conditons 100% gravel, some rough, but becoming smoother with time

Jonathan Kennett

Otago's Rail Trail experience includes several impressive viaducts.

Bookings If you want someone to organise your trip along the Rail Trail, contact Trail Journeys in Alexandra. They organise bikes, accommodation, meals and transport. Their website is www.trailjourneys.co.nz. Altitude Adventures in Alexandra offer a similar service (email bookings@altitudeadventures.co.nz).

Notes There are motor camps and motels at Alexandra.

There is also a short but sedate tidbit of Rail Trail between Clyde and Alexandra (the Anniversary Track is much more fun; see above). Pick up the free Otago Central Rail Trail pamphlet, which includes a good map, from any local information centre.

12 **Dunstan Trail**

Dunedin to Alexandra

INTERMEDIATE

Grade 3+, 2–4 days, 170 km ★★

This trip is a collection of quiet gravel roads, 4WD tracks and old wagon trails pioneered as a bike route by gnarly cycle tourers in the 1970s.

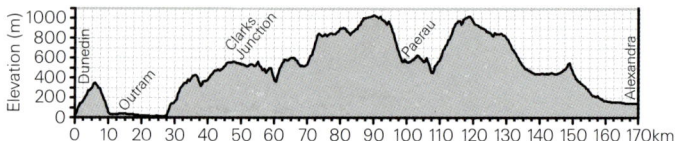

Route description To leave Dunedin by the shortest possible route, cycle straight up Stuart Street from the Octagon and veer right onto Taieri Road, which turns into Three Mile Hill Road. Soon after crossing Silver Stream, turn right onto Milner Road. Carry straight on and you'll reach Highway 87 a few kilometres north of Mosgiel. It's mostly uphill cycling, northwest on Highway 87, to Clarks Junction about 30 km away. It costs around $60 to shuttle this first section.

The Old Dunstan Road turns off to the left here, and you head into an isolated and barren Central Otago landscape. From Clarks Junction, it is 48 km of up and down (but mostly up) to the abandoned Paerau (called 'Styx' by the locals) where there is an esplanade reserve by the Taieri River. The jail there has a fireplace that may be useful if it's raining or snowing. If you go any further than the river, you will be on private land.

It's a hard 71-km day from Paerau to Alexandra with a lot of uphill and heaps of downhill. Cycle north out of Paerau on the Styx-Patearoa Road for 1.5 km. A fence heads off to the left 150 metres after a hay shed. The next 800-metre section of the old trail you're looking for has been ploughed up, but if you cycle along the northern side of the fence up towards the hills, you'll soon pick up two historic cartwheel ruts in the grass. They're marked on the map as a 4WD track and lead to a derelict house on Linnburn Runs Road, 7 km away. In this stretch, you'll need a compass to avoid drifting onto new 4WD tracks.

Simon Kennett

The most remote part of the Dunstan Trail.

From there, head north for 300 metres before turning west onto another 4WD track, which is also part of the original Dunstan Trail. After 3 km, this track meets up with the Old Dunstan Road. Route finding from here on is relatively easy. From Poolburn, it's 50 km mostly downhill to Alexandra.

Track conditions 35% sealed rd, 45% gravel rd, 20% 4WD track

Notes The historic Dunstan Trail was the route originally used by goldminers in the 1860s to travel from Dunedin to the goldfields in Central Otago. This area experiences extremes of weather any time of year, so go well prepared. In wet conditions, parts of the trail are unrideable because of sticky mud.

Topomaps H42 Waipiata and H43 Middlemarch are essential to follow the Dunstan Trail proper as the existing road diverts from it twice. During a northwesterly wind, it is easier to do this trip in reverse, from Alexandra to Dunedin.

If it's wide open spaces free from man-made structures that you're after, get in quick. The area is earmarked for large-scale windfarm development.

13 Government Track

40 km west of Dunedin

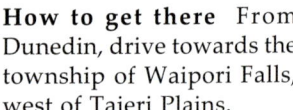

INTERMEDIATE

Grade 3, 3–5 hours, 23 km ★★★

Government Track is a classic, pre-mountain biking single track through beautiful native forest.

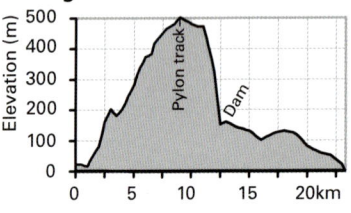

How to get there From Dunedin, drive towards the township of Waipori Falls, west of Taieri Plains.

Route description Start from the picnic area, which is marked on the map beside Waipori Falls Road, 2 km after entering the bush. Cycle back down the road for 1 km before turning left onto Government Track. This old coach road sidles its way up to a wide pylon track on top of the ridge. Most of the track runs through beech forest, but about 30 minutes into the climb, you'll reach a patch of farmland where navigation is tricky. Dip down to the left very briefly at the 'Track' arrow sign and then just keep climbing gradually through the paddock. A stile awaits at the other side of the paddock. We found the climb to be about 90% rideable.

From the gravel road at the top (by the 'Government Track' sign), you have two options. Either turn right and continue on to Lake Mahinerangi via the forestry roads, then cross the dam and go back along Waipori Falls Road, or go left for a short cut to Waipori Falls township (as per the altitude graph). The latter route turns into a steep single track, which is unrideable for a minute near the bottom. A permit is required to head through the exotic forest to the lake. Visit Wenita Forest Products Ltd in Harstonge Ave, Mosgiel, phone (03) 489 3234 or go to their website: www.wenita.co.nz

Track conditions single track, pylon track and gravel road

Notes Expect to encounter windfalls if you're heading in after a big blow; these are normally cleared in early autumn. Government Track can be covered by snow in winter. Walkers also use this track, so be wary. Take Topomap H44 Lawrence.

Dunedin

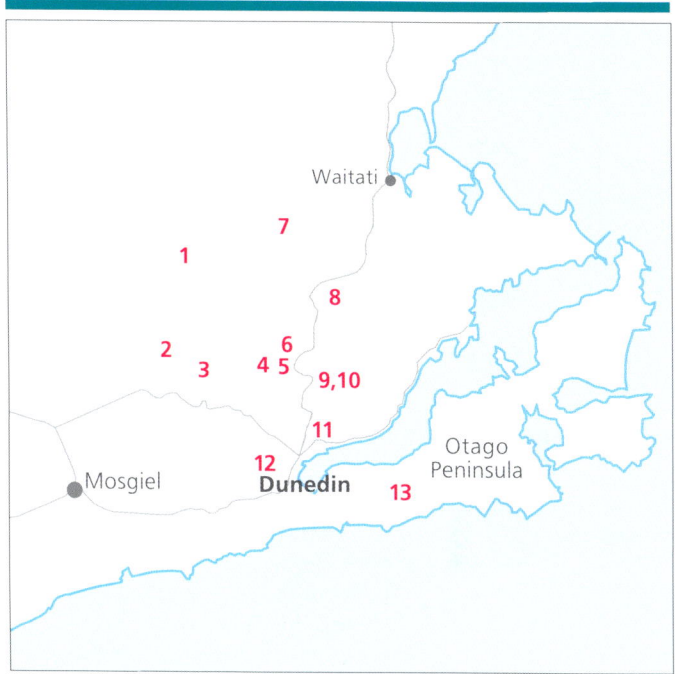

1	Pulpit Rock	**8**	Waitati Loop
2	Racemans Tracks	**9**	Forresters Track
3	Whare Flat	**10**	Bethunes Gully
4	Swampy Summit	**11**	Signal Hill
5	Switchback Track	**12**	Jubilee Park
6	Burns-Rustler Circuit	**13**	Otago Peninsula Backroads
7	Green Hill		

DUNEDIN HIGHLIGHTS

Dunedin is a mixed bag. In summer and autumn, you can get out there and thrash yourself on some of the best purpose-built single track in the country. In wet winter conditions, many tracks are not worth riding, so we've included a couple of gravel-road rides to keep you rolling.

1 Pulpit Rock

INTERMEDIATE

15 km west of Dunedin

Grade 3+, 5–8 hours, 48 km return ★ ★

Without a church in cooee, this old-school enduro ride leads you into the depths of the remote Dunedin outback; you'll return converted.

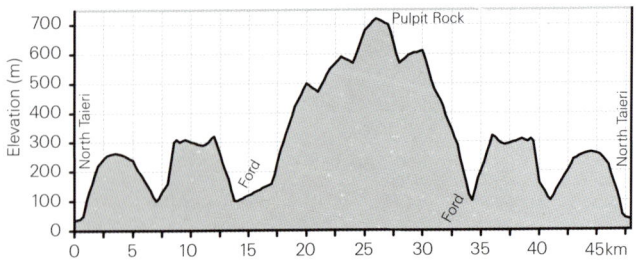

Landowners Wenita Forestry, phone (03) 489 3234–a permit is essential. To get hold of one, pop into the Wenita Forestry office on Harstonge Ave in Mosgiel (turn off Gordon Rd at the New World) or try their website: www.wenita.co.nz

Route description From North Taieri, head up Taioma Road. From the top, stay on the main gravel road for the next 10 km and at the bottom of the second long downhill, you'll reach a four-way intersection, next to Big Stream. Hop over a gate to your right and cycle up beside Big Stream. After 4 km, turn right onto a steep, somewhat overgrown 4WD track heading up into pine forest. If it's wet, expect a fair bit of walking. Zigzag up this rutted track to a gravel road on a ridge, then turn left.

You can see Pulpit Rock in the distance, about 6 km away as the cyclist pedals. If the weather is fine, it's worth climbing the last 50 metres up to the rock–leave your bike near the gate below the top and walk up a little track on your left.

Continue north from Pulpit Rock. After 1 km, you'll pass a turn off on your right, which leads to Mt Silverpeak (777 m), the highest spot in the Silverpeaks. Head west along the ridge, passing several turn-offs, for almost 7 km until you reach a sharp left turn signposted 'Boggy Burn'. This drops you back down to Big Stream. Watch out for the spiked gate at the bottom. From there, head back out the way you came in.

Track conditions 10% sealed road, 65% gravel, 25% 4WD track

Notes This forest is being logged and is only open to riders during the weekend. The first 12 km of this trip can be driven, but beyond that, it's a bit rough for most 2WD cars.

The Silverpeaks area is very exposed to bad weather. (In '86 Paul got lost somewhere around here and spent a miserable night curled up inside a plastic survival tube. Now he writes guidebooks?!) Warm clothes and Topomap I44 Dunedin are essential.

2 Racemans Tracks

ADVANCED

15 km northwest of Dunedin

Grade 4, 2–3 hours, 13 km return ★ ★

A well-graded, technical track through native forest. Best ridden when dry.

How to get there Drive out of Dunedin on Stuart Street, then Taieri Road and then Three Mile Hill Road. When you are 10 km from the Octagon, turn right onto Silverstream Valley

Jonathan Kennett

Scott Farmer launches into the Racemans Track.

Road and go for another 5 km. Stop at an obvious parking area that is 200 metres past the Scout Camp.

Route description From the car park, pass the gate and continue up the road, across a ford and look out for the signposted Racemans Track on your right. There is a little bit of walking to get up to the actual tail-race, but then the riding improves. There are still a few short walking sections, but after about 1 hour, you will reach the top weir.

After a rest, head back from the weir the way you came until you reach the signposted intersection where you can turn off down to the Powder Creek Track. This provides a 15-minute diversion from the Racemans Track. Then you will cross a ford and be back at the gravel road you cycled in on, only 5 minutes from the car park.

Track conditions 40% gravel road, 60% single track

Notes You can pick up a pamphlet on this area from the Dunedin information centre at the Octagon. The tracks in this area can be very boggy and slippery after rain, and tree falls are common after storms.

3 Whare Flat

ADVANCED

8 km from central Dunedin

Grades 4–5, 1–3 hours, 12 km ★ ★ ★

People who enjoy technical challenges will want to spend all day on the fun and freaky tracks at Whare Flat.

How to get there From the Octagon, head up Stuart Street and over Three Mile Hill. After 5.5 km, turn right onto Flagstaff Whare Flat Road and drive 2.5 km up to the Bull Pen.

Route description Head west on a main gravel road (Longridge Road). At the summit, go to the far end of the clearing on your left. After 300 metres, turn right and follow a steep motorbike track down to Laings Road. (Local mountain bikers are building an alternative to this track, which we've marked on our map.)

Once on Laings Road, you'll find a sweet single track called Snakes and Ladders only 40 metres away on your left.

Jonathan Kennett

See Gareth saw on The Third Place.

Snakes and Ladders leads on to The Third Place, which leads to The Green Mile. All three together are 5 km long and are smattered with dozens of interesting obstacles. Some are grade 5, and not all have bypasses, so treat with respect. The track is grade 4 if you don't take on any obstacles.

There are big rock drops, seesaws, log rides, and of course, ladders. No snakes yet, but the track is still under construction. If you like a technical challenge, you will love this track. None of the built obstacles are over 1 metre high.

The Green Mile leads to Surge Tank Road. Follow it to the right to Burma Road, then take the next two left-hand turns. You will climb back up to Laings Road, not far from Whare Flat Road. The Bull Pen is 5 minutes ride further on.

Track conditions 30% forestry road, 70% single track

Notes The tracks must be dry to really enjoy them; otherwise your tyres will clog up with mud, making it impossible to ride the difficult obstacles. There are plans to gravel the climbs in future. There are also plans to have a new downhill track built between Longridge Road (near the Bull Pen) and Laings Road—wahoo!

For updates on tracks at Whare Flat and a map check out www.mountainbikingotago.co.nz

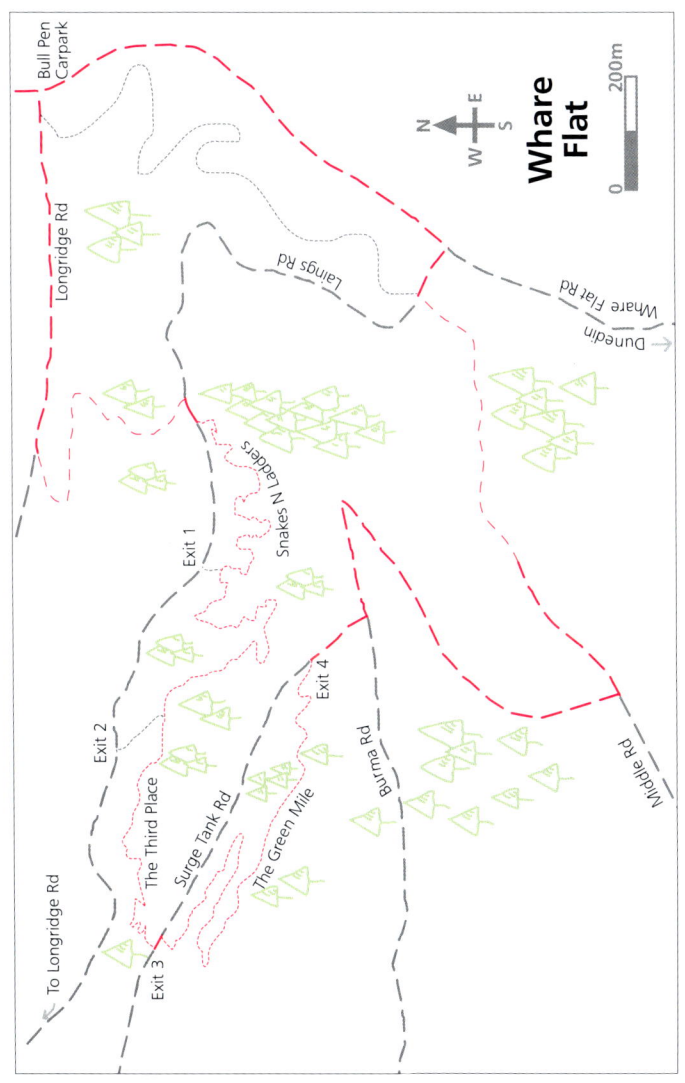

Whare Flat

N W E S

0 200m

4 Swampy Summit

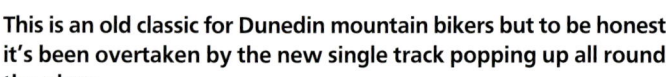

8 km northwest of Dunedin

Grade 2+, 2–4 hours, 19 km ★★

This is an old classic for Dunedin mountain bikers but to be honest it's been overtaken by the new single track popping up all round the place.

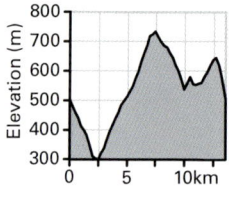

How to get there Ride out of Dunedin on Stuart Street and then Three Mile Hill Road. One kilometre past Halfway Bush, you'll reach Flagstaff Whare Flat Road on your right, next to a reservoir. Climb up Flagstaff Whare Flat Road till you reach the 'Bull Pen' car park.

Route description From the Bull Pen, continue straight ahead on the gravel road, and enjoy a fast 5-minute downhill. Turn

Easy riding near the top of Swampy Summit.

right at Rollinson Road and then settle in for a steady half-hour climb to the Swampy Summit.

Turn right at the ridge and pass the Doppler radar, which looks like a UFO. Turn right at the next two intersections, and watch out for the nasty rut on the way down. Then you'll be

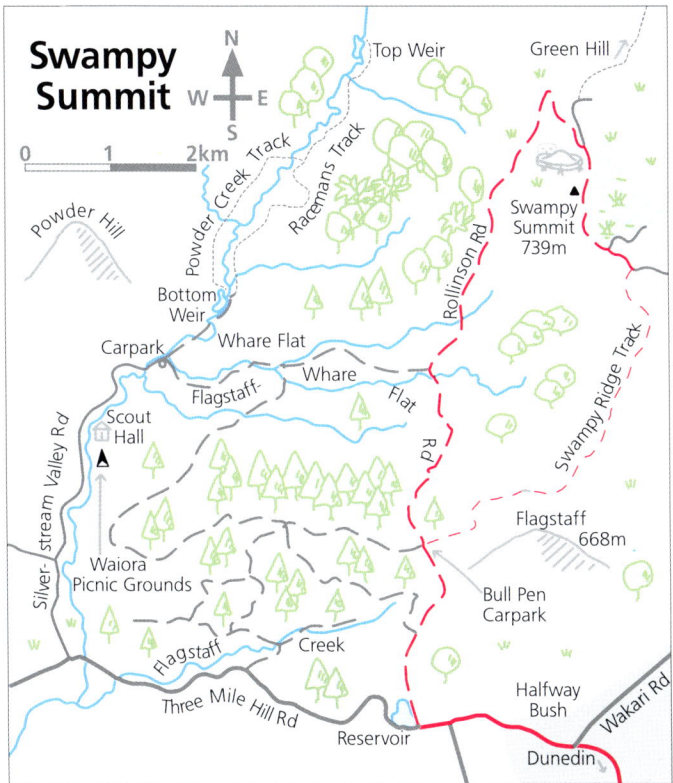

riding along the ridge, past the turn-off to the Switchback Track (which will be the best way back to town when it's finished in late 2009—see below).

Take the next two right-hand turns to return to the Bull Pen (but don't turn right down a really steep track near the end). This last stretch was bulldozed in 2008 and becomes unrideable porridge when wet (damn it).

Track conditions 50% gravel road, 25% 4WD track, 25% grassy single track

Notes The Pineapple Skyline Walkway also starts from the Bull Pen, but be warned: This is the sole domain of pavement plodders and the haunt of old ladies (with thermos flasks and woollen mittens) who lie in wait for law-breaking mountain bikers, with the intent of shoving their ivory-handled walking sticks through the offending spokes and then trampling the hapless rider under slippered feet. This walkway is a high conflict track—best to leave it alone.

5 Switchback Track

INTERMEDIATE

Dunedin to Swampy Summit

Grade 3, 1–2 hours, 9 km when finished ★ ★ ★

Once completed, this single track will be by far the best way to ride between Dunedin and Swampy Summit.

Route description In 2008, the first 5 km of this track were completed, and it looked like another 3 km would be needed to connect up with the Swampy Summit ridge.

From Dunedin, head up Leith Valley Road roughly 1 km and stop at a small bridge across Nicols Creek. The track starts

Jonathan Kennett

Switchback Track by night.

Jonathan Kennett

Hamish Seaton test rides one of his switchbacks.

10 metres past the bridge on your left. The first couple of kilometres have been gravelled and ride brilliantly. From there on, the track narrows a bit and can be muddy in winter.

After climbing 5 km from Leith Valley Road, the mountain bike track stops and meets up with the Nicols Creek walking track, which we pushed our bikes up for half an hour to reach Swampy Summit ridge. At the ridge, turn right to go to the summit or left to go to Whare Flat. The MTB track will be extending towards the ridge throughout 2009.

To do it the other way round, ride from the Bull Pen at Whare Flat up the 4WD track towards Swampy Summit for 3 km, then look out for a minor track on your right (it's at the top of the second crest along the ridge). The walking track section at the top is mostly rideable downhill and will be replaced with mountain bike track soon.

Notes What a mission! Hamish Seaton has been leading the charge, both designing and building this track, since 2005. It might be finished in late 2009.

6 Burns-Rustler Circuit

8 km from Dunedin

Grade 6, 2–3 hours, 10 km

These two tracks are signposted with mountain bike symbols, but they are actually unrideable tramping tracks. Avoid unless you love carrying your bike.

Route description The Burns-Rustler tracks start a few hundred metres north of Swampy Summit and drop down to Waitati Road. They are well signposted at the top and bottom, and both involve difficult bike carrying sections.

Just north of Swampy Summit, the Burns and Rustler tracks start together, but after 10 minutes, they split apart. At that point, you are better to take the Rustler. It spits you out onto the Pipeline Track. Turn right and after about 1 km you'll meet the bottom of Burns Track. From there, you can see Waitati Road just a few hundred metres away.

Track conditions rough semi-rideable tramping track

Notes Walk them first, before deciding if you really want to 'ride' them. Avoid when wet.

7 Green Hill

10 km northwest of Dunedin

Grade 4, 2 hours, 10+km ★ ★

This is an old-school ride for those who love the outdoors. The track must be dry to be fully rideable.

How to get there The best way is to ride up to Swampy Summit and then continue north on the Swampy Ridge Track for another 4 km. Alternatively, drive over to Blueskin Bay and head up Double Hill Road and Semple Road for about 7 km.

Route description If riding, do the first half of the Swampy Summit ride (see above), then, when you reach the ridge, turn left at the signposted 'Swampy Ridge Track' and ride

Julian Cox branches off the Green Hill track.

north for 4 km. Then, turn left again at the 'Green Hill' sign.

The next 4 km is reasonably technical single track. Stop at the old Green Hut clearing for a breather before heading back the same way.

If driving, park at the roadside clearing opposite the 'Green Hill' signpost along Semple Road. The first part of this track is badly rutted by motorbikes. You will have to walk some of it.

On the way down, you can come out on the signposted 'Mountain Road' track, which is more rideable and then ride along the road for just over 1 km to get back to your car.

Track conditions 99% rideable single track when dry, 70% rideable when wet

Notes Green Hill is only 1 km from Pulpit Rock, but the track is an unrideable slog.

This is a remote area, so it's best to go well prepared for bad weather and mechanicals. Take Topomap I44 Dunedin just to be sure.

8 Waitati Loop

Dunedin

Grade 1, 2–4 hours, 41 km ★

This is a popular, mud-free winter ride. It's all on public roads–no challenges technically but a good bit of exercise all the same.

Route description Head out of Dunedin city on Malvern Street and cruise up Leith Valley Road. Cross Highway 1 on an overbridge and continue up a gravel road before crossing the highway again–there's no overbridge this time, so be careful.

Now you get to fly down Waitati Valley Road. At the bottom, dice with the highway one more time and cross onto Donalds Hill Road. After another 300 metres, turn left and ride up the hill for about 1 km before turning right onto Mt Cargill Road.

After about 10 km on Mt Cargill Road, you'll reach a T-intersection where you can follow North Road left and cruise back into the city via North East Valley, or you can turn right and take Clava Street and Norwood Street down to Bethunes Gully (see below).

Track conditions All gravel and sealed road

Notes This route is shown on the Dunedin City Council cycling pamphlet.

9 Forresters Track

Dunedin

Grade 2, 15–20 minutes, 2.5 km ★★

This is a great beginner's ride or warm-up for Bethunes Gully (just across the road).

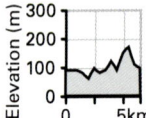

How to get there Head out to North East Valley and cruise up Norwood Street. About 100 metres past the last house, turn right at Forresters Park (signposted).

Route description Forresters Track skirts around the back of the playing field, then the back of the Dog

Club building, before entering the pine forest and squiggling through this small block of trees. After 5 minutes you'll pop out, back near the top and can ride across the BMX track towards Bethunes Gully (see below).

This is an ideal ride for young kids just getting started.

Track conditions 100% single track

10 Bethunes Gully

Dunedin

Grade 3, 1 hour, 5 km ★ ★ ★

This area has some awesome single track built for XC racing through the forest, and more is likely to be added to the network soon.

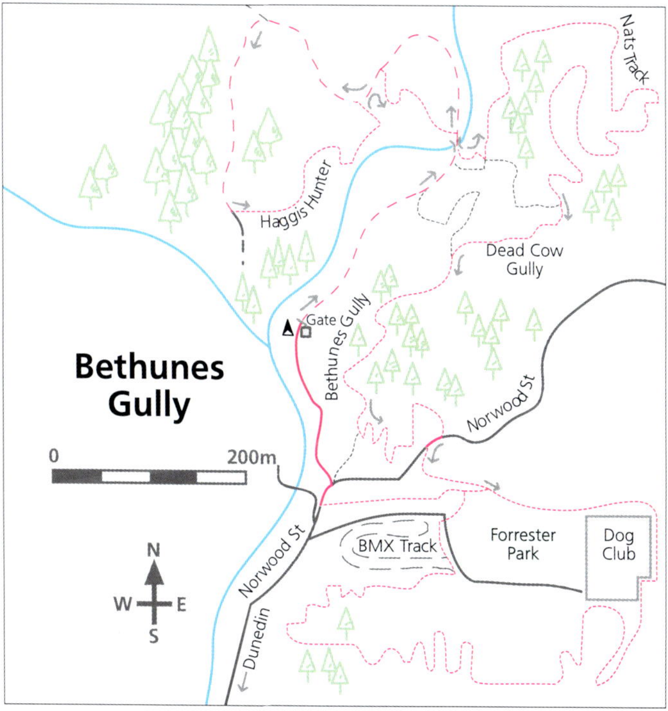

Nats Track

Haggis Hunter

Dead Cow Gully

Bethunes Gully

Gate

Bethunes Gully

0   200m

Norwood St

BMX Track

Forrester Park

Dog Club

N
W   E
S

Norwood St

Dunedin

How to get there Start with a warm-up on Forresters Track (see above for directions).

Route description After Forresters Track, cross Norwood Street and ride up to the Bethunes Gully picnic area. Check out the signboards, and the map in this book. Now ride up the gravelly Mt Cargill Walkway for almost 1 km before turning left at some recently felled pines (it should be signposted). Follow this forestry track for 300 metres then turn left again onto some purpose-built single track called the Haggis Hunter. Och Aye!

This brings you back to the walkway, but not for long. After recrossing the main stream at the bottom, look out for the start of the Nats Track on your left. This climbs up to a clearing then rewards you with a fun descent through pines. It will spit you back out onto Norwood Street.

Track conditions mostly purpose built single track

Notes Respect the 'walking-only' status of the upper Mt Cargill Walkway.

11 Signal Hill

Dunedin

Grades 2–5, 1–2 hours, 5+ km ★ ★

This scrub and pine forest bears some of the oldest MTB single track in Otago with famous rock-garden sections.

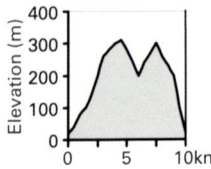

How to get there Start by heading to the information centre in the Octagon to pick up a pamphlet on Signal Hill. From the Octagon, head up George Street, past the northern end of the Botanic Gardens and climb Opoho Road followed by Signal Hill Road all the way up to the Centennial Memorial where excellent views await.

Route description With pamphlet in hand, womble around the warm-up track and then head into the forest to follow the route you've planned. We started with the Zig Zag, the Contour and the Haggis Basher–all good tracks but quite short. All the XC tracks (a dozen or so) are on the top half of the hill and can be ridden within 2 hours.

Once you're done with the XC tracks, start heading downhill to Logan Park. Aim to emerge at the playgrounds behind Logan Park High School, then take the main school driveway out to Butts Road. Watch out for killer jumps on the way down to the park.

If you are approaching this ride from Ravensbourne, check out the access off Rimu Street (which is off Junction Road).

Notes Part of Signal Hill had been logged in 2008, and had that depressing bomb-site feel to it.

Bike limbo gone horribly wrong.

Scott Farmer

12 Jubilee Park

Central Dunedin

Grade 2+, 10 minutes, 1 km ★

The shortest ride in town, and the closest to the city centre.

How to get there Ride up Serpentine Ave (1 km southeast of the Octagon), turn right onto Maori Road and after only 100 metres you will see the entrance to Jubilee Park on your right.

Route description Check out the map at the park entrance and plan how to do the mountain bike track as a clockwise loop. We just took every right-hand turn.

There is one set of downhill steps and two short steep climbs. Otherwise the ride is easy.

Keep an eye out for walkers–this is a popular park.

Notes This ride is known by some as Trev's Track after a legendary local mountain biker. It's short but sweet. Thanks Trev.

13 Otago Peninsula Backroads

Dunedin

Grade 2+, 1–2 hours, 10–15 km ★

We were about to axe this ride from the book when local riders told us emphatically that it had to stay in because it's a good ride if you want to avoid mud. So here you are.

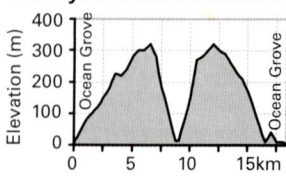

Route description From Ocean Grove, just east of St Kilda, ride east on the main road. This soon becomes Centre Road and climbs steadily up to the main ridge of the Otago Peninsula.

From there, take your pick of the rough Karetai, Buskin and Paradise roads. The map overleaf gives some idea of where you're heading.

Track conditions 20% sealed road, 20% gravel road, 25% 4WD track, 25% single track, 10% unrideable sand

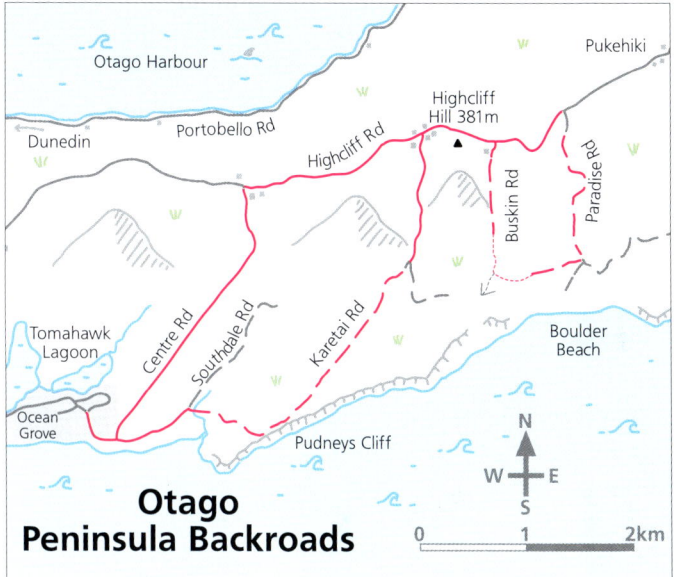

Otago
Peninsula Backroads

Notes Boulder Beach is only 300 metres from the farmhouse at the bottom of Paradise Road; check it out.

Dave Mitchell

Welcome to Southern Lakes.

Southern Lakes

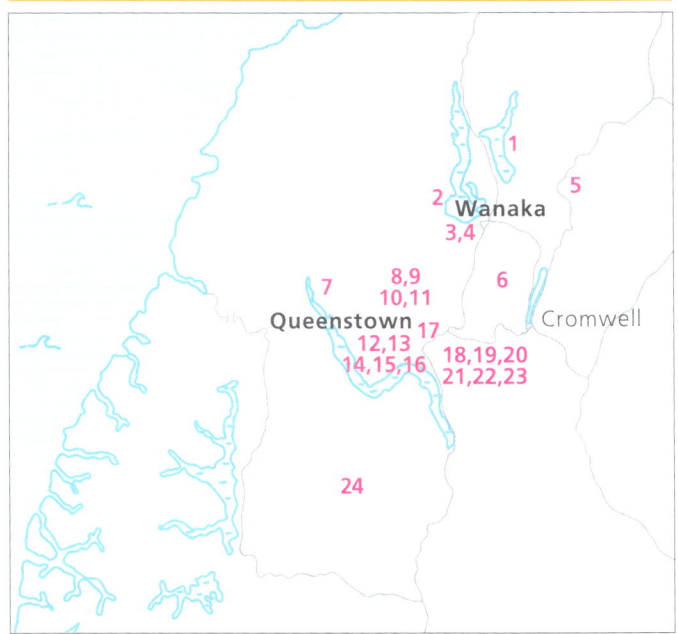

1	Lake Hawea Circuit	**13**	Lake Dispute
2	Minaret Burn Track	**14**	Queenstown Lakefront
3	Wanaka Lakefront Tracks	**15**	Seven Mile MTB Area
4	Plantation Trails	**16**	Fernhill and Vertigo
5	Lindis Loop	**17**	Lake Hayes
6	Pisa Range	**18**	Deer Park Heights
7	Whakaari	**19**	Frankton Walkway
8	Skippers Canyon	**20**	Kelvin Peninsula Track
9	Mt Dewar	**21**	Jacks Point
10	Motatapu Valley	**22**	Ben Cruachan
11	Macetown	**23**	Mt Rosa, Coal Pit Saddle
12	Moke Circuit	**24**	Mavora Lakes

SOUTHERN LAKES HIGHLIGHTS

Nowhere are you more spoilt for choice than Queenstown and Wanaka. There are loads of stunning old walking tracks, purpose-built single tracks, challenging free-riding and several gnarly all-day missions in the mountains.

1 Lake Hawea Circuit

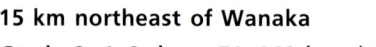

15 km northeast of Wanaka

Grade 2, 1–2 days, 71–148 km ★★

Add a few extra bananas to your packed lunch and head for the great outdoors on this lakeside epic.

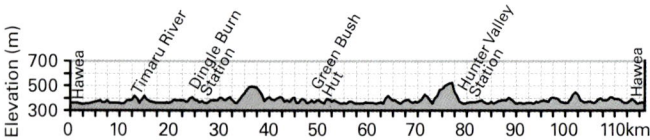

Landowners To complete the full loop of the lake, it is essential to obtain permission in advance from Mr or Mrs Cochrane (or Penn or Taff) at Hunter Valley Station, phone (03) 443 1241. You will be expected to state your trip intentions quite clearly and then stick to them.

Permission will not be granted in winter or during lambing (June to mid November). Only groups of up to four riders are allowed through at a time.

You don't need landowners permission to follow the right-of-way up the eastern side of the lake and back.

How to get there Normally this is a 148-km, 2-day trip, but if you get dropped off at Timaru River and picked up at Kidds Bush (and skip Ferguson Hut) it is a 71-km, 1-day trip. We'll

Dingleburn bound betwixt bluff and blue.

write it up here as if you were cycling the whole way.

Route description From the Lake Hawea dairy, cycle east and take the following roads: Lakeview, Muir, Cemetery, Gladstone and Timaru. It's 15 km to Timaru River and then another 100 metres to a turn-off down to a picnic/camping area.

Another 14 km on from Timaru River, you'll reach Silver Island Bay—hang left to follow the new peninsula track, past the Turihuka Conservation Area and onto a 4WD track that becomes rougher and rougher as it sidles up and down beside the lake.

If you don't have the 'OK' from Hunter Station, stop at the head of the lake and return the way you came.

If continuing, go well past the head of the lake, and then pick your way carefully across the braided Hunter River. This is only possible during low river flow. You can take a side trip north of here for about 16 km before backtracking—the scenery is stupendous in this section of the Hunter Valley, and Ferguson Hut (DOC) is a great overnight destination.

After crossing the Hunter River, cycle south. Hunter Valley Station is 25 km away (5 km before Kidds Bush—a scenic DOC camping area). Highway 6 is only 6 km on from Kidds Bush. Lake Hawea township is a further 24 km to the south.

Track conditions 60% sealed and gravel road, 40% 4WD track

Notes Once a year, you can ride this as a part of the Lake Hawea Epic, which is run in April. See www.lakehaweaepic.co.nz

The Cochranes may ask you to use their huts for a charge of $10 per night as they would rather people didn't camp because of the fire risk. Remember, it's easier for farmers to give a blanket 'no' than to allow difficult cyclists across their land. Call at least a day in advance. Refer to Topomap G38 Haast Pass and Kiwi Pathfinder Queenstown.

2 Minaret Burn Track

20 km northwest of Wanaka

INTERMEDIATE

Grade 3+, 3–6 hrs, approx 34 km return ★★

Another little beauty courtesy of the High Country Tenure Review; this ride provides breathtaking views across the lake.

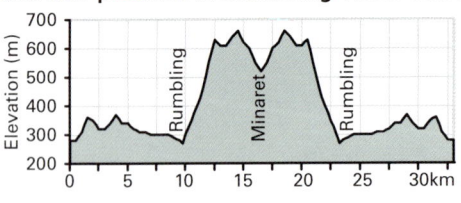

How to get there Head west out of Wanaka. Four kilometres past Glendhu Bay, turn right onto West Wanaka Road, and after another 5 km look out for the DOC car park at Homestead Bay.

Route description Follow the DOC markers over a rambling mix of single track and farm track. You'll reach Rumbling Burn after 10 km—if you're not bursting with energy, this is a good spot to check out the beach and then turn back.

From Rumbling Burn, the track climbs to a high terrace and traverses it before dropping down to Minaret Burn. We went just far enough to get a view up the valley, then headed back the way we came. Refer to DOC's Minaret Burn Track pamphlet.

Track conditions 95% 4WD track, 5% single track

Minaret Burn Track above Lake Wanaka

Dave Mitchell

3 Wanaka Lakefront Tracks

Wanaka

Here are two great rides to do from Wanaka. Load up on coffee and buns before hitting the trails. It's worth picking up DOC's *Wanaka Walks and Trails* brochure on the way out of town.

Wanaka Outlet Track
Grade 1+, 1–2 hours, 18-km loop ★ ★ ★ ★

BEGINNER

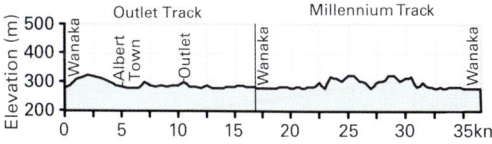

Ride from Wanaka to Albert Town via Highways 84 and then 6. Turn left off Highway 6 onto Alison Ave (signposted) and follow it for 1 km to a DOC signpost at the end of the avenue (and the start of Gunn Road). Follow the signs along a choice single track to the lake outlet. From the end of this track, follow the main gravel road beside the lake. After 200 metres, it becomes a 4WD track that leads to Beacon Point and Penrith Beach (great swimming spot), from where another signposted single track leads to Bremner Bay.

At the end of this track, follow the road, either straight ahead or to the right, back to Wanaka township. If you head right, through the pines, you connect up with a third section of single track.

Notes If you want to avoid the road riding, simply ride the single track there and back. Expect to see walkers and runners along the way.

Millennium Track

Grade 2, 1–2 hours, 10 km return ★ ★

EASY

This track was originally called Waterfall Creek Track. From Wanaka township, head west on the track between the road and the lake front to Glendhu Bay. Five minutes on from the Wanaka shops, you'll pass a 'Waterfall Creek 20 min' sign. From there, it's buffed single track most of the way to Waterfall Creek Reserve 3 km away. Sweet!

From the sign board at the reserve car park, the Millennium Walkway heads further around the lake. This track has been upgraded and is worth riding for another 3 km. Turn around once it becomes unrideable and head back the same way.

Notes This is a popular walking track, so take it easy and ride elsewhere during busy holiday times. The route is shown on DOC's *Wanaka Walks and Trails* brochure.

4 Plantation Trails

Wanaka

INTERMEDIATE

EXTREME

Grades 3–6, 1–4 hours, 10–30 km exploring ★ ★ ★

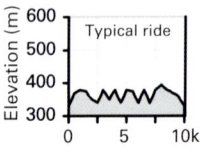

How to get there From the Wanaka Info Centre, ride north to the end of Rata Street, 3 km away.

Simon Kennett

The joys of an autumn ride at Wanaka.

Route description A maze of fantastic trails has been built above the Wanaka Outlet Track—but before you jump on your bike, go to one of the bike shops in town or the info centre and see if you can get a map of the tracks. Without it, you're lost.

Simon Kernett

Bloody mountain bikers ... always cutting up the tracks!

From the end of Rata Street, on the edge of Wanaka town, we recommend the following intro for intermediate riders: Ride up Hoe Down (1), along Easy Street (3), down Venus (8), then up Cranking Fine and down the track just to the right of 10– it's very cool. Now you're at 'The Hub', which offers a smorgasbord of track beginnings and ends. We headed up Scooby (7) a couple of times to ride tracks 9, 10 and 11 and treated ourselves to Venus again. A guaranteed fun way to finish is to Hoe Down (1) back to Rata Street. Yeehaa!

Track conditions 15% 4WD track, 85% single track

Notes In 2008, the status of these trails was up in the air, as the ownership of the land was being reviewed. Most of the structures had been removed after a safety audit. It was hoped that the local council might purchase the land for its reserve values. Visit the Wanaka Information Centre to check out the latest. The less developed tracks in Hikuwai Reserve to the east of the Plantation are on DOC land. These can be accessed from the Outlet Track (see Wanaka Lakefront Tracks above), adjacent to the Clutha River.

5 Lindis Loop

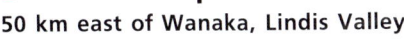

50 km east of Wanaka, Lindis Valley

Grade 2+, 4–8 hr, 53 km ★★

This road and farm-track loop offers fantastic views, a historic site and one awesome descent through iconic high country.

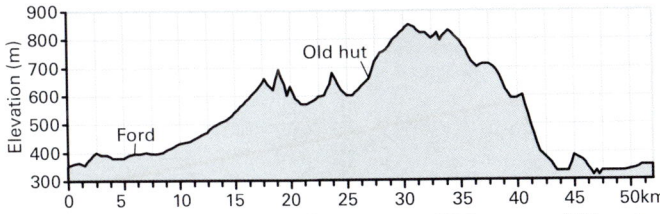

How to get there Head north from Tarras (33 km east of Wanaka) on Highway 8 for 17.6 km and park on the left at the start of Old Faithful Road.

Route description Ride up Old Faithful Road to the derelict Lindis Pass Hotel (a good camping spot). Then carry on to the Lindis River ford.

After crossing the ford and joining the highway again, head south for 1 km before turning left onto Goodger Road. Follow this road past Tim Burn and Pleasant Valley car parks on to the base of McPhies Ridge. By now, the route follows DOC markers along faint grass 4WD tracks.

Climb up onto McPhies Ridge, past the high point of 836 m, along the tops and finally down a fast, silky smooth descent to Lindis River. Cross the river bridge, climb a few hundred metres up to the highway and turn right. Eight fast kilometres on the road will lead you back to where you started.

Clean sky over McPhies Ridge.

Notes Check out the DOC pamphlet *Lindis Valley Tracks*. This area is closed from June to 5 December due to wicked winter weather and then lambing. Be prepared for cold weather at any time of the year. The neighbouring Lindis Peak and Chain Hills tracks are extremely steep.

6 Pisa Range

Between Lake Wanaka and Queenstown

The Pisa Range is a massive yet benign-looking set of hills. It provides the highest altitude cycling in New Zealand but is subject to polar weather conditions for half the year.

How to get there A couple of pamphlets promote mountain biking on several access roads and tracks up to the Pisa Range. The tracks are nearly all too steep to ride up (eg, the Roaring Meg access leads to an unrideable poled route). The best access up is via the snow farm road or off Crown Range Road Saddle (described below).

Tuohys Gully

Cardrona, 24 km south of Wanaka
Grade 4, 3–5 hours, 27 km ★★★

ADVANCED

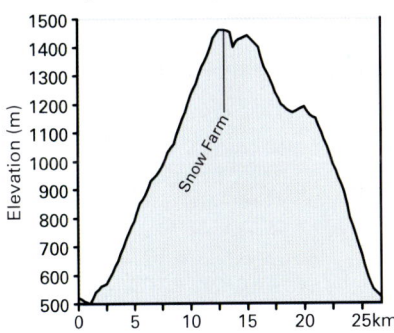

How to get there From Wanaka, head 20 km south on the Cardrona Valley Road (Highway 89). Soon after passing a Cardrona Alpine Resort sign, turn left at the Waiorau Snow Farm sign, then right at the Roaring Meg Pack Track car park sign.

Route description From the car park, backtrack to the snow farm entrance and follow the main snow farm road up the hill for 12 km. There are marker posts every kilometre.

At the 12-km marker post, you should turn right and ride past the building closest to you (this is the edge of the snow farm). Ride along a straight flat for 100 metres, then follow a 4WD track to the bottom of a ski tow in the gully on your right. Climb out of the small gully and across to the high point 1460 marked on the topomap. Veer right again towards some transmitters, hop

Sweating the big stuff on the Pisa Range.

Dave Mitchell

over a gate and then turn left just before the transmitters. There has been development around here, so you'll need the map to confirm you're heading in the right direction.

Now follow the main farm track all the way to Tuohys Saddle, which is signposted. The ride from here on is very cool indeed.

From Tuohys Saddle, you can nip over to Meg Hut (DOC), 2 km away, or turn right and follow a fast and furious track down the gully to the car park you started from. Red waratahs mark the way. About 500 metres before the car park, you have to veer right, off the farm track and across a flattish paddock to a stile. It's marked but easy to miss if you're blazing.

Track conditions 40% gravel road, 60% farm track

Notes This track is impassable in winter due to snow, but you can hire skis up at the snow farm instead. Throw plenty of warm clothes and extra food into your pack at any time of year.

If you are feeling fit and don't mind some road riding, start by riding 17 km up to the top of the Crown Range Road and from the Crown Range Saddle head to Tuohys Gully via Mt Hocken, Mt Allen, and Quartz Knoll (1593 m)—fine test of the old ticker! Topomap F41 Arrowtown is essential.

Pisa Range Snow Farm
Grade 3, 1–4 hours, 55 km ★★

INTERMEDIATE

From December to April, you can drive up to the snow farm lodge (13 km up from the valley floor) and explore 55 km of ski trails by bike. They are cross-country ski trails, so the riding is easy, and the scenery is fantastic. If the weather is perfect, ride up to Mt Pisa. At 1963 m, it is the highest fully rideable mountain in New Zealand.

You must check in at the lodge office before starting your ride. There is a fee of $10 per adult for 'Area usage' and 'Trail fees'– it's less for families and children.

Notes The lodge also has an up-to-date map of the trails and hires out bikes as well as offering meals and accommodation. For more information, check out www.snowfarmnz.com or phone (03) 443 7542.

Cardrona-Cromwell Pack Track

Here's a great wilderness trip in the Pisa Conservation Area. It's a full-day, grade 4+ ride. From the very top of Mt Pisa, follow a 4WD track south along the main range for about 12 km to connect up with the Cardrona-Cromwell Pack Track. This rough track heads west to Meg Hut (DOC) and involves some walking through speargrass as well as some primo stretches of riding.

From Meg Hut, a 2-km 4WD track leads up to the saddle above Tuohys Gully. Take the steep track down to the car park in Cardrona Valley (at the bottom of the snow farm road).

Notes This is big country. For further information about the 22,000 ha Pisa Conservation Area, contact the DOC office in Wanaka. Definitely take Topomap F41 Arrowtown, lots of water and warm clothing. If you are at all unsure of the weather, also carry a compass or GPS, extra food and a survival blanket.

7 Whakaari

INTERMEDIATE

43 km northwest of Queenstown

Grade 3+, 2.5–6 hrs, 14–20 km ★ ★ ★

Here's a new conservation area loaded with interesting historic mining sites and old access tracks.

How to get there Just 2 km short of Glenorchy, on the road from Queenstown, park up at the main entrance to the Whakaari Conservation Area (altitude 390 m).

Route description Head past the display panels and up, up, up to top out nicely with the Bonnie Jean Hut (940 m). The first and last kilometres are very steep, but much of the rest is good satisfying riding. You'll want to walk the last few hundred metres from the stream to the hut. Check out the displays and return down the way you came up.

If you are feeling in the zone and ready for some hike 'n' bike, try the loop up to Heather Jock Hut at 1300 m (via Bonnie Jean Hut) and back via Jean Hut.

Track conditions 95% 4WD track, 4% single track, 1% walking

Notes This is a BIG climb—be prepared for a change in weather at any time of year. Check out DOC's wee booklet on this area for a small map and brief history tour; available from the DOC office above Outside Sports in Queenstown. The track conditions above are for the return trip to Bonnie Jean Hut only. Jean and Bonnie Jean Huts are uninhabitable.

8 Skippers Canyon

Queenstown

Grades 2–4, 2 hours–3 days, 10+km ★★★

As the name suggests, this is dramatic, steep and rocky terrain. The area's long history of mining and farming has left a network of old 4WD tracks waiting to be explored.

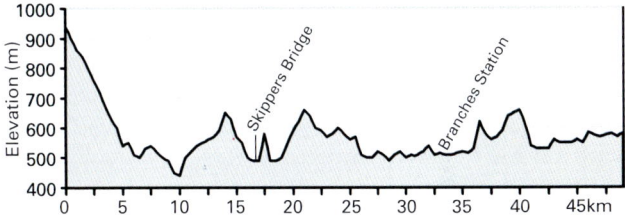

How to get there Ride north from Queenstown on Gorge Road. After 12 km, turn left up the Coronet Peak ski-field road. After another 4 km, turn left again onto Skippers Road.

Route description From Skippers Saddle, either continue down Skippers Road or dive down the Skippers Pack Track.

Skippers Pack Track

This superb single track starts at Skippers Saddle and meets up with Skippers Road after 5 km. The round trip down the track and back up the road to the saddle takes about 1 hour. The track is too rough for fully laden bikes.

Skippers Ghost Town

Almost 16 km down from Skippers Saddle, you can turn left and drop 1 km down to Skippers Bridge and then climb 500 metres to a picnic/camping area near Mount Aurum Station. There are several excellent interpretation boards and a water supply here.

A couple of great bike 'n' hike trips start from the camping area. Try riding and then walking up to Dynamo Flat or the Phoenix Battery. Both routes were much-travelled goldminers' trails back in the old days and are steeped in fascinating history.

Branches Station

To ride on Branches Station, phone the managers on (03) 441 8421. From Skippers Bridge, it is 17 km to Branches Station. The road is no longer suitable for 2WD cars but is great fun on a bike. Snow and slips close the station off every winter and spring.

From the station homestead, there are two good rides. An interesting 2-hour trip is to ride via The Amphitheatre to The Neck to explore a diversion tunnel. Be careful not to fall in the water at the tunnel entrance—it plunges over a waterfall at the exit!

To do a full-day trip, ride up valley via The Island, Polnoon Burn and Sixteen Mile Gorge. Keep going until you feel like a break for lunch then head back the same way. You should easily make it to the impressive gorge swing bridge and back (30 km return).

This is excellent country for exploring by bike as the farm tracks marked on the topomaps are 99% rideable and the scenery is outstanding. Make sure you talk to the station managers before your ride. They are mines of information.

Accommodation   Contact DOC in Queenstown, phone (03) 442 7935, to book one of the huts next to Mount Aurum Homestead.

The managers of Branches Station sometimes allow people to stay in the old homestead near the road end. It is similar to a tramping hut and makes a good base to explore the valley from. In return, a sensible koha, such as fresh fruit and vegetables or an up-to-date newspaper, wouldn't go amiss.

Track conditions   Mostly rough gravel road and 4WD track, some single track

Other users   Farmers and tourists

Notes Scary drops off the edge of the road end in the Shotover River hundreds of metres below. Topomaps E41 Queenstown and E40 Earnslaw are essential for trips beyond Skippers Bridge. F40 Wanaka is needed for a trip past Branches Station.

Zoot Track

If you are riding back to town from Skippers Saddle, check out the 1-km Zoot Track, south of the saddle. It's a short cut down to the sealed Skippers Road. Be prepared for lots of ruts and jumps—best take it real easy your first time down.

9 Mt Dewar

INTERMEDIATE

Skippers Saddle, Queenstown

Grade 3+, 2–4 hours, 20 km ★★

A classic back-country trip with a little bit of everything—ups, downs, arounds, great views, interesting navigation.

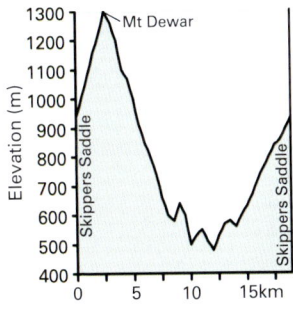

How to get there From Queenstown, drive north towards Coronet Peak. After 12 km, turn left at the Skippers Road sign, drive for another 600 metres and park at the saddle.

Route description A DOC map board at the saddle shows the route you are about to take. Start by tackling the half-hour climb up to Mt Dewar (1310 m). From the top, you can just about see Sydney (on a fine day).

Now follow a steep 4WD track down to the huts beside the Shotover River. Watch out for the bike-bucking water bars.

From the huts (one old and one new), a rough track takes you past a slip face to Butchers Point. The track then veers away from the Shotover and joins up with Skippers Road just a few hundred metres from the bottom of the Skippers Pack Track (it's too steep to ride up). From there, the well-graded but rough Skippers Road leads back up to Skippers Saddle. It's only a 300 m climb; should take about half an hour.

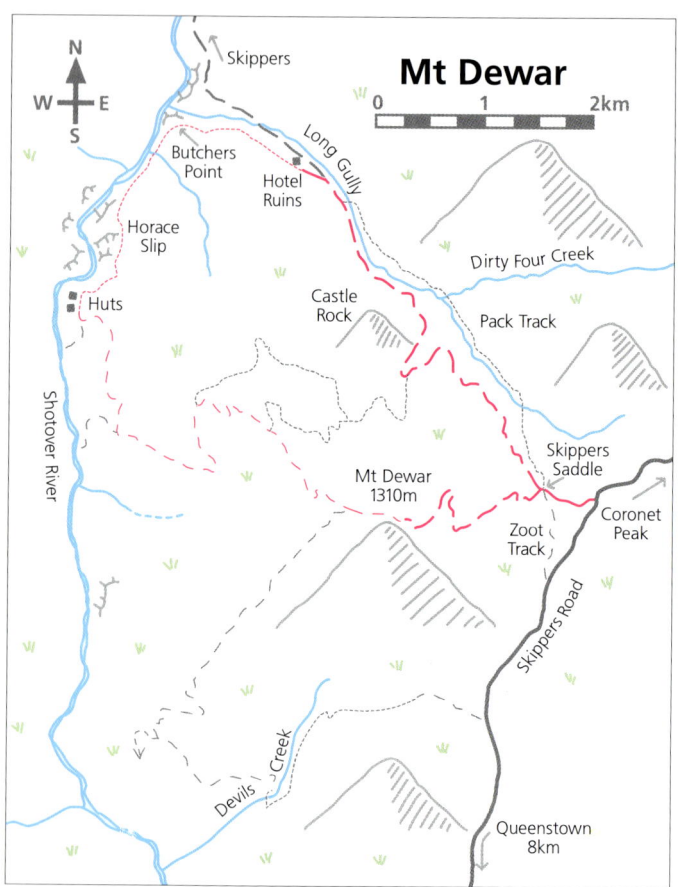

Track conditions 34% rough dirt road, 50% 4WD track, 15% single track, 1% unrideable

Notes This ride is on retired high-country leasehold land now administered by DOC. Don't forget your jacket and Topomap E41 Queenstown (or Terramap *Queenstown & Cromwell Recreation Areas*).

Mt Dewar to Devils Creek

Grade 3+, 3 hours, 20-km loop from Arthurs Point ★ ★

From the top of Mt Dewar, you can also ride southwest to an intersection at grid reference 677 743, then drop down to Devils Creek. The climb out of the creek is only slightly hellish and won't take an eternity. From a small saddle, an old farm track leads back down to Skippers Road, a few kilometres north of Arthurs Point, which is just north of Queenstown.

10 Motatapu Valley

10 km west of Wanaka

Grade 3, 3–6 hours, 50 km ★ ★

The ride from Glendhu Bay to Arrowtown via Motatapu Valley passes through three private properties and is not generally open to the public. There is an exception ...

Once a year, in mid-March, the Motatapu Icebreaker mountain bike event passes through this area. The entry fee in 2009 is $115. For more information on this opportunity, contact Iconic Adventures, email info@iconicadventures.co.nz, phone (03) 441 1025 or visit www.iconicadventures.co.nz/Motatapu

11 Macetown

Arrowtown

Grade 2, 2–4 hours return, 30 km ★ ★ ★

Macetown is a great ride for a group with riders of all abilities. The track is generally easy, and there is an interesting destination to aim for.

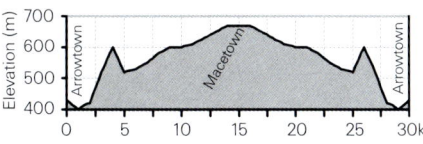

Route description

From the west end of the Arrowtown shops, you'll see a 'Macetown' sign 100 metres away. From this sign, a slightly confusing jumble of tracks heads into the valley. Follow the main 4WD track northeast (to your right).

En route, you'll cross the Arrow River over a dozen times. There are small yellow pegs along the way marking points of interest—for the self-guide brochure describing these points contact the Lakes District Museum in Arrowtown or DOC in Queenstown.

At peg '3', make sure you turn right.

At peg '14', you should follow the main 4WD track as it turns left to cross the river and then heads up the obvious side valley to Macetown.

At the Macetown Historic Reserve, there are interpretation boards and loads of great picnic spots. You can continue a further 2 km up valley to check out the Anderson Battery if you're interested in that sort of thing. Return the same way.

Track conditions 95% 4WD track, 5% water

Other users 4WD vehicles, motorbikes, equestrians, walkers

Notes Best done on a stinking hot day. There are loads of stream crossings—take a big bottle of oil. DOC's Arrowtown walks and trails pamphlet and Topomap F41 Arrowtown show the route (or Terramap *Queenstown & Cromwell Recreation Areas*).

12 Moke Circuit

Queenstown

Grade 3+, 3–6 hours, 33 km ★ ★ ★

Moke Circuit provides a quiet yet challenging journey by bicycle through the rustic Ben Lomond Station.

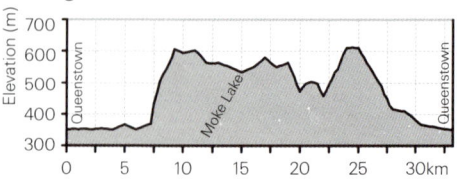

Landowners For access permission, call John Foster of Ben Lomond Station, phone (03) 442 8893.

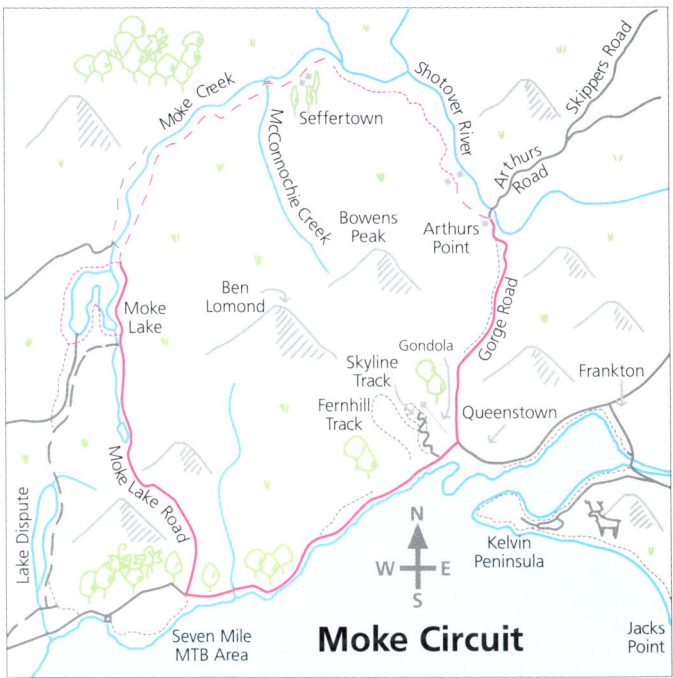

Moke Creek

Seffertown

McConnochie Creek

Shotover River

Skippers Road

Arthurs Road

Bowens Peak

Arthurs Point

Gorge Road

Ben Lomond

Moke Lake

Gondola

Skyline Track

Frankton

Fernhill Track

Queenstown

Lake Dispute

Moke Lake Road

N
W   E
S

Kelvin Peninsula

Seven Mile MTB Area

Moke Circuit

Jacks Point

Route description Head southwest out of Queenstown and cycle around the lake front for 7 km. Turn right at the 'Moke Lake' signpost and follow the road to Moke Lake. The gravel road leads past the lake to a fence with an 'Arthurs Point' sign on it. Climb over the stile and continue for a few minutes before hopping over a fence beside two gates and riding up valley on a well-formed gravel road. There is also a 4WD track on the other side of the valley that provides a longer alternative to this trip.

After a few kilometres of sidling around the hill high above Moke Creek, you'll pass a small car parking area and drop steeply down to the valley floor only to climb straight up again after crossing a side stream.

Soon after passing 'Sefferstown', the track becomes narrow and technical, and a bit of bike carrying is necessary. Most intersections are signposted, and before long, you'll start descending to Arthurs Point. The last few kilometres of single track are used for horse trekking and may be rather churned up. After passing a few turn-offs to farmhouses, follow your nose through a new subdivision, down to Arthurs Point pub. Queenstown is 5 km down the road.

Track conditions 40% sealed road, 40% 4WD track, 20% single track

Other users Walkers and horse riders

Notes This area is scenically similar to Skippers Canyon. If you are an average rider and do this trip in the other direction, you'll have to walk most of the single track. However, if you are an expert rider, the single track is an excellent challenge and, by doing this loop in an anticlockwise direction, you can add in the Lake Dispute track at the end as the icing to top the cake.

For a shorter trip, ride up and around Moke Lake and back via Lake Dispute (see below). Take Terramap *Queenstown & Cromwell Recreation Areas*.

During winter 2008, a large slip forced DOC to close the Moke Circuit. We hope it will be re-opened by the end of 2008. To be sure, call DOC Queenstown on (03) 442 7935.

13 Lake Dispute

INTERMEDIATE

7 km west of Queenstown

Grade 3+, approx 1.5 hours, 13 km ★★

Although the track is fairly tame, this is a fun wee ride if you enjoy exploring new areas.

Route description Head southwest out of Queenstown and cycle around the lake front for 7 km. Turn right at the 'Moke Lake' signpost and follow the road to Moke Lake—a fairly stiff climb. Immediately before the lake, leave the road at the DOC signpost, following a single track with many boardwalks to your left. Continue following the DOC signs and markers to Lake Dispute. Some of the riding is slow going through lumpy grassland, but you'll pick up an easier gravel road shortly before the lake. Then, not far past the lake, the DOC signs will direct you off to a steep single track descent back to the main road. Turn left to head back to town.

Track conditions A little bit of everything.

14 Queenstown Lakefront

From Queenstown, a series of single tracks leads southwest around Lake Wakatipu for 17 km. These tracks provide a good ride in their own right or an excellent way to get to the Seven Mile MTB area or the Lake Dispute or Moke Circuit rides.

Sunshine Track

Grade 3-, approx 20 min, 2 km ★★

This is the first single track heading along the lakeside west of Queenstown. It is very steep and technical in places but worth the effort.

Route description Start from the Fernhill roundabout, a few hundred metres southwest of central Queenstown. Simply follow the single track heading away from town. Expect walkers around any corner.

From the end of Sunshine Track, you can spin round the lakefront road for a couple of kilometres to Seven Mile Point or climb up Fernhill Road and Arawata Terrace for 500 metres to do the Arawata Track; depends on how much of a hurry you are in to get to the Seven Mile MTB tracks.

Arawata Track

Grade 3, approx 30 minutes, 2 km of single track ★★

Route description From number 45 Arawata Terrace, ride down to the end of the drive, and onto a sweet single track that leads you down to the Glenorchy Road about 4 km from Queenstown (to your left) and 1.5 km from the Seven Mile Point Track (turn right—see below).

Seven Mile Point Track
Grade 4-, 40 min, 3.5 km ★★★

Route description About 6 km from Queenstown, turn left off Glenorchy Road at the 'Seven Mile Scenic Reserve' sign. You can follow a single track back around to Glenorchy Road at Wilson Bay. The reserve has also become a major mountain biking area, with a dozen great tracks crammed into it. Check out Seven Mile MTB Area below.

From the end of Seven Mile Point Track, you can cycle along the Glenorchy Road for 2 km to the start of the Twelve Mile Delta track.

Twelve Mile Delta
Grade 2+, approx 50 minutes, 6.5 km ★★

Route description This track is signposted 'Twelve Mile Delta', about 11 km west of Queenstown on the Glenorchy Road. From the Glenorchy Road turn-off, head down a gravel road for 600 metres, veer right and follow the main 4WD track for 300 metres. This then becomes a single track.

There are two historic stone kilns worth checking out along the way. After 5 km, you'll reach a fork in the track; turn left to extend the ride by 5 minutes or right for a short cut.

Then drop down to Bobs Cove (see below for another riding option) and take three consecutive right-hand turns to return to Glenorchy Road.

Bobs Cove
Grade 4, approx 20 mins, 1.5 km ★

Route description Lying just west of Twelve Mile Delta (see above) and 13 km from Queenstown, this is the last in the series of single tracks that lie to the southwest of Queenstown.

It's short and not 100% rideable but goes through some splendid native forest. In fact, it's also a nature trail, with some trees labelled for your edification. You might want to ditch the bike partway and join the leaf peepers.

www.jumpingjimflash.com

Structures as 'art' at Seven Mile.

15 **Seven Mile MTB Area**
Queenstown

Grades 2–5, 20 min–2 hours, 1–12 km ★ ★ ★ ★

Since 2005, the Seven Mile area has exploded into one of New Zealand's best mountain biking spots. There are now 11 tracks packed into this DOC recreation reserve. The tracks are managed by the Queenstown MTB Club. Get hold of a copy of their MTB trail guide from a bike shop in town (cost $4 in 2008).

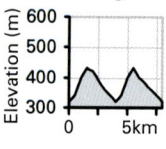

How to get there From Queenstown, ride out of town on the road to Glenorchy for about 6 km before heading into the Seven Mile Point Track, which is 2-way and dual use. Alternatively, drive 8 km from town to the Wilsons Bay parking area. Then make your way up to 'The Hub', where there's a large map and groovy wooden structures to try stunts out on—a great place to meet other riders.

Route description From The Hub, we recommend checking out Cool Runnings, Kirks Terrace, Kachoong, and Grin & Holler (with a detour through Fruit Loop). After that, you'll either be finding your bearings or totally confused. Regardless; we guarantee you'll be wanting more. These are some of the best flowing tracks anywhere!

Notes If, like us, you are not a big jumper, take it easy on your first run down these tracks. If the largest jumps in this area leave you wanting more, check out the Wynyard Freestyle Terrain Park off Wynyard Terrace, Fernhill, Queenstown.

Remember to expect to meet walkers on the original DOC track.

16 **Fernhill and Vertigo**
Queenstown

Grade 4, 1–2 hours, 5–10 km ★ ★ ★

These are both fantastic tracks, highly rated by locals and visitors alike for their good views and great downhill riding.

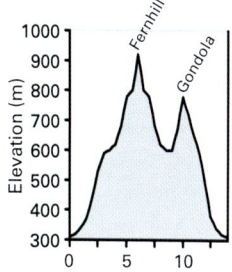

Route description From downtown Queenstown, cruise round to the bottom of the Skyline/Gondola Vehicle Track, on Lomond Cres. It's a 5-minute ride to the track, and there's a 'Ben Lomond Walkway' sign at the bottom.

From the sign, climb the main gravel road for 1.5 km. Then you will see the 'Original Mountain Bike Trail' sign on your left—that's the way you'll head back. A stone's throw up from that turn off is the Fernhill track on your left. Climb up through beech forest and onto tussock country for an awesome view, then head back the same way.

When you get back to the Skyline/Gondola Vehicle Track, either head down the signposted 'Original Mountain Bike Trail' or nip up to the gondola and try the flowing Vertigo track first.

Vertigo

Ride up the gravel road to the building at the top of the gondola. Check out the awesome view from the balcony then backtrack for 50 metres to the red 'Original Mountain Bike Trail' sign. This grade-4 downhill flows like water. There are scary alternatives branching off it every now and again. Just stick to the main track and follow the occasional red sign. After crossing the Skyline/Gondola Vehicle Track a couple of times, you'll find yourself back at the bottom of the Fernhill track. Now bomb down the signposted 'Original Mountain Bike Trail' to the bottom of the vehicle track.

Ben Lomond Loop

From the gondola, you can climb up the Ben Lomond Track for 10 minutes until you reach a 'No Mountain Bikes beyond this point' sign at a fork in the track. Turn left and within 10 minutes you will connect with the lower part of the Fernhill Track. This is a short but sweet way to get above the tree line. Follow the Fernhill track and the 'Original Mountain Bike Trail' back into Queenstown.

Track conditions 25% gravel road, 75% single track

Notes These tracks have been built by local mountain bikers and DOC. They are steep in places and therefore prone to damage by skidding tyres. If you haven't got the skills to avoid skidding, then stick to gravel roads. The Skyline/Gondola Vehicle Track is a private road with a locked gate at the bottom.

17 Lake Hayes

11 km northeast of Queenstown

Grade 2-, 40–60 mins, 9 km ★★

Lake Hayes offers a quick, easy, single-track spin around a beautiful lake–ideal for a family outing.

Route description From Queenstown, head northeast on Highway 6. A couple of kilometres past the Shotover River bridge, turn into the signposted car park on the left. Ride down to the lake and complete a lap in either direction. Apart from a couple of stiff wee climbs, this ride makes for an easy, good time for the whole family.

Notes Best ridden in autumn when the leaves are turning. Avoid this ride in weekends and public holidays when it will be swarming with tourists and dog walkers. This ride can also be accessed from Arrowtown via the Lake Hayes Road.

18 Deer Park Heights

Queenstown

Grades 2–3, 1.5 hr, 10–13 km ★★

Here's a ride to knock the socks off all you animal lovers.

How to get there From Queenstown, cruise round to Kelvin Heights via the Frankton Walkway and Kelvin Peninsula Track (see below). When you reach a jetty at a recreation reserve, leave the track and follow a short street up to the Peninsula Road. Follow Peninsula Road to your left for 500 metres where you will find the signposted entrance to Deer Park Heights.

Route description This interesting animal farm is open every day until dark, and car access costs $20—but bikes cost nothing! Give yourself at least an hour to ride the gravel road to the top of the hill and take in the 360° panorama.

From the top, explore the single tracks around the Korean film set that still exists on the eastern summit.

Notes For a gold coin, you can buy a can of pellets and get mobbed by a variety of four-legged mammals. Vertigo (phone 0800 VERTIGO) run guided bike trips through the park.

19 Frankton Walkway

Frankton

Grade 1+, 45 minutes, 9 km ★★

This track follows the edge of Frankton Arm from Kawarau River Bridge to the Botanic Gardens in Queenstown and has several entry/exit points. It's used a lot by local walkers and bikers, so take it easy.

Route description From the Kawarau River Bridge at Frankton, hop up to the turbine and follow a short track down to the lake edge 100 metres away. Turn right and follow the gravel road for a few hundred metres before veering left onto a gravelled track. From here, the walkway is a mixture of single track, 4WD track, gravel and sealed road. Just after passing the wooden boat club, cycle up Park Street to cruise into the centre of Queenstown.

20 Kelvin Peninsula Track

Frankton

Grade 2, approx 1.5 hours, 15-km loop ★★

This ride comprises some brilliant single track, but it's quite a populated area and best avoided during busy times.

Route description From the southern end of Kawarau River Bridge just out of Frankton, drop down to the water's edge, hang a left and follow the single track close to the lake front.

After about 20 minutes, you'll come to a playground and golf course. From here, you can either backtrack or carry on around the golf course to the very end of the peninsula.

After riding around the peninsula, head left up the first road you reach, and you'll soon see the playground again, only 300 metres away. Cruise back to Frankton by the main road or the track.

Alternatively, carry on around the lake to Jacks Point (see below). **Track conditions** Mostly fun single track.

21 Jacks Point

Frankton

Grade 3-, approx 1.5 hrs, 12 km return ★★★

If the Kelvin Peninsula Track (see above) left you champing at the bit, then you'll enjoy this technical and scenic single track.

Route description From the Peninsula golf course, head southeast around the lake to the impressive rock outcrops of Jacks Point. From the lookout, head back the way you came.

The first kilometre from the golf course to Jardines Park is tight and technical, but the track beyond there was being upgraded to a width of 1 metre in 2008. There are still some steep sections to test expert riders and fine scenery for all. **Notes** You can avoid the most difficult part of the track by starting from Jardines Park.

22 Ben Cruachan

Gibbston, 30 km east of Queenstown

Grades 4–5, 4–7 hours, approx 44 km ★★★

Pick a fine day, and this ride will take your breath away; it's one of the most sustained climbs, and descents, in the country.

From Gibbston, 30 km east of Queenstown, follow Coal Pit Road for 7 km, climbing 700 vertical metres to Coal Pit Saddle. From the saddle, an easy water-race track heads southwest around the hills for 4.5 km. A steep 2-km-long track then climbs up to a 4WD track on the main ridge. You can follow this track over Mt Salmond and all the way to Ben Cruachan (1895 m). Turn around when you feel like it to enjoy the massive downhill.

Remarkables–Ben Cruachan

Alternatively, if you're feeling wired, ride up to the Remarkables Ski Field from Queenstown and hoof it across rough terrain to Ben Cruachan. This takes up to an hour of tramping over steep rocky slopes, so you will have fully earned the 1500 m downhill to Gibbston. The key to this route is riding to the top of the eastern ski tow and then picking a good line to carry your bike up to the prominent ridge. Aim for a spot about 500 metres south of high point 2057. From there, it is 50% rideable over to Ben Cruachan, which sets you up for the massive downhill. The scenery will blow your mind.

Off piste between the Remarkables and Ben Cruachan.

Notes If you're feeling lazy, give Vertigo a call on 0800 VERTIGO. They can transport you to Coal Pit Saddle or Ben Cruachan and from Gibbston back to Queenstown. Topomap F41 Arrowtown, extra food and clothes and gallons of water are essential.

23 **Mt Rosa, Coal Pit Saddle**

26 km west of Cromwell

Grade 4, 3–5 hours, approx 23 km ★ ★

If you're one of those rare riders who enjoys grinding their granny gear up the side of a mountain for a couple of hours, you'll love this ride.

How to get there   Twenty-five kilometres from Cromwell up the Kawarau Gorge Road, you will cross the gorge. About 2 km past the bridge, stop at the DOC car park on the left.

Route description   Ride up Kawarau Gorge Road for 2 km before taking the Gibbston Back Road to Coal Pit Road. Shed a layer (or two) and climb on up to Coal Pit Saddle. Then catch your breath and keep climbing, east up to Mt Rosa (1322 m).

Shortly after the summit, cross a stile onto a faint old 4WD track and drop steeply towards Mt Mason. After a short climb near the top of Mt Mason, pick up a 4WD track that sidles south of the summit before diving down towards the Kawarau Gorge. After passing under a high voltage power line, keep your eyes peeled for the orange markers that will guide you through a couple of tricky turns, back to the DOC car park.

Be prepared for some bike pushing on this half-day 'mini epic'.

Notes   Refer to Topmap F41 Arrowtown. The Wentworth Track is also open to mountain bikes. It's a there-and-back trip, heading south from Coal Pit Saddle. Allow a full day to explore all of the Wentworth Track.

24 **Mavora Lakes**

Between Queenstown and Te Anau

Grade 2, 2 days, up to 160 km return ★ ★

Mavora Lakes are a great destination for fat-tyred cycle tourers. The roads and 4WD tracks are quiet and the scenery stunning.

How to get there   From Queenstown, catch the steamboat Earnslaw across Lake Wakatipu to Walter Peak (phone 0800 656 501 to book in advance). One adult and bike cost $34 one

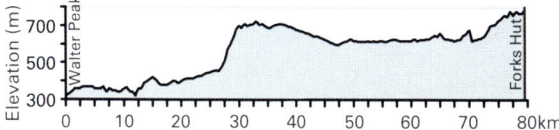

way in 2008. Over summer, the Earnslaw is scheduled to leave
Queenstown at 10am, 12noon, 2pm, 4pm, 6pm and 8pm. We
don't recommend doing this trip in winter.

Alternatively, you can drive/ride east from Te Anau for 30 km
on Highway 94 before turning north onto the Mavora Lakes Road,
38 km from the lakes.

Route description From the jetty at Walter Peak, cycle 12 km
round to Mt Nicholas Station, then head south on the quiet Von
Road for almost 40 km. Turn right at Mavora Lakes Road and
within 8 km you'll reach the official road end at the second lake.

From the road end, follow the 4WD track beside North Mavora
Lake for about an hour to Carey's Hut. 4WD vehicles have thrashed

Heading for home from Mavora Lakes.

the track in places, so you'll have to nip out to the lake edge from time to time to avoid some boggy sections. Carey's hut (DOC, 6 bunks) is a good place to shelter from either rain or sandflies.

If you're keen to explore further, you can ride for another hour up to Boundary Hut (DOC, 6 bunks; no fireplace) or 2 hours up to Forks Hut (DOC, 4 bunks).

From the huts, turn around and backtrack to Mavora Lakes. You can then either head back to Lake Wakatipu and Queenstown, or ride south to Te Anau.

Track conditions sealed and gravel roads and 4WD tracks

Notes This ride is particularly popular with Southland-based riders and is a great place to go camping ($5 per tent site). In winter, take your snow tyres. Refer to Topomaps D42 Livingstone and E42 Walter Peak.

Riding high in the mountains beyond Skippers Canyon.   Dave Mitchell

Southland

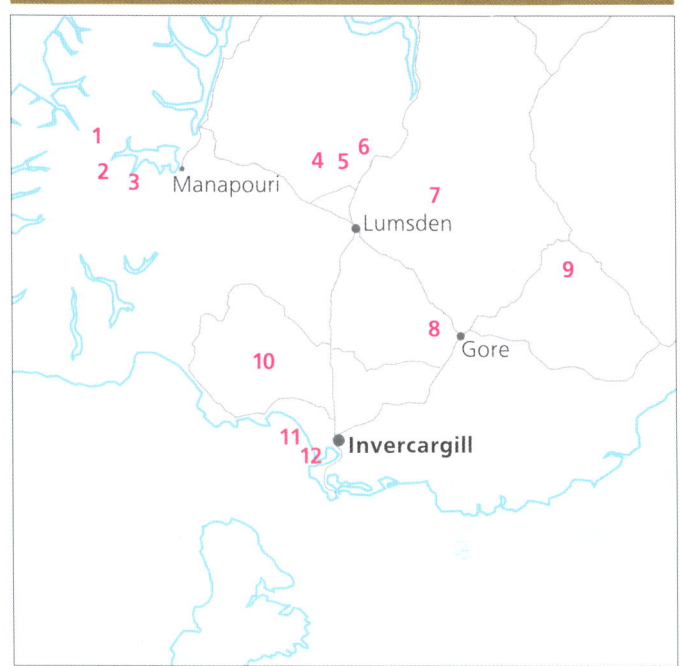

1	Doubtful Sound	**7**	Waikaia Bush Road
2	Percy Pass	**8**	Hokonui MTB Track
3	Borland Lodge	**9**	Blue Mountains Classic
4	West Dome	**10**	Bald Hill
5	Mt Bee	**11**	Oreti Beach
6	Dog Box Hut	**12**	Sandy Point

SOUTHLAND HIGHLIGHTS

For a short ride close to Invercargill, the tracks at Sandy Point are good fun. For hard-core adventurers, the magnificent Percy Pass is a must. For something in between, the Eyre Conservation Area has a few intermediate rides with fine scenery.

1 Doubtful Sound

INTERMEDIATE

Manapouri, Fiordland

Grade 3, 4–8 hours, 70 km ★★

This there-and-back ride follows New Zealand's most remote public road, through our largest National Park.

How to get there Catch the tour boat across Lake Manapouri to the hydro power station at West Arm. A one-way ticket cost $38 (plus $7 for a bike) in 2008. Phone Real Journeys on (03) 249 6602 to pre-book.

Route description Hop off the boat and ride away from West Arm on the only road there is. Ignore the right-hand turn to the power station and then the left-hand turn to the hostel. It's 22 smooth gravel kilometres over Wilmot Pass (670 m) and down to Doubtful Sound. The climb back the same way is from sea level and is relentless.

  The dreamy scenery includes stunning waterfalls, which are accessible via short walks from Deep Cove, where there is a hostel that is open to the public when school kids aren't using it. Ask Fiordland Travel about it when booking the ferry.

Track conditions 100% gravel road

Notes There is a DOC hut 10 mins up the road from West Arm.

2 Percy Pass

Manapouri, Fiordland

Grade 5, 8–12 hours, 70 km ★ ★ ★

This is the stuff that epics are made of! Long miles, a difficult and remote bike carry section, unpredictable and often wild weather... Even if everything goes according to plan, it's a hard ride, but like all good adventures, very rewarding.

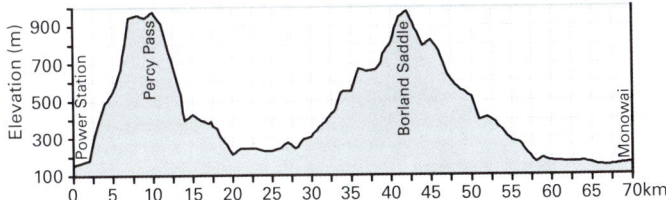

How to get there Catch the tour boat across Lake Manapouri to the hydro power station at West Arm. A one-way ticket cost $38 (plus $7 for a bike) in 2008. Phone Real Journeys on (03) 249 6602 to pre-book.

Route description From the wharf, ride past the right-hand turn-off to the power station. After a few minutes, take the left-hand turn across the Spey River and towards the power station hostel. Turn left just before the hostel garages and hop over a gate. From here, recalibrate your pain-metre as you climb, climb, climb for an hour or two until you reach a wide hanging valley. Cross this valley and climb just a wee bit more to the top of Percy Pass, next to a telecommunications hut.

From here, the power transmission line, which is your guide for most of this ride, dives down to another hanging valley almost 300 m below. There is a basic route heading left, then down, marked with a handful of waratahs and cairns. You must carry your bike across steep scree slopes and through thick native bush for around an hour before reaching the pylon track that leads to Monowai.

Simon Kennett

Approaching the top of Percy Pass.

Note that the marked route wisely stays just above the bushline for as long as possible before diving down to the far pylon. That way it avoids any crazy bush-bashing. Travel light or you'll be making two trips down this tricky route.

Next comes a rocky descent with numerous switchbacks down to a river. Cross the river and take the left fork, past pylon 30. Continue to a T-intersection beside Grebe River. If you're looking for a campsite, turn left at the bridge and ride a few kilometres to the South Arm of Lake Manapouri, where there are toilets and flat land for camping.

Otherwise, turn right to carry on to Monowai. A gravel road follows the bush-clad valley floor for almost 15 km before climbing steeply up to Borland Saddle, way off in the distance. From here, it's a long gentle descent to Monowai, 25 km away.

From Monowai to Manapouri it's an extra 42 km of quiet sealed road through rolling farmland.

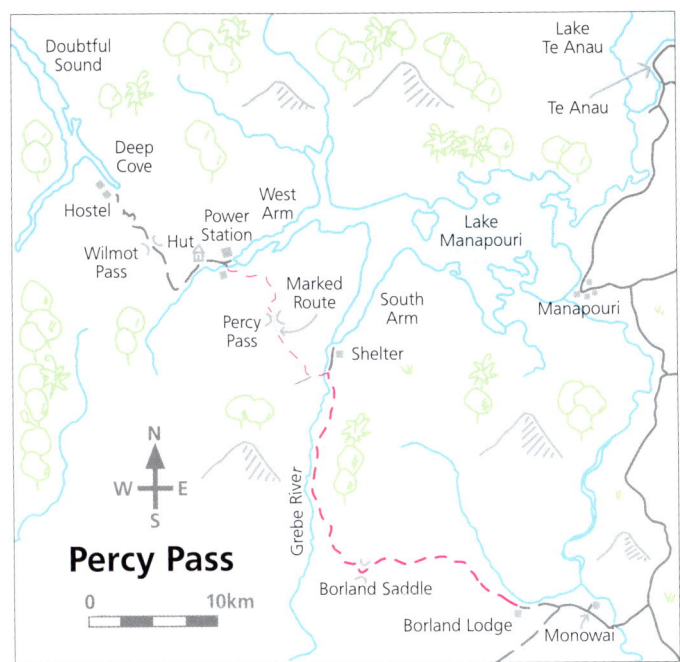

Percy Pass

0   10km

Track conditions 80% rough gravel road, 18% 4WD track, 2% unrideable

Notes Manapouri township has the only shop anywhere near this route–stock up well. Insects in this area are so fierce that power station workers receive a special 'sandfly allowance'!

There is a DOC hut near West Arm (Lake Manapouri) and backpacker accommodation at the far end of the ride at Monowai Lodge and Borland Lodge.

The hydro power station is worth a visit–it's New Zealand's largest, built 200 m underground into solid rock. Take topomaps C43 Manapouri and C44 Hunter Mountains.

Two less arduous alternatives to Percy Pass are the Borland Lodge or Doubtful Sound rides.

3 Borland Lodge

50 km from Manapouri, Fiordland

Grade 2–3, 2–7 hours, 34–70 km ★

This primo old-school ride follows an isolated pylon access road into the spectacular Fiordland National Park.

Route description This is the cruisy second half of the Percy Pass epic (see above). From Borland Lodge (8 km west of Monowai), head up the road to Borland Saddle for a picnic. The view of Fiordland from here is a feast that will fill your soul. This is roughly 34 km return.

To turn it into a 70-km day-ride, carry on to Lake Manapouri's South Arm and back. Borland Saddle is at the top of the only big hill. Remember to bring insect repellant.

Track conditions 100% remote gravel road

4 West Dome

32 km northwest of Lumsden

Grade 3+, 4–8 hours, 41 km return ★ ★

A forestry road, followed by a tramping track, leads to the remote and scenic Windley Bivouac.

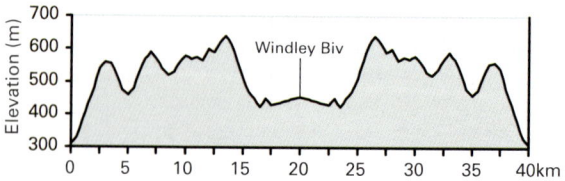

Landowners Before your ride, you need to get a permit from Rayonier Forestry, 176 Spey St, Invercargill.

How to get there From Mossburn, head northeast on the Mossburn Five Rivers Road for 6 km. Turn left onto Hilla's Road and drive for 5.6 km to a fork in the road. There will be a bridge on your right and a 'West Dome Block' sign on your left. Park here.

Route description Ride west on the forestry road and after 800 metres, at a second forestry sign, go straight ahead. Follow this hilly road, through a mixture of pines, scrub and tussock, as it arcs around the flanks of West Dome. There are great views along the way. Eventually the forestry road descends to Windley River.

When you reach the river, follow a 4WD track up valley for 2.5 km. (Hint: for the first few hundred metres, the track is 30 m above the river, not right beside it). This track is difficult to follow in places, so keep the map handy. The track ends 1 km before the biv. We left our bikes and made a beeline for the biv on foot. First we crossed a grassy dell and then followed a vague track that weaved through beech forest and led right to the small, well-hidden hut. It has two bunks (with mattresses) and is situated in an idyllic spot on the edge of the forest, looking towards the river.

Now that you have the route sussed, the return trip will be a breeze.

Track conditions 83% forestry road, 12% 4WD track, 5% semi-rideable

Notes If you are into technical riding, try pedalling all the way to the biv. It's mostly rideable–on a good day. Topomap E43 Eyre is essential.

5 Mt Bee

ADVANCED

21 km north of Lumsden

Grade 4, 2–5 hours, 18–32 km ★ ★

A huge climb up onto the tops is rewarded by fantastic views, improved fitness and a long descent back the same way.

How to get there Head north from Lumsden for 13 km on Highway 6, then turn left at Five Rivers. Cruise towards Te Anau for 3 km before turning right onto Irthing Road. Park by the DOC sign at the end of Irthing Road, almost 5 km away.

Route description At the end of Irthing Road, hop over a gate and follow a farm track north across the paddocks for 2 km.

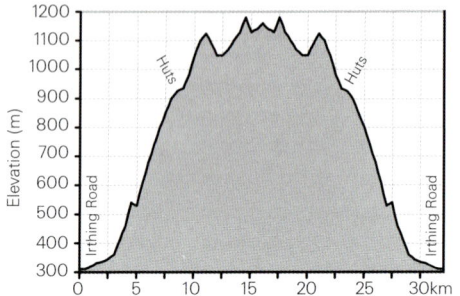

The track then veers left and enters a Rayonier NZ Ltd pine forest (which was being milled in 2008). The track you're after then starts climbing seriously – whenever it forks, take the high road. The Mount Bee huts are just over 9 km (and 600 vertical metres) from the road end.

Mt Bee, beyond the huts.

Simon Kennett

From the huts, the track deteriorates as it climbs another 300 m up the spine of Mount Bee. The views are fantastic, but watch out for the razor-sharp rocks around here. As the topomap shows, the track finishes just short of spot height 1203. The downhill back to Irthing Road is a blast.

Track conditions 100% 4WD track

Notes Mount Bee Huts have eight bunks and four mattresses. DOC has no plans to maintain this track. There is an official camping area beside Mulholland Road, 2 km north of the start of the ride. Refer to Topomap E43 Eyre.

6 Dog Box Hut

INTERMEDIATE

120 km north of Invercargill

Grade 3, 2.5–5 hours, 30 km return ★★

This ride follows the Eyre Creek Valley into the Eyre mountains, through an interesting mix of farmland and native forest.

How to get there From Highway 6, 1.5 km west of Athol, turn up Eyre Creek Road. About 5 km from the highway, there is a DOC sign at the Eyre Creek Station boundary. There are frequent farm gates for the next 5 km (If you're driving by yourself, it would be easier to ride this stretch). After another 5.5 km, the gravel ends at the Glen Eyre Station boundary.

Route description Follow the orange marker poles along the easement to the park boundary and continue up the 4WD track to the 'three-star' Shepherd Creek Hut.

The next 5 km to the historic Dog Box Hut offer difficult riding in places, but you won't want to slow down for long—the sandflies are as ferocious as a swarm of hungry flying piranha.

Dog Box Hut is perched above the track on the right, just past Dog Box Creek. Return from here the way you came.

Notes Mataura River, just to the north, provides an alternative ride, but both the track and scenery are better on the Dog Box Hut ride. There are some handy maps in DOC's 'Eyre Mountains/Taka Ra Haka Conservation Park' pamphlet. Alternatively, refer to Topomap E43 Eyre.

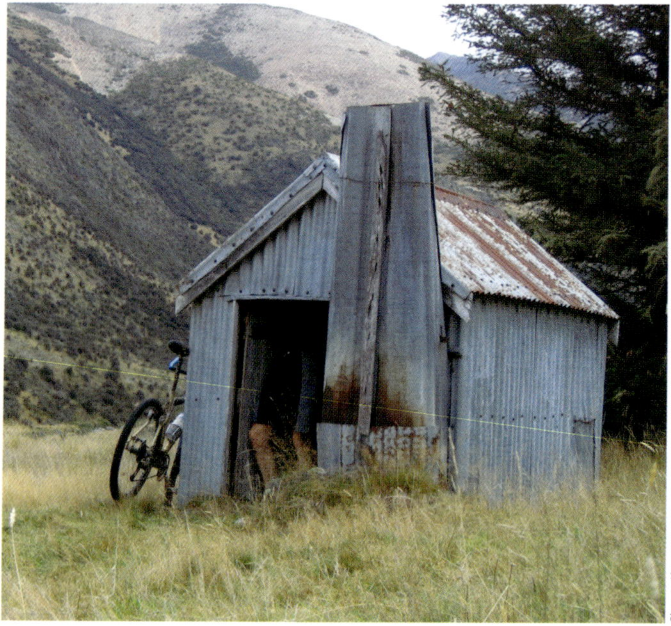

Dog Box Hut.

7 Waikaia Bush Road

80 km north of Gore

Grade 3, 2–4 hours, 24–40 km ★★

Although starting out on a scenic gravel road suitable for the whole family, don't be fooled; this ride eventually ends up tackling an extreme 4WD track on the Old Man Range.

How to get there From Gore, head northwest to Riversdale then north, past Waikaia, to Piano Flat Camping Area.

Route description Park at the DOC camping area and ride northeast on a quiet dirt road through pristine native forest with a few chunky hills for 12 km. A few hundred metres after emerging from the bush you'll reach a group of large signs (the derelict Christies Hut is half a kilometre away).

From the signs, you can give yourself a serious workout by heading east, straight up towards a high point on the Old Man Range (1366 m). The first couple of kilometres are super steep and rutted but the views just get better and better the higher you climb, and the gradient mellows out a bit after halfway.

Head back the same way for some great downhills, but beware of 'Mystery Corner', which according to MTB folklore takes out half the riders who race their way back to Piano Flat. It is closely followed by 'Death Corner'!

From the fork by the gates, you can also drop down to Canton Bridge, 1 km away, for a look at the upper Waikaia River. There is a locked gate at the bridge, and from there a 4WD track heads west over some massive hills to Blue Lake 20 km away. Get the OK from Glenary Station, phone (03) 202 7898, before heading past the bridge.

Notes The road above the bushline is closed from 10 May to 18 October due to extreme weather. See Topomap F43 Garvie.

8 Hokonui MTB Track

INTERMEDIATE   EXPERT

6 km from Gore

Grade 3–5, 30–60 mins, approx 3 km ★

The Gore MTB Club have been busy building a gnarly wee single track through native bush near Dolamore Park.

How to get there Drop into the Gore information centre for a map, then head west out of town on Reaby Road. Just over 6 km from downtown Gore, turn right onto Pope Road at the 'Hokonui MTB' sign. There's a DOC sign and car park 700 metres up the road.

Route description Another 500 metres further on, you'll cross a stile and enter the bush. When you come to a fork, veer right and try creating an anticlockwise loop. There's a map in the trails section of www.southlandmtbclub.co.nz

Notes Some of this track is very steep and best avoided when wet. Near the top of the track you'll see some grade-5 launch ramps. These structures have been built with dodgy, untreated native timber—'ride at your own risk'!

9 **Blue Mountains Classic**

45 km northeast of Gore

Grade 4, 2–3 hours, 21 km ★★

Once used as a mountain bike race course, this ride is still a great test of lungs and legs.

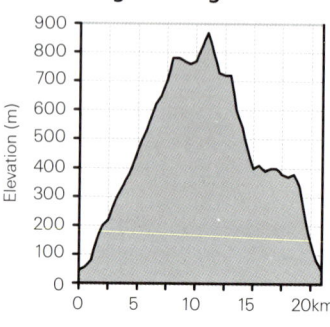

Landowners Check with Ernslaw One Forestry, phone (03) 204 8061, for permission to cross their land, before heading off.

How to get there From Beaumont on Highway 8, head down Beaumont Rongahere Road for 6 km to the 'Blue Mountain Recreational Hunting Area' sign, just after crossing a small bridge.

Route description Turn right at the sign, then left after 20 metres to follow the main gravel forestry road. After 6 km of steady climbing, turn right to follow the power poles at the 'No Exit' sign. You will soon have to hop over a locked gate and then 400 metres later should spot a vague 4WD track heading off on your right.

If you're keen, follow the main track up to a TV transmitter 1.5 km away on the main ridge of the Blue Mountains. There are fantastic views of Southland and Otago from up there, and you can even continue along the ridge for several more kilometres before the track peters out.

The classic loop, however, heads off down the 4WD track to the right and along to an obvious knob with a trig on it. At the trig, veer right down a major spur. Route finding becomes difficult the further down you go; just stick close to the crest of the ridge and you will pop out onto the sealed road 100 metres from the sign at the start of the ride.

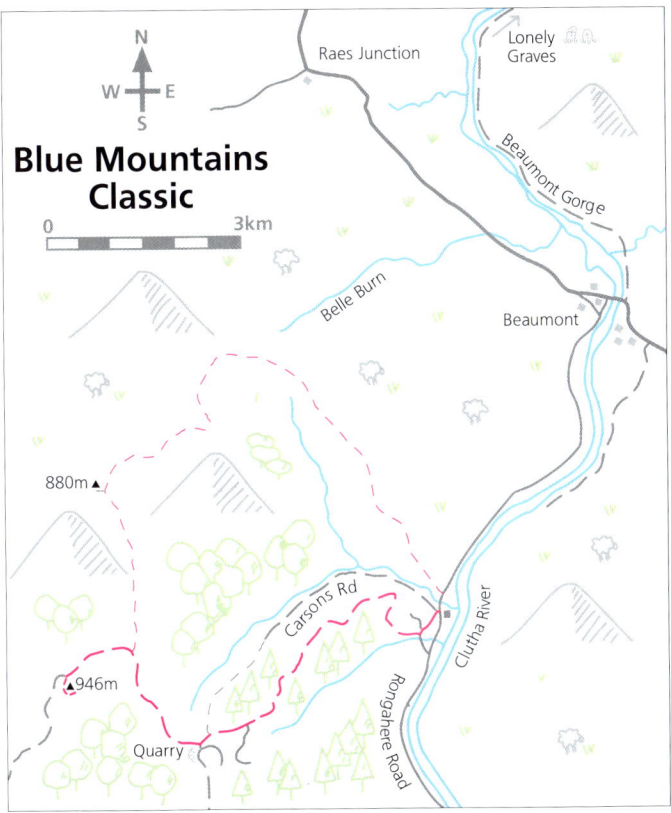

Blue Mountains Classic

Track conditions 35% gravel road, 65% 4WD and single track (some of the muddy farm sections are unrideable when wet)

Notes This mountain range is very exposed to high winds, rain and snow from the southwest. Heavy mists can hinder navigation. It is advisable to carry warm clothing and extra food. Also take spare tubes as the speargrass is very sharp. Take Topomap G44 Beaumont.

10 Bald Hill

40 km northwest of Invercargill

Grade 3, 3–6 hours, 47 km ★★

INTERMEDIATE

This ride climbs through Longwood Forest to the very top of Bald Hill. At 804 m, this is the highest point on Longwood Range and one of the best lookout points in Southland, with views of Fiordland, the Southland plains and Stewart Island.

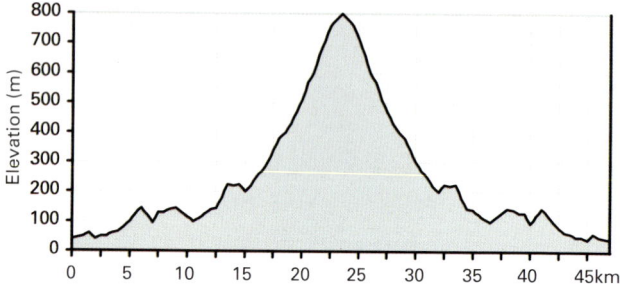

Landowners You will need to pick up a forest permit from Rayonier Forestry, 176 Spey St, Invercargill–it's free.

How to get there From Invercargill, set your car's trip meter to zero to follow these directions. Drive out of Invercargill on 'North Road'. At 5 km, turn left towards Riverton on Highway 99. At 25.9 km, turn right at 'Thornbury Rd'. At 35 km, turn left onto 'Omutu Rd'. At 40.1 km, turn right onto 'Ermdale Rd'. At 42.5 km, park at the first right turn, which is Harrington Road.

Route description From your car, pedal up Harrington Road. At the first two intersections, just go straight ahead. After 6.4 km, you will reach a 3-way intersection where you should veer right (left goes to the Pourakino Picnic Area). Stay on Harrington Road at the next intersection, then, 9 km into the ride you should veer left at 'Mill Rd'.

Stay on Mill Road and climb up to a large gravel pit. This is where the fast riders practise jumps while waiting for the rest of the group. It's a relatively sheltered spot.

From the gravel pit, it's another 20 minutes climbing to the Telecom buildings on top of the rounded Bald Hill. This is a scenic alpine zone with massive views. We would have spent hours up there, if a storm from Antarctica hadn't arrived at the same time.

The ride back takes an hour. Watch out for the treacherous ruts and occasional vehicles.

Notes It's very exposed above the gravel pit. Take Topomap D46 Riverton.

11 Oreti Beach

10 km west of Invercargill

Grade 1, 2–4 hours, 35 km ★

The ideal beginners' ride. Oreti Beach is wide and the sand firm, during low tide.

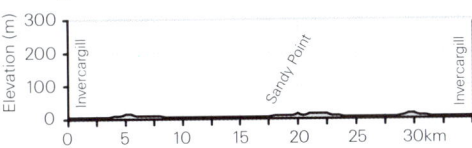

Route description Ride west from Invercargill on Stead Street and then Dunns Road. The route is signposted 'Oreti Beach 10 km' from Dee Street, just south of the town centre. Cross Oreti River and continue straight ahead for another 3 km till you hit sand. Turn left and cycle down the beach–ideally one hour before low tide. The surface above high-tide mark is too soft for good cycling.

Ride round to Sandy Point, 10 km away and then head off the beach onto a sandy 4WD track. You'll pass a couple of houses and reach a gravel road. Continue north on the main road–it turns into Sandy Point Road and leads back to Dunns Road. You'll pass several picnic spots and the Sandy Point mountain biking area (see below). Do this loop in reverse if a southerly is blowing.

On the way back, try the signposted 'McShanes Track'. This 4WD track weaves through a mixture of totara and pine forest and brings you back to the main gravel road. It's named after an infamous bootlegger who collapsed drunk beside his fire and cooked one of his own legs–it had to be amputated!

Track conditions 50% sealed road, 20% gravel road, 30% sand

Notes Clean your bike thoroughly after this ride as salt and sand are a corrosive combination. This makes for an enjoyable moonlight ride, but do it in reverse at night as there is a street light at the Dunns Road exit to guide you off the beach. Refer to Terrainmap 16 Invercargill.

12 Sandy Point

10 km west of Invercargill

Grade 2, 1–2 hours, 6+km ★ ★ ★

The Invercargill City Council has designated part of the Sandy Point Recreation Area for mountain bikers, and the local club has done a great job of building tracks there. They've built two more tracks here since the 6th edition went to print.

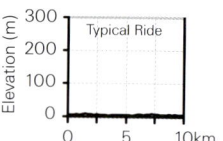

Route description From Invercargill, head towards Oreti Beach for 7 km. After crossing Oreti River, turn left onto Sandy Point Road. After another 3 km, you'll see a 'Mountain Bikes' sign on your right.

This is the start of several handmade single track loops. There is a map board at the parking area, and the tracks are well marked. We started with the Yellow Trail. It was a fun 6-km twisty track; about grade 2. The Red Trail explores more of the forest and is a better option if you really want a workout.

Track conditions 35% grassy 4WD track, 65% single track

Note The area is sheltered from bad weather, so it's good to ride here any time. To check out a map of the area before your visit, click on 'Trails' at www.southlandmtbclub.co.nz

Index

Jonathan Kennett

Notes:

Also from the Kennett Brothers
New Zealand Cycling Legends Series

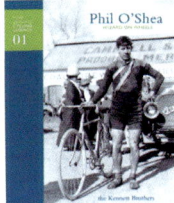

Phil O'Shea: Wizard on Wheels $17.00

The original champion of champions, Phil O'Shea's consistent victories, from quarter-mile sprints to 265-kilometre road races, earned him the moniker of 'New Zealand's Greatest All-Round Cyclist'.

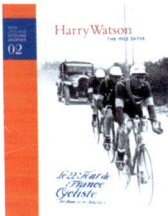

Harry Watson: The Mile Eater $24.90

Harry Watson has long been considered New Zealand's greatest endurance rider. In 1928, he was the first Kiwi to race the Tour de France. That year many stages were over 300 km long on gravel and cobbled roads.

Bill Pratney: Never Say Die $20.00

Tagged 'The Ironman', Bill Pratney became New Zealand's greatest Maori cyclist, after defying death and winning titles from 1 mile to 120 miles. His cycling career spanned an astounding seven decades.

Warwick Dalton: The Lone Eagle $20.00

Warwick Dalton was a champion all-round cyclist. He won major races on road and track in New Zealand, Australia and Europe, including the British Milk Race green jersey.

Gear checklist

For every trip take:
- [ ] landowner's permission
- [ ] pump
- [ ] puncture repair kit
- [ ] spare tube (or two)
- [ ] tyre levers
- [ ] multi-tool
- [ ] cycling shoes
- [ ] cycling shorts
- [ ] cycling gloves
- [ ] helmet
- [ ] food
- [ ] water bottle or camelbak

On day trips add:
- [ ] rain jacket
- [ ] spare warm top
- [ ] money, ID, etc
- [ ] sun block & lip balm
- [ ] sunglasses
- [ ] chain tool
- [ ] spoke tool
- [ ] tyre boot
- [ ] first aid kit
- [ ] maps and compass/GPS
- [ ] backpack
- [ ] cell phone
- [ ] this book

For overnight trips add:
- [ ] lots more food and drink
- [ ] rear carrier
- [ ] spare carrier bolts
- [ ] panniers
- [ ] billy and cooker
- [ ] plastic bowl
- [ ] cutlery
- [ ] lighter/matches
- [ ] sleeping bag
- [ ] sleeping mat
- [ ] 2 x thermal tops
- [ ] fleece jacket
- [ ] thermal tights
- [ ] thin hat or balaclava
- [ ] spare socks
- [ ] torch (& spare batteries)
- [ ] bungy cords
- [ ] duct tape and wire
- [ ] mini-tool with pliers
- [ ] tent or hut pass
- [ ] small bottle of chain oil
- [ ] toiletries (incl. paper!)

Optional extras:
- [ ] extra clothes and footwear
- [ ] camera
- [ ] towel
- [ ] bike lock
- [ ] travel tickets/booking numbers
- [ ] water filter or tablets
- [ ] nylon cord
- [ ] spare brake pads
- [ ] spare derailleur cable
- [ ] rear derailleur hanger
- [ ] crank tool (or 8 mm Allen key)
- [ ] suspension pump
- [ ] ground sheet
- [ ] ear plugs
- [ ] bike bag
- [ ] insect repellent